TOURING NAM

TOURING NAM

The Vietnam War Reader

**Edited by
MARTIN H.
GREENBERG
and
AUGUSTUS
RICHARD
NORTON**

William Morrow and Company, Inc.
New York

Library of Congress Catalog Card Number: 84-62022

ISBN: 0-688-03463-2

Printed in the United States of America

First Edition

1 2 3 4 5 6 7 8 9 10

BOOK DESIGN BY JAMES UDELL

Contents

Introduction

There was something surreal about the war we went off to fight. There was no hoopla, no band, just a set of orders. I remember going to a nightclub in San Francisco the night before I was scheduled to leave for Vietnam from Travis Air Force Base, California, in 1968. Chatting with a comely young lady, I was sure that all sorts of sensual gifts would await me when I announced that I would be off to war the next day. Instead, my announcement was met with studied nonchalance. It was as if I had said that I was going to a Giants game at Candlestick. Maybe my romantic charms were at fault, but somehow I think the young woman's apathy reflected a society's unconcern. America seemed to scarcely care, sending its young to war as if it were sending a problem child to summer camp.

The next day, after the hurry-up-and-wait drill at Travis, I boarded a charter airplane with two hundred other men and I was on my way to a steaming land of pajama-clad enemies, punji stakes, and a personal war for survival (most of us did not have a very sophisticated understanding of Vietnam). The dreary, cramped, and overcrowded flight seemed designed to be so tedious that we would all be thankful to leave the plane in Bien Hoa. After passing through what seemed to be a hundred time zones, puzzling over the concept of the international date line, and eating endless bland airline meals, we landed. Four hundred eyes surveyed the drab airfield. The panorama was all in shades of brown and green, and a hazy fog of heat seemed to hug the ground. As we descended from the plane, the heat hit each of us like a body block.

Those first few days in the Repo-Depot (90th Replacement Depot–Long Binh) were filled with empty hours, boring briefings by bored briefers, and finally, on the third or fourth day, orders. It was only now that most of us discovered where we would fight our small share of the war. Indeed, the shares could be very different. Fighting with the 1st Cav meant extravagant helicopter support and hot meals every night. The Third Herd, the 173d Airborne, offered the prospect of learning the meaning of humping the bush in the Central Highlands. The Ninth Division offered a potpourri of experiences in the water-logged Delta, where contact was sometimes as regular as leech bites. Vietnam was many wars, and for the survivors it was always fascinating to learn that cohorts in other units seemed to be fighting a different war in a different country. In I Corps, the marines' environ, combat often came in big doses, thanks to the large numbers of enemy regulars in the area (as opposed to the guerrillas, who were often the major problem in other parts of Nam). Only a fraction of us would actually see the cutting edge of course. Many of those in the Repo-Depot would spend their 365 days cooking, clerking, driving, flying, or supplying the cumbersome war effort. For us grunts (infantrymen), everyone else was an inferior being—maybe more comfortable, better fed, and safer, but still inferior. The grunts' simple vocabulary said it all. Non-grunts were wimps, REMFs (rear-echelon mother fuckers), glory hounds, and PX cowboys. Whatever our station in the war, we were off to our units.

At some point in the process of joining our unit we were issued about a hundred pounds of equipment. Some of this stuff was essential, rifles and canteens for example, but some of it was garbage. Fancy mosquito net hats that some slick defense contractor (whose son was probably scarfing up an Ivy League education) had sold an overweight procurement officer, who probably couldn't tell an entrenching tool from a GI tablespoon. The multiple sets of fatigues, great for the REMFs, but any grunt who fought in Vietnam will tell you that you didn't load yourself down with extraneous stuff like a change of clothes (every week or so we would get a semiclean uniform to replace a funky one). Underwear. Show me a man who wore underwear in Nam and I'll show you a man who never left the air-conditioned offices of Pentagon East (the MAC-V headquarters near Saigon). And then the piece of equipment we couldn't discard—that devious item of tubular aluminum construction, cleverly decorated with an OD (olive drab) nylon—the rucksack. This was the essential luggage that allowed us to carry fifty to sixty pounds of chow, bullets, mortar rounds, canteens, poncho, entrenching tool, grenades, air mattress (if we were lucky), and other wartime toys. Opinions may vary, but I came to hate my rucksack. After it dug into my shoulders for ten or twelve hours, I was more than pleased to cruelly dump it after a day's hump.

And so our wars began. In this book we have tried to include factual and fictional accounts that capture what it was really like to fight and serve in Nam. At times the invented may seem hard to distinguish from the real, but it was so in Vietnam as well. Some of the stories may seem farfetched, and some are, but others have a special ring of authenticity that I found compelling. There is no way a book can substitute for a year of war, but if some of the smells and emotions are communicated, then maybe Vietnam can begin to be comprehensible.

Remembering an odd war evokes odd memories. I remember how I came to despise the constant wetness. The sweat would run in gallons off a man who was standing still. Wetness rendered the simplest scratch or cut a potentially serious infection. Wetness was every grunt's enemy; we fought it continuously but almost always unsuccessfully. Bone-weary and drained from my daily trek in the jungle, the prospect of sleep was a magnet, and yet riverlets flowing down my back often stole the escape of sleep, substituting fatigue and meanness. With the omnipresent moisture came the leeches that disgusted as they discoagulated. Vietnam was a year of being wet.

Then there were the body bags. We all lost friends, but the loss that leaves me feeling an overwhelming sadness is that of a soldier killed by a single mortar round on an otherwise quiet night on the Bong Son plain. He was not even in the unit long enough for me to know his name. He is only a statistic, a man erased by the war.

Yea though I walk through the Valley of the Shadow of Death I fear no evil, because I'm the meanest son of a bitch in the valley.

—Inscribed on a grunt's lighter

FNGs
(FUCKING
NEW GUYS)

After a tiring flight to Vietnam, replete with testy stewardesses, bland food, and cramped seating that increased profits while eliminating comfort, the newcomers faced their first ordeal—inprocessing. Tense and uncertain about the twelve months to follow, each man had a few days to listen to inbriefings, sign a few dozen forms, draw equipment . . . and listen to war stories (of which a few were even true).

David Reed

The Beginning

It was night, cold and rainy, when the hundred and sixty-five soldiers boarded the chartered Boeing 707 jet at Travis Air Force Base near San Francisco. The plane whisked them across the Pacific at nearly the speed of sound. It had stopped briefly to refuel in Hawaii and the Philippines, and now, more than twenty hours after leaving Travis, it was landing at Bien Hoa Air Base, just north of Saigon.

When the soldiers disembarked, they felt faint from the hundred-degree heat, the suffocating humidity, and the blinding glare of the Vietnamese afternoon. "Kinda warm here, ain't it?" a nineteen-year-old draftee said, but none of his buddies replied. The men were tired from their long journey and they were dazed and frightened by the prospect of what lay ahead. They had been sent to Vietnam as replacements for soldiers who had fallen in battle or who had completed their tours of duty and been sent home. The newcomers would serve exactly one year in Vietnam and then they, too, would be rotated home. But it was a mathematical certainty that some of them would never make it.

"Okay, gentlemen, let's get into the buses," a sergeant shouted. The Army has come a long way since other wars and now even enlisted men are addressed—sometimes at least—as "gentlemen." The soldiers piled into four buses. Two jeeps with machine guns mounted on them took up positions in the front and rear, and then the convoy moved out, bound for the camp of the 90th Replacement Battalion at nearby Long Binh Junction.

The road to Long Binh Junction was lined with shanties. Naked children played in putrid ditches. Peasants in black pajamas struggled with water buffalo in plowing muddy rice paddies. The soldiers stared at the squalor incredulously. They had never seen anything like it in their lives.

Most of the soldiers were very young, some only eighteen or nineteen, too young to shave daily, too young to vote or drink whisky legally in most states, too young to affix their signatures on legal documents. But they were brave and they did not complain, and they faced what lay ahead with a mature acceptance far beyond their years.

An eighteen-year-old draftee from New York State said he was worried that he might be killed. Then he added wistfully: "A lot of guys do come back okay from here, though." A twenty-year-old infantryman from South Carolina said, "I'm scared, but I'm kind of looking forward to combat—I want to see what my reactions will be." And a twenty-two-year-old Ohioan said, "I volunteered to come here for one reason—my kid brother just got drafted and I don't want him over here." Under military policy, brothers are not sent to Vietnam at the same time.

Some of the men believed fiercely in the war. A thirty-six-year-old sergeant from Georgia said, "I'm not a hero. I'm not longing for any medals, but I feel my place is here. The more you get those creeps in the streets back home, the more I was determined to come here. I could have had a dream assignment—ROTC instructor at Georgia Tech—but I gave it up to come here. I'm here for my wife and son and country."

And a twenty-four-year-old draftee from Maryland said, "I feel that I live in the United States and I have an obligation to defend it. The only thing that bothers me is that some others ought to be here, too."

When the buses reached the replacement depot at Long Binh Junction, explosions were heard. "I don't know if it's practice firing or the real thing," an officer said. The men shuffled into a wooden building to indulge in the old Army game of filling out forms. Then they took off their starched khaki uniforms and changed into baggy green fatigues—the clothing they would wear for the next year. A sergeant took them to the mess hall for an orientation talk. "Gentlemen, school's out," he barked. "This is war! The time has come when you will put into practice all that you have learned." While jet fighter planes roared overhead, the sergeant lectured them on heat exhaustion ("Take plenty of salt and water"), on malaria ("You start freezin' to death in Vietnam, you better head for the dispensary"), and on other health problems ("We got women in Vietnam who are VC agents and we also got women who are VD agents").

In an air-conditioned building not far from the mess hall, a stack of punch cards was whirring through a computer, assigning the men to various units all over Vietnam. In twenty-four hours the men would be moving out by plane and truck to their new outfits. In twenty-four hours some of them would come under enemy fire.

Elsewhere in the camp there was another group of men. They were bronzed and lean. They laughed, joked, and indulged in horseplay. They were dressed in freshly starched khakis, and many of them were heroes, with new decorations on their chests. They had completed a year in Vietnam and now were waiting to board buses for the ride to the airport.

The war was over for them. For the newcomers it was just beginning.

Don Porsché

Evenings in Europe and Asia

The youth hostel at Avignon is on an island in the Rhône River. During my first visit there, in May or early June of 1963, I had a long talk one evening in the embankment by the edge of the water with a young man, a German, of about my own age. We were both in our early twenties, born at the beginning of the Second World War. He had hitch-hiked from Hamburg and was going, I believe, to Marseille.

As often happens in such conversations, there was a quick establishment of trust, and we were soon talking about personal topics. He asked me about my early childhood; I said my first memories were of a porch full of toys at a friend's house around the corner, and tarred alleys and running under the hose in the summer.

"You were in the States, I suppose, all during the war?"

I said yes, I was born and grew up there.

"And the war didn't make much impression on you, as a small child?"

"No. I'm not sure I even knew there was a war going on. I don't remember anything about it except V-J day; there was a parade. And ration stamps, but I guess my memories of ration stamps are from afterwards. There was an embarrassing moment in kindergarten or the first grade when it developed that I didn't really know the difference between ration stamps and money."

He smiled.

I asked if he had been in Germany during the entire war.

"Yes. My earliest memories are of the air raids: sirens in the night, running down stairs, explosions in the distance. Waiting, everybody frightened. Sometimes nearby explosions and crumbling walls. My father was killed on the Russian front and my cousin, one of my older cousins, died in an air raid a few blocks from where I was. It was terrible. I dreamed about it for years afterwards. Sometimes I still do."

My first impulse—and it was a foolish one, I admit—was to envy him for his early memories. I thought vaguely that it might be better to begin one's life with something decisive, something that cut into the depths of existence, rather than the trivial embarrassments I remembered from my suburban childhood in the United States. I had the idea that I was living only on the surface of my life and that my shallowness was partly the result of a banal childhood. My German friend appeared neither shallow nor trivial.

We went on to talk about Germany in the years immediately after the Second World War, and I tried to imagine the feeling of waking up after the end and finding oneself still alive. We also talked about the German Youth Movement: its beginnings in the early part of this century, and what's left of it now. When we got back to our own travels I said I had spent the winter in Spain and was now on my way up the Rhône, by bicycle, going to Germany. By the third week of June I had to be in Frankfurt, to take a pre-induction physical at a U.S. Army hospital. If I passed, as I surely would, I expected my induction notice by the end of the summer.

"Are you going to let yourself be drafted?"

I said yes, I didn't like the idea but there wasn't much I could do about it.

"You could refuse."

"And go to jail? I suppose I could, but that would be even worse than being in the army. And it wouldn't really accomplish anything."

"At least you wouldn't kill anyone."

I scoffed. "I won't kill anyone in the army, either. I'll be given a desk job, I'll put in my two years of mindless busywork, and that will be that. The only thing that remotely resembles a war right now is in Vietnam, and all we've got there are a few 'military advisors.' They're all volunteers, career men. Marines and such." I had read articles saying they weren't sending any American draftees over there because the Vietnamese were doing all the fighting. Like most people in 1963, I had only a vague idea where Vietnam was and what was going on there.

The sun had set behind us, and its glow was fading from the massive stone palace of the medieval popes, across the river to the east. Now the pale aluminum light from a half moon was reflected in the swiftly moving water between us and the *pont d'Avignon,* the remains of the bridge that was danced upon in the French folk song.

"I know so many people," he said, "who have drifted into the army—various armies—thinking the same thing. 'There's no war. I'll have a desk job. I'll just serve my time.' And then they find themselves in the middle of something they want no part of. When my father was drafted there was no war, and everyone said there wouldn't be one, *der Führer* wouldn't allow it. I never knew my father, but I'm told he had no intention of fighting. He just got entangled in the military, and then it was too late."

I nodded, but said nothing.

"Suppose you *do* find yourself in a war," he said. "Suppose someone was aiming a gun at you. Would you kill him?" My answer was that I really didn't know. After a pause he said: "Actually I shouldn't have asked you that. It's the sort of question they ask at hearings for conscientious objectors, to determine if you're 'really' a pacifist: 'What if someone attacked your grandmother on the street?' Any way you answer is wrong."

I asked if he was a conscientious objector himself.

"Inside, yes. But if you mean do I have the official status of a C.O., no I don't, not yet. I've applied, and had some hearings and appeals, but nothing's settled yet. Of course I haven't served and don't intend to. If all else fails I'll stay out of Germany, or go to jail. I haven't really decided if a direct refusal is essential, or if it's enough simply to avoid service by whatever means. Maybe I'll just move to West Berlin. We have that advantage, in the Federal Republic, that if we move to Berlin we can no longer be inducted. But of course you Americans have no such island."

I said I had considered just staying in Europe. "In many ways I prefer Europe to the States, anyway . . . But still, it *is* my native country, and if I could never go back there it might be quite a hardship."

He asked if I had considered conscientious objection, and I said I hadn't, as it was very difficult in the States except for members of certain religious groups. But I wasn't religious, and couldn't really claim to have any great moral principles. "No," I went on, "the one possibility is being deferred as a student, and I've done that to the point where I just can't go on doing it any more. I've graduated from college in the States, I've studied in Switzerland and Paris, and last fall I enrolled at Barcelona but I couldn't go through with it. I rode around Spain on my bicycle all winter instead. The trouble is that by now I *know* what I want to learn and I know how to go about learning it. The more I study in universities, the more they seem to get in the way. I'd have given up on universities a year or two ago, except that I wanted to stay out of the army. But now I'm so sick of doing pointless things to avoid it that I think I'll just let myself get drafted, serve my two years, and have done with it."

"Of course, that's just the way they want you to feel."

"I suppose. Or it may be that they don't care how you feel, just so they get you one way or another."

The moon had risen higher in the sky. It was nearly closing time for the youth hostel, and groups of people were drifting inside.

"I know how you feel," said my German friend, "but if I were you, I wouldn't do it. Somehow, I'd refuse."

Later, when I was in Vietnam, I often thought of our conversation by the river in Avignon. I wished I had written down his name and address, so I could write him a letter.

One thing I was right about: I didn't kill anybody. At least I didn't kill anybody directly, personally, with my own hands or my carbine. Like everyone else, though, I was involved in complex processes that resulted in people being killed—many more people than I could possibly have killed just by shooting them.

Sometimes when I was working nights in the radio shack at Ngheo Nan there was a light observation plane overhead, and the pilot would call me on the radio and say: "This is Hawk one-seven. I see some lights, they look like campfires, by a bend in a small river south of your location. I believe they're within your artillery radius. The coordinates are . . ." and he would give me six numbers indicating the location on the map. Occasionally I thought of changing the numbers in some way before passing them on, but I never did it. Mainly I was afraid of getting caught, I suppose, but another reason was that I didn't know the area well enough, and I was afraid I might bring down artillery fire on some innocent people, other than those the pilot had in mind. At any rate I plugged a jack into a hole marked "ARVN OCC" on the field switchboard, turned a crank to ring a phone on the other side of the compound, and read the six numbers to an American lieutenant on the other end. "ARVN OCC" meant "Army of the Republic of Vietnam, Operations Control Center." Why the people at OCC couldn't have had their own radio and talked to the pilot directly I don't know, but they didn't. The American lieutenant who took my call had to give the numbers to a Vietnamese lieutenant who in turn had to phone them out to the Vietnamese artillery crew. Usually everyone at the artillery position was asleep, and the Vietnamese lieutenant had to go out and wake them up.

After a while the pilot called again: "Are those people ever going to fire?" I said I'd ask, and then I called the American lieutenant over at OCC, who said: "Beats me, I gave them the coordinates and that's all I know. Hold on a second." Then I would hear the American lieutenant calling to the Vietnamese lieutenant: "Hey, Thieu Uy, why aren't they firing?" Pause. "They're sleeping? Then why don't you go wake them up?" Pause. "Well? Why don't you?" Pause. "Do you want me to go with you?"

Most of the Vietnamese lieutenants were city boys from well-to-do families in Saigon. They appeared to be afraid of the dark or afraid of the enlisted men in their own units, or both. Sometimes the Vietnamese lieutenant would leave the room (ostensibly to wake up the artillery men), remain outside for a few minutes, then return and slip behind his desk without saying anything. "Well?"——"They no wake up? How come they no wake up? Did you yell at them? Did you shake them? You tell them you're the Thieu Uy, they damn well better wake up." Some of the American lieutenants were infuriated, some only amused, depending on their temperament.

Even I got impatient sometimes, because all this talking back and forth on the radio and telephone was keeping me from my reading. I kept telling myself I should encourage inefficiency; at least no one was getting killed while the Vietnamese were sleeping and fooling around. But I was worried (as the U.S. command doubtless wished me to be) that this habitual inattention might be the death of us all, in case we ourselves were ever attacked.

Some nights, in spite of everything, the artillery eventually fired.

"Hawk one-seven, this is Tunafish Control," I said over the radio. "One round on the way."

"Roger. About time. I'm getting low on fuel. Stand by to adjust fire." I clicked my microphone button twice, which meant all right.

Our call sign had been "Tunafish Control" for so long that no one found it the slightest bit odd. Eventually it was changed to "Able Mable" and still later to "Antique Bed Five-Zero."

Soon I heard the pilot's voice again: "Up two hundred, right three fifty." "Roger." I relayed the instructions to the American lieutenant, who told the Vietnamese lieutenant, who phoned the artillery crew. A moment later there was another loud bang. "Hawk one-seven this is Tunafish Control, another round on the way." "Roger." He gave a further adjustment, I relayed it, another round went off. Invariably I felt an odd satisfaction now that everything was finally clicking, now that the system was finally working the way it was supposed to. Somewhere I once read that rhythmic interdependent motions performed by a group of people, such as workers in a factory, can be satisfying regardless of what is being accomplished. In my case, this was certainly true. I didn't like what was being accomplished, but I couldn't help enjoying the rhythm of doing it. "Tunafish Control, this is Hawk one-seven, they're putting out some of those campfires. Tell them up fifty and fire for effect." I relayed the message and soon heard a series of explosions: boom-boom, boom-boom, boom-boom. . . . There were two artillery pieces that fired one right after the other, then reloaded and fired again. It always reminded me of a Gregory Corso poem: *Boom-bam ye rivers, Boom-bam ye jungles*. . . . Boom-bam ye Vietnamese peasants who happen to be in the way.

Some nights the colonel, who lived in an adjoining building, came over in his pajamas to see what was going on. He was small, grey-headed, and slightly pigeon-toed, but even in his pajamas he somehow managed to look authoritative, at least to me. "What was that artillery a while ago? Just H-and-I?" That stood for Harassment and Interdiction; it meant firing a few rounds at random into the jungle. "No, sir. Hawk one-seven was up, and he spotted some campfires to the south." "Any trouble with the artillery?" "No more than usual." The colonel nodded, glanced at the radio log on my clipboard, and then said: "Very good. Tomorrow I'll try to talk my counterpart into sending a battalion or two in there, to see if we hit anything. Maybe we can at least get a body count."

His counterpart was Colonel Quan, the South Vietnamese zone commander, an enthusiastic tennis player. Our colonel's job, as Colonel Quan's advisor, was to advise him over and over again to *do* something: strengthen the defenses, conduct an operation, send out patrols, anything besides play tennis. When I was running the switchboard I often listened to their conversations: ". . . oh, yes, Colonel Williams, we do that right away, maybe middle next week." "I really think, Colonel Quan, that since your last operation was, ah, such a success, you really should, er, strike again while they're still off balance." "Oh, yes, but men tired. All the time operations. . . ."

My own attitude toward Colonel Quan was problematical. Emotionally I found myself identifying with Colonel Williams's anger and frustration—identifying with aggressive American know-how against dark-skinned native sloth—even though I knew perfectly well, intellectually, that playing tennis was more rational than leading hundreds of men around the countryside trying to shoot people. I also knew that these "operations" did nothing to increase our own security; on the contrary, at that particular stage of the war the local Viet Cong seemed generally content to leave us alone, provided we did the same to them. But my emotional response often refused to agree with my intellectual understanding.

I worked the evening or night shifts whenever I could. Between calls I read books, looked up words in my foreign-language dictionaries, drank tea that I made from an immersion heater plugged into the wall, wrote letters, and did calisthenics under the breeze of the ceiling fan.

In the rainy season there were swarms of insects, especially in the first few steaming hours after a heavy downpour. They came in an astounding variety, big and small, flying and crawling, biting and nonbiting. Somehow, in my previous experience, large numbers of insects had only come at me in homogeneous hordes, one species at a time, for instance mosquitoes in Maine so thick you couldn't take a breath without inhaling a few of them, or tiny hard-biting black flies in Canada, or plagues of grasshoppers in Colorado, where one summer a local radio station offered a free "Purple People Eater" record to anyone who brought in a quart jar of grasshoppers to the studios. Fortunately in Vietnam the biting insects were in a minority, outnumbered by the moths and stink-beetles and especially by the clumsy golf-ball-sized monsters I privately called "Caribous" because they were slow and awkward like the fat two-engine Caribou airplanes that brought us our mail and beer and Coca-Cola every day from Saigon. These "Caribou" insects lumbered around the room, crawled all over the switchboard and the radios, flew around your face, smacked into your head and arms, fell into the tea-water and drowned, landed on the light bulb and singed themselves to death, blundered onto your open book and crawled across the line you were trying to read. Once when I was on a three-day pass in Saigon I looked through several book stores on the Boulevard Le-Loi trying to find a guide to Southeast Asian insects, but I never found one and so I never learned the official name for these monstrous flying bugs. Sometimes I closed the doors of the radio shack to keep them out, but that made the room too hot, and they got in anyway through the holes that had been drilled in the walls for antenna cables and telephone wires. It helped somewhat to turn off all the lights except the little fluorescent lamp on the table in front of me; then at least the light wasn't visible from so far away, and that seemed to keep the numbers down. But of course those insects that were already in the room all congregated around me and my lamp. Inevitably I got annoyed and started swatting at them with a rolled-up newspaper, and before long the cement floor was littered with dead insects.

There was a spray can on the shelf, but I never used it. I insisted on swatting each insect individually with a newspaper, both because I didn't like the smell of insecticide and because of something I called "refusal to kill with technology." One night I was explaining this to someone when Colonel Williams came in, and to my surprise he smiled in his grim way and said: "Well, I'm glad someone has some comprehension of what's involved over here." He never elaborated, and I'm not sure his comprehension was the same as mine, but at least he gave me credit for some sort of understanding, and I reluctantly did the same for him.

To be consistent I should have put the newspaper aside and killed each insect with my bare hands, but I was too squeamish for that. To be absolutely consistent I shouldn't have been there at all.

An often told story.

David Reed

The Way
It's Done

The colonel puffed a cigar and said, "Hear the story about the eager young communist in Hanoi who is given two mortar rounds? Well, he starts off, swimming rivers where the bridges are blown and walking along busted roads at night. He crosses into Laos and he spends ten days coming down the Ho Chi Minh Trail. Finally he gets to South Vietnam and he spends another ten days, traveling at night to avoid air attacks, until he gets to a place where the North Vietnamese and the Americans are having a big battle. An NVA sergeant takes the two rounds and shoots them off. 'Okay,' says the sergeant, 'now go back and get two more.'"

After the visitor had chuckled, the colonel said, "As a matter of fact, I don't think that's too far from the truth."

CONTACT

Tim O'Brien

Days

"**I**t's incredible, it really is, isn't it? Ever think you'd be humping along some crazy-ass trail like this one, jumping up and down out of the dirt, jumping like a goddamn bullfrog, dodging bullets all day? Don't know about you, but I sure as hell never thought *I'd* ever be going on all day like this. Back in Cleveland I'd still be asleep." Barney smiled. "Jesus, you ever see anything like this?"

"Yesterday," I said.

"Yesterday? Shit, yesterday wasn't nothing like this."

"Snipers yesterday, snipers today. What's the difference?"

"Guess so," he said. "They'll put holes in your ass either way, right? But shit, yesterday wasn't nothing like this."

"Snipers yesterday, snipers today," I said again.

Barney laughed. "You don't like snipers, do you? Yesterday there were snipers, a few of them, but Jesus, today that's all there is. Can't wait 'til tonight. My God, tonight will be lovely. They'll really give us hell. I'm digging me a foxhole like a basement."

We lay next to each other until the volley of bullets stopped. We didn't bother to raise our rifles. We didn't know which way to shoot, and it was all over anyway.

Barney picked up his helmet and took out a pencil and put a mark on it. "See," he said, grinning and showing me ten marks, "that's ten times today. Count them—one, two, three, four, five, six, seven, eight, nine, TEN! Ever been shot at ten times in one day?"

"Yesterday," I said. "And the day before that and the day before that."

"Oh, it's been worse today."

"Did you count yesterday?"

"No. Didn't think of it until today. That proves today's worse."

"Well, you should have counted yesterday."

"Jesus," Barney said. "Get off your ass, let's get going. Company's moving out." Barney put his pencil away and jumped up like a jumping jack, a little kid on a pogo stick, then he pulled me by the hand.

I walked a few steps in back of him. "You're the optimistic sort, aren't you, Barney? This crap doesn't get you down."

"Can't let it get you down," he said. "That's how GI's get wasted."

"What time is it?"

"I guess about four, judging by the sun."

"Good."

"What's good about four, you getting tired? I'll carry some of that stuff for you."

"No, it's okay. We should stop soon. I'll help you dig that basement."

A shrill sound, like a woman shrieking, sizzled past our ears, carried on a waft of the day's air.

"Jesus Christ almighty," Barney shouted, already flat on his belly.

"Jesus Christ almighty," I said, kneeling beside him.

"You okay?"

"I guess. You okay?"

"Yeah. They were aiming at us that time, I swear. You and me."

"They know who's after them," I said. "You and me."

He giggled. "Sure, we'd give 'em hell, wouldn't we. Strangle the little pricks."

"Let's go, that wasn't worth stopping for."

The trail linked a cluster of hamlets together, little villages to the north and west of the Batangan Peninsula. It was a fairly wide and flat trail, but it made dangerous slow curves and was flanked by impenetrable brush. Because two squads moved through the tangle on either side of us, protecting the flanks from close-in ambushes, the company moved slowly.

"Captain says we're gonna search one more ville today," Barney said.

"What's he expect to find? Whoever's there will be gone long before we come."

Barney shrugged, walking steadily and not looking back.

"Well, what *does* he expect to find? Christ, Charlie knows where we are, he's been shooting us up all day."

"Don't know," Barney said. "Maybe we'll surprise him."

"Who?"

"Charlie. Maybe we'll surprise him this time."

"Are you kidding me, Barney?"

He shrugged and chuckled. "I don't know. I'm getting tired myself. Maybe we'll surprise Charlie because he's getting tired, too."

"Tired," I muttered. Wear the yellow bastards down, right?

"Actually, this trail seems pretty good. Don't you think? Been on it all day and not a single mine, not a sign of one."

"Good reason to get the hell off it," I said.

"What's the matter, you want to be the one to find a mine?"

"No, I didn't mean that."

"Well, it's a damn good trail around here if you don't hit a mine."

"It means we'll find one sooner or later. Especially with Charlie all over the place."

The company stopped moving. The captain walked to the front of the column, talked with a lieutenant and moved back. He asked for the radio handset, and I listened while he called battalion headquarters and told them we'd found the village and were about to cordon and search it. Then the platoons separated into their own little columns and walked into the brush.

"What's the name of this goddamn place?" Barney asked.

"I don't know. I never thought of that. Nobody thinks of the names for these places."

"I know. It's funny, isn't it? Somebody's gonna ask me someday where the hell I was over here, where the bad fighting was, and, shit, what will I say?"

"Tell them St. Vith," I said.

"What? That's the name of this fucking place?"

"Yes," I said. "That's the name of it. It's here on the map. Do you want to look at it?"

He grinned. "What's the difference, huh? You say St. Vith, I guess that's it. I'll never remember. How long's it gonna take me to forget *your* name?"

The captain walked over and sat down with us, and we smoked and waited for the platoons to fan out around the village.

"This gonna take long, sir?" Barney asked.

Captain Johansen said he didn't think so.

"Don't expect to find anything—right, sir?" Barney said.

Johansen grinned. "I doubt it."

"That's what O'Brien was saying. But like I told him, there's always the chance we can surprise the gooks."

"My God, Barney, they were shooting at us all day. How the hell are you going to surprise them?" I was indignant. Searching the ville, the whole hot day, was utterly and certainly futile.

The platoon finished the cordon, tied it up neatly, then we joined the first platoon and carefully tiptoed through the little hamlet, nudging over a jug of rice here and there, watching where we walked, careful of mines, hoping to find nothing. But we did find some tunnels, three openings behind three different huts.

"Well, should we search them?" a lieutenant asked.

"Not me, sir. I been shot at too much today, no more luck left in me," Chip said.

"Nobody asked you to go down."

"Well, don't ask me either, sir," another soldier said.

Everyone moved quietly away from the lieutenant, leaving him standing alone by the cluster of tunnels. He peered at them, kicked a little dirt into them and turned away.

"Getting too dark to go around searching tunnels," he said. "Somebody throw a grenade into each of the holes. Make sure they cave in all the way." He walked over to the captain and they had a short conference together. The sun was setting. Already it was impossible to make out the color in their faces and uniforms. The two officers stood together, heads down, planning.

"Blow the goddamn tunnels up," someone said. "Christ, let's blow them up before somebody decides to search the damn things."

"Fire-in-the-hole!" Three explosions, dulled by dirt and sand, and the tunnels were blocked. *"Fire-in-the-hole!"* Three more explosions, even duller. Two grenades to each tunnel.

"Nobody's gonna be searching those tunnels now."

Everyone laughed.

"Wouldn't find anything, anyway. A bag of rice, maybe a few rounds of ammo."

"And maybe a goddamn mine. Right?"

"Not worth it. Not worth my ass, damn sure."

"Well, no worry now. Nothing to worry about. No way anybody's going to go into those three tunnels."

"Ex-tunnels."

Another explosion, fifty yards away.

"Jesus, goddamn you guys," the captain shouted. "Cut all the damn grenade action."

Then a succession of explosions, tearing apart huts; then yellow flashes, white spears of sound, came out of the hedgerows around the village. Automatic rifle fire, short and incredibly close rifle cracks.

"See," Barney said, lying beside me, "we did find them."

"Surprised them," I said. "Faked them right out of their shoes."

"Incoming!"

"Incoming!"

"Jesus," Barney said. "As if we didn't know. Incoming, my ass." He looked over at me. "INCOMING!"

"Nice hollering."

"Thanks. You hurt? I guess not."

"No. But I'd guess someone is hurt. That was a lot of shit."

The company, the men on the perimeter of the village, returned fire for several minutes, spraying M-16 and M-70 and M-14 and M-60 fire down the trail, in the direction of the enemy fire, in the direction from which we'd just come.

"Why don't they stop shooting?" I said.

"Why not?"

"Well, for God's sake, they aren't going to hit anything."

"CEASE FIRE," Captain Johansen shouted. "Cease fire, what's wrong with you guys? Stop wasting the goddamn ammo. CEASE FIRE!"

"Cease fire," the lieutenants hollered.

"Cease fire," the platoon sergeants hollered.

"Cease the goddamn fire," shouted the squad leaders.

"That," I told Barney, "is the chain of command."

Bates, one of our buddies, ran over and asked how we were. "Somebody had to get messed up during all that," he said. He peered down at us. He held his helmet in his hands.

"We better look over there," I said. "That's where the grenades came in."

"Grenades?" Bates looked at me. "You sure you're not a sailor?"

"Not altogether."

"Not altogether, what?"

"Not altogether sure I'm not a sailor, for Christ's sake."

"Damn straight, not altogether," Bates said. "Those were mortar rounds coming down on us. Eighty-two millimeter mortar rounds."

"You sure?" Barney always asked people that question.

"Well, pretty sure," Bates said. "I mean, I was a mortar man before they made me a grunt. Those were mortar rounds."

"It's gonna be a nice night," Barney muttered, smiling like a child. His face had the smooth complexion of a baby brother. "Just as I was saying before. We aren't gonna get much sleep."

We walked to where the mortar rounds had exploded. Some soldiers from the third platoon were standing there, in the wreckage of huts and torn-down trees, looking at four holes in the dirt. "Nobody's hurt over here," one of them said. "Lucky thing. We were all sitting down, resting. Anybody standing when that stuff came in would be dead. I mean really dead." The soldier sat on his pack and opened a can of peaches.

The captain ran over to us and asked for casualties, and the same soldier told him there were none. "We were all sitting down, sir. Resting. Pretty lucky for us. We should rest more—right, sir?"

"Okay, that's good," Captain Johansen said. He told me to call battalion headquarters. "Just inform them that we're heading off for our night position, not a word about the little fight just now. I don't want to spend time playing with gunships, and that's what they'll make us do."

We hefted our packs and guns and straggled in a long line out of the village. It was only a two-hundred-meter walk to the little wooded hill where we made our night position, but by the time the foxholes were dug and we'd eaten cold C rations, it had been dark for a long time. The night was not as frightening as other nights. Sometimes there was the awful feeling in the air that people would die at their foxholes or in their sleep, but that night everyone talked softly and bravely. No one doubted that we would be hit, yet in the certainty of a fight to come there was no real terror. We hadn't lost anyone that day, even after eight hours of sniping and harassment, and the presence of the enemy and his failure during the day made the night hours easier. We simply waited. Taking turns at guard, being careful not to light cigarettes, we waited until nearly daybreak. And then only a half-dozen mortar rounds came down, none of them inside our circle of foxholes.

When it was light Bates and Barney and I cooked C rations together.

"You need a shave," Bates told Barney.

"I need R & R. And a woman; a lay's what I need. She can take me with or without the whiskers."

"You haven't got whiskers," Bates laughed.

Barney rubbed his face, feeling for hair. "Well, Jesus, why do you say I need a shave?"

"Do you ever shave?"

"Not often." Barney stirred his bubbling ham and eggs.

Slowly, the camp came alive. The heat was what woke us up, cooking through the poncho liners. Then flies. Everyone stirred slowly, lay on their backs for long minutes, talked in little groups. At that hour no one really kept guard. A look out into the brush now and then, that was all. A cursory feign.

It was like waking up in a cancer ward, no one ambitious to get on with the day, no one with obligations, or dreams for the daylight.

"That wasn't a bad night, really," Barney said. "I was looking for the Red Army to come thunking down on us. A few measly mortar rounds."

"Maybe they're out of ammo," Bates said.

"Could be." Barney looked at him, wondering if it were a joke.

"Sure, we just put their little town in siege and wore them down. A war of fucking attrition, what."

Barney stared at him. "Well, they probably got some ammo left."

"Probably."

"Did you sleep last night?" I asked Barney.

"Sure, I guess so. You know, you get tired walking the whole damn day, so not even the Red Army could keep me from my Z's. You sleep? You looked like you were sleeping; I saw you on guard."

"What? I wasn't sleeping on guard."

"I didn't mean that," Barney said, feeling good about inadvertently drawing some blood. "I mean while I was on guard. I saw you sleeping pretty well."

"Until two hours ago. Something woke me up, sounded like someone trying to kill me."

"Must have been a dream." Bates turned away.

"Ah, that wasn't anything," Barney said. "They'll go away soon. We better get saddled up, Johansen looks like he's fixing to move out."

We gathered up our gear, stuffed it inside green packs and found our places in the single-file line of march off the hill and into the first village of the day.

The tedium of the infantryman's routine was often broken by heliborne assaults. Flying in formation, each Huey loaded with five or six grunts and accompanied by gunships that would soften up the landing zone, the choppers would swoop down as every man hoped that the red smoke grenades used to signal a "hot" LZ would not have to be used.

Tim O'Brien

Assault

On the twelfth day of April, Erik wrote me, and on the sixteenth day I sat on a rucksack and opened his letter. He was at Long Binh, working as a transportation clerk. I was on a hill. It was a hill in the middle of the dead, cancered, bomb-grayed Batangan Peninsula, at a place we called Landing Zone Minuteman.

April 16 was hot, just as every day in April had been hot. First, in the April mornings, came the signs of the day. An absolutely cloudless, silent sky crept out of the dark over the sea. The early mornings were clear, like a kind of distorted glass. A person could see impossible things. But the sun mounted, and the sky focused it on LZ Minuteman. By ten o'clock each morning, the rifles and uncovered canteens and ammo were untouchable. We let the stuff lay.

Sometimes, before the tepid swamp of air moved into its

killer phase, Captain Johansen would move us off LZ Minuteman and we would sweat out the April morning on the
march. We would search a hamlet carelessly, hurrying to get
out of the sun. We would taunt some Vietnamese, applaud an
occasional well or creek, find nothing, and finally retire to the
top of our hill for the worst of each day.

We ignored the Viet Cong. We fought over piles of dead
wood. We hacked poles out of the stuff, rammed them into
the ground, and spread our ponchos over the poles, forming
little roofs. Then we lay like prisoners in the resulting four
square feet of shade.

The sun owned the afternoon. It broiled Alpha Company,
that dusty red hill the skillet. We came to accept the sun as our
most persistent and cunning enemy. All the training and disci-
pline and soldierly skill in the world shriveled and decomposed
during those April afternoons. We slept under our shelters, off
guard, and no one cared. We waited for resupply. Occasionally a patrol would go down the hill to search out water. I sat
with the radio, prodding and sometimes begging the rear to
speed things up. Alpha was a fat company. We took our
oranges and sacks of cold Coke for granted, like haircuts and
bullets. There could be no war without them.

During those April afternoons Captain Johansen or the artillery officer would call for the chess set, and we passed time
watching my white, clean army succumb. We wrote letters.
We slept. I tried poetry and short stories. Other times we
talked, and I tried to pry Johansen into conversation about the
war. But he was an officer, and he was practical, and he would
only talk tactics or history, and if I asked his opinion about the
politics or morality of it all, he was ready with a joke or a
shrug, sending the conversations into limbo or to more certain
ground. Johnasen was the best man around, and during the
April afternoons it was sad he wore his bars.

The rest of the men talked about their girls, about R & R
and where they would go and how much they would drink
and where the girls performed the best tricks. I was a believer

during those talks. The vets told it in a real, firsthand way that made you hunger for Thailand and Manila. When they said to watch for the ones with razor blades in their vaginas—communist agents—I believed, imagining the skill and fright and commitment of those women.

We lay under our shelters and talked about rumors. On the sixteenth of April the rumor was that Alpha Company would be leaving soon. We would be CA'd into Pinkville. Men uttered the rumor carefully, trying to phrase it in more dramatic ways than it had come to them. But the words were drama enough. We feared Pinkville. We feared the Combat Assault. Johansen gave no hints, so we waited for resupply and hoped it wasn't so.

At three in the afternoon my radio buzzed and word came that resupply was inbound. Johansen had us spread out security for the chopper. When the pile of sacks and jugs and boxes was tossed off the bird, he hollered for everyone to stop clustering around the stuff. It was the big moment of April 16, and we were nothing but the children and hot civilians of the war, naked and thirsty and without pride. The stuff was dispersed. By three-thirty we had returned to our shelters, swearing that if the sun were our worst enemy, then the Coca-Cola Company certainly snuggled in as our best friend. Next in order was the mail. And Erik:

> Unclothed, poetry is much like newspaper writing, an event of the mind, the advent of an idea—bam!—you record it like a spring flood or the latest quintuplets. Which, after a sorely strained metaphor, brings me to the subject of the poems you sent me. If Frost was correct when he said a poem must be like a cake of ice on a stove, riding on its own melting, then the *Dharma* poem rides well indeed. I especially like the lines "truly/brutally/we are the mercenaries of a green and wet forest"; also, the juxtaposi-

tion of the last line to the whole of the poem is so effortless, so ephemeral, like the last ice crystal made liquid, that I can't help but regret its melting: "Moksa, which is freedom."

Of the rather limited reading I've done lately, I've discovered how meek a poet Robinson Jeffers is. I'm surprised he's not better respected. The fellow makes me think of April, I can't say why, and April turns me to *The Waste Land*, and for a reason which I do understand, the first lines of *The Waste Land* turn my thoughts not to England, rather to you, here, in Vietnam. Take care. For it is not a fantasy:

April is the cruelest month, breeding
Lilacs out of the dead land, mixing
Memory and desire, stirring
Dull roots with spring rain.

April went on without lilacs. Without rain. When the choppers came in, they scooped dunes of red dust off LZ Minuteman, stirring the soil in their rotor blades, spewing clouds of rust color for a hundred yards. We learned to hide when the choppers made their drops. We stuffed our clean paper and clothes and apples into plastic bags. Minuteman was like the planet Mars. The place was a perfect mist of red soot. It was desolate, hostile, utterly and vastly boring.

The days in April multiplied like twins, sextuplets, each identical. We played during the days. Volleyball. Gin. Tag. Poker or chess. Mad Mark had fun with his riot gas grenades, tossing them into a bunker and watching the artillery officer scramble out in tears. Captain Johansen and the battalion commander, Colonel Daud, flew overhead in a helicopter, dumping gas grenades onto the LZ. It was a training exercise. The idea was to test our reaction time, to make sure our gas masks were functioning. Mostly, though, it was to pass away the month of April.

At night we were supposed to send out ambushes, orders of Colonel Daud. Sometimes we did, other times we did not. If the officers decided that the men were too tired or too restless for a night's ambush, they would prepare a set of grid coordinates and call them into battalion headquarters. It would be a false report, a fake. The artilleryman would radio phony information to the big guns in the rear. The 105's or 155's would blast out their expensive rounds of marking explosives, and the lieutenant would call back his bogus adjustments, chewing out someone in the rear for poor marksmanship. During the night's radio watch, we would call our nonexistent ambush, asking for a situation report. We'd pause a moment, change our voice by a decibel, and answer our own call: "Sit Rep is negative. Out." We did this once an hour for the entire night, covering the possibility that higher headquarters might be monitoring the net. Foolproof. The enlisted men, all of us, were grateful to Alpha's officers. And the officers justified it, muttering that Colonel Daud was a greenhorn, too damn gung-ho. Phony ambushes were good for morale, best game we played on LZ Minuteman. The rumors persisted. Near the end of the month they picked up steam; they became specific. Alpha Company would be CA'd into the My Lai area. A long operation. The helicopters would carry us to Pinkville before the end of the month. But the rumors had no source. To ask for a source was folly, for you would eventually be referred to the sun or to the rice or to a man who would have to ask someone else. Johansen only shrugged.

Four days before the end of the month, we were pulled off LZ Minuteman. We were given three days of rest in Chu Lai, a sprawling and safe military base along the South China Sea. Drinking, whistling, and gaping at the women in the floor shows, we killed the days and nights. On the final day of rest, Colonel Daud confirmed it. He played a strong but loving father. He drew Alpha Company into a semicircle and told everyone to be at ease.

"You're going after the VC Forty-eighth Battalion," he

said. He was a black man, a stout and proper soldier. He
didn't smile, but we were supposed to like him for that. "The
Forty-eighth Battalion is a helluva fighting unit. They're
tough. Some of you have tangled with them before. They're
smart. That's what makes them tough. They'll hit you when
you're sleeping. You look down to tie your boot laces, and
they'll hit you. You fall asleep on guard—they'll massacre
you. You walk along the trails, where they plant the mines
because Americans are lazy and don't like to walk in the rice
paddies, and they'll blow you all back to the world. Dead."

Colonel Daud seemed to think we were a bunch of mo-
rons. He thought he was teaching us, helping us to live. And
he was sending us out there anyway.

"Okay. So you gotta be smart, too. You gotta be smarter.
You're American soldiers. You're stronger than the dink.
You're bigger. You're faster. You're better educated. You're
better supplied, better trained, better supported. All you need
is brains. Common sense will do it. If you're sleepy on guard,
wake up a buddy, have him take over. Be alert while you're
on the march. Watch the bushes. Keep an eye out for freshly
turned earth. If something seems out of place, stay clear of it
and tell your buddy to stay clear. Okay? Pinkville is a bad
place, I know that. But if you're dumb, you'll die in New
York City."

Daud flew away in his helicopter. "Christ, what a pom-
pous asshole." It was an officer. "Sends us to Pinkville and
says we'll be okay if we're smart. New York City, my ass."

I wrote a letter to Erik. Then there was a floor show. A
Korean stripper started in her black evening gown and silver
jewelry. She did it to Paul Simon and Arthur Garfunkel's music. *Homeward bound, I wish I was, homeward bound.* She had big
breasts, big for a gook everyone said, damn sure. Pinkville.
Christ, of all the places in the world, it would be Pinkville.
The mines. Sullen, twisted dinks.

The Korean stripped suddenly, poked a tan and prime-lean
thigh through a slit in the black gown. She was the prettiest

woman in the Orient. And her beastly, unnaturally large breasts quivered.

The men cheered when the gown slid by wonderful accident from her shoulders.

It seemed to embarrass her, and she rolled her back, turning slightly away from Alpha Company and flexing her shoulder blades.

She was in time with the music. She unwrapped herself. She took up a baton, and she prodded herself with it.

The band played Beatles music, *Hey, Jude, don't be afraid. Take a sad song and make it better. Remember.* The girl finished stripping and sang the words. *And anytime you feel the pain, Hey Jude, refrain, don't carry the world upon your shoulder.*

Everyone sang, slowly and with an ache, getting drunk, and the Korean beat time against her brown leg.

On April 29 we were on the helipad before dawn. With a hangover and with fear, it is difficult to put a helmet on your head. The helmet seems heavy and awkward. It is painful, in a slow and torturous way, to stumble to the pad under a sixty-pound rucksack, not easy to tote a rifle.

We lay in private groups on the tarred parking lot of an airfield. The black soldiers joked and were too loud for the early morning. They had their own piece of the helipad, and only officers would interrupt them. Out over the sea the sun began to light the day. Captain Johansen talked with his lieutenants; then he lay on his back. We smoked and thought about the Korean stripper and about hometowns. I made a communications check with battalion headquarters, wiped off my M-16, and put oil on the working parts. Some of the men complained about having to carry extra M-60 ammunition. The squad leaders were harsh, trying to be leaders in the morning. We exchanged cans of C rations, turkey loaf for pork slices, applesauce for peaches. All the noise ruined the early morning, the time when pure silence is only right and the time that is for thought alone.

With the first sunlight, Colonel Daud flew over. He ra-

dioed down. The first formation of choppers had an ETA of
0605 hours; they would arrive in four minutes. The landing
zone in Pinkville seemed quiet, he said. Fourteen miles to the
south, the villagers of My Khe were sleeping.

Then the helicopters came in. They carried the day's hard
light with them. It was already hot. Third Platoon and the
command unit waddled to the birds and climbed in. We knelt
or sat with our legs dangling over the open lips of the choppers. We shouted, trying to cheer up our friends. The helicopters roared, rose very slowly, dipped their noses forward, and
climbed.

It was a short, hopelessly short, ride. Chu Lai and the jets
and PX's and clubs and libraries and USO and friendly
beaches were down there; then there were the guard towers
and fences; and then came the countryside. Clusters of
hamlets, paddies, hedgerows, tunnel openings. Riding along,
we watched for movement along the trails. It was too early.

You begin to sweat. Even with the rotor blades whipping
cold air around like an air-conditioner, you sweat. You light a
cigarette, trying to think of something to say to someone. A
good joke would help, something funny. Laughing makes you
believe you are resigned if not brave. You stare at the faces.
The Vietnamese scout, a kid who looked younger than my
fourteen-year-old brother, was scared. Some of the other men
seemed unconcerned. I felt tired, thinking I should be in bed,
wondering if I were ill.

Johansen pointed down. It was an expanse of rice paddy,
bordered on one side by a ridge of forest and on the other side
by one of the villages of My Khe. "That's the place," he said.
"When we begin the descent, grab my shoulder harness and
hold on. If I'm hit, I don't want to fall out of this chopper."

We started to go down. The worst part of the Combat
Assault, the thing you think about on the way down, is how
perfectly exposed you are. Nowhere to hide your head. You
are in a fragile machine. No foxholes, no rocks, no gullies.
But the CA is the army's potent offensive tactic of the war, a

cousin to Hitler's blitzkrieg. The words are "agile," "hostile," and "mobile." One moment the world is serene, and in another moment the war is there. It is like the cloudburst, like lightning, like the dropping of the bomb on a sleeping Hiroshima, like the Nazis' rush through Belgium and Poland and Czechoslovakia.

You sit in your helicopter, watching the earth come spinning up at you. You jam your magazine into the rifle.

We came in at tree level, and the helicopter's machine guns opened up on the forested ridge, spraying down protective fire.

I held on to Johansen's shoulder straps. We waited for the crack of enemy fire, trying to hear above the sound of the bird and our own fire. The helicopter nestled into its landing area, hovering and trembling over the paddy, and we piled out like frantic rats. We scrambled for paddy dikes and depressions and rocks.

Bates lay beside me. "Jesus," he whispered, "I got a fire burning in my gut, I'm so scared. A big fire right in my gut."

There was no incoming fire, a cold LZ. Johansen waited until the helicopters were in the sky again. Running and waving, he got us to our feet, and we raced to search out the village. Someone spotted Vietnamese running from the village on the northern edge. We chased them. We felt confident and happy to be alive, and we felt brave. Simply surviving the assault was blessing enough, something of a mandate for aggressiveness, and we charged like storm troopers through My Khe.

It ended with two dead enemy soldiers and one dead American, a fellow I clobbered in Ping-Pong back in Chu Lai.

More Combat Assaults came in the next days. We learned to hate Colonel Daud and his force of helicopters. When he was killed by sappers in a midnight raid, we heard the news over the radio. A lieutenant led us in song, a catchy, happy, celebrating song from *The Wizard of Oz:* Ding-dong, the wicked witch is dead. We sang in good harmony. It sounded like a choir.

Lucky to be alive is a phrase that often had real meaning in Vietnam. Raymond Nutter is just one example.

David Reed

The Raid

When Maj. Raymond T. Nutter, the leader of a helicopter gunship platoon, came in over the rice paddy at a low altitude, his stomach knotted. Below, he saw that the Viet Cong had two Green Berets and nearly thirty Nungs (mercenaries of Chinese origin) pinned down by heavy fire from eight .50-caliber machine guns. Several of the men were sprawled lifeless in the paddy. Nutter realized that unless something were done at once, all would be annihilated in a few moments.

"Viking Lead!" a Green Beret shouted on the radio—that being Nutter's call sign—"we're being torn to pieces. Are you going to get us out?"

The thirty-seven-year-old Nutter, who hails from Bowling Green, Kentucky, gave an order, and he and two other gunships wheeled and made five firing runs just ten feet above the VC. The VC blew out the windshield of Nutter's ship with machine-gun fire. Mortar shells burst directly beneath it, tossing it about violently. One man in each of the other two ships was wounded, and the ships, having used up their ammunition, flew off to rearm and get treatment for the wounded. Then two more gunships as well as two dustoff helicopters appeared. While the three gunships laid down a blistering cover fire, the dustoff ships tried to dart down and pick up the doomed men. But they were riddled with bullets and driven off.

The Green Beret was frantic now. "Viking Lead, are you going to get us out?" he screamed.

Nutter could have refused. With eight heavy machine guns down there, it was almost suicidal. But Nutter was a brave man and an honorable one, and he felt that he could not turn his back on the cry for help.

He turned to the copilot. "Do you think we can get in and out?" he asked on the intercom in his soft Kentucky drawl.

"What difference does it make? You're going to go in anyway," the copilot said with a grin. And those were the last words he ever uttered—a few moments later he was dead.

Nutter turned to the two door gunners—Staff Sgt. Roger I. Swindler, 33, of Lakeland, Florida, and Spec. 5 David N. Olson, 22, of Jackson, Minnesota. "How about it?"

The men gave the thumbs-up sign.

The Green Beret was back on the radio. "I'm wounded and the other American is dead," he said.

"I'll get you out," Nutter replied.

As Nutter headed the ship down, a Nung got on the radio. "We need chopper!" the man screamed.

Nutter's ship came in at a hundred knots, with a gunship on each side. All three were firing every weapon they had. The VC responded with the fifties and with mortars. Holes appeared one after another in Nutter's ship. He flew directly across the paddy, did a quick 180-degree turn, and came almost to a hover, ten feet above the ground.

Looking down, he got a jolt: the Nungs and Americans

were lying face down in the paddy. Every one of them seemed dead.

"We're being blasted apart," a crewman shouted in the intercom.

Nutter took off. He gained forty feet of altitude and sixty knots of speed when the controls were shot out. The ship careened wildly, then crashed in a grove of twenty-foot-tall mangrove trees.

The men in the escorting gunships winced. They were sure that their platoon leader and his crew had been killed in a valiant but futile effort to save the lives of the Green Berets and Nungs. But three of the men were alive. And now began what rates as one of the fantastic escape stories of this or any other war.

Nutter was out of his ship. He was knee-deep in water. He was in a daze. He had a nasty leg wound, a big gash on the lip, and a badly wrenched ankle. He was trying to pull the copilot from the wreckage. "Sir, he's dead," Swindler was saying. Nutter was trying to find the copilot's pulse. Swindler was shaking the major roughly and saying, "He's dead and the Charlies are closing in on us."

Nutter's head cleared. He saw that ten to fifteen VC were approaching through the mangroves only fifty yards away. A group of eight or nine VC was coming from another direction. As bad luck would have it, the Americans had crashed in the midst of two VC battalions—some one thousand men.

The Americans had the presence of mind to grab weapons from the wrecked chopper. Nutter, who had had infantry training and was a master parachutist in addition to being a helicopter pilot, made sure that he had his survival knife—a dagger eight inches long. As it turned out, this would be a most important item. The men ran forty yards through the mangroves, up to their knees in water, then froze: a third group of about ten VC was closing in on them from that direction.

It looked as if it were all over. Then Nutter saw a mangrove thicket close by. He dived into it and, followed by the two gunners, bulled his way deeper into it. Suddenly Nutter fell into a little stream. He waded down it for a hundred yards in water up to his armpits. The two enlisted men were right behind him.

Any moment, the men thought, the VC would be on them. They saw a clump of lily pads and Nutter had an idea; the men crawled under the pads with only the tops of their heads above water.

"Ole—get your red hair out of sight," Nutter whispered fiercely to Olson. "Charlie will see you for sure." Nutter piled lily pads on Olson's flaming red hair in an effort to camouflage him, then pushed Olson's head deeper into the water.

"Sir, you're going to drown me," Olson wailed.

The men remained hidden under the pads for nearly an hour. Leeches attached themselves to their bodies, but the men nevertheless remained very still.

As the minutes ticked by, Nutter thought bitterly about the events of the day. His platoon of five gunships had been ordered to escort 17 slicks (troopships) that were to carry out a commando raid near the town of Vi Thanh in the Mekong Delta. The slicks carried 120 Nungs, who had been recruited by the Green Berets for just such missions, and ten Green Berets. Their mission was to try and free an American soldier who, Intelligence had heard, was being held prisoner by the VC in a nearby village. It was said that the American was a Negro, that he had been held captive for two years, and that the VC had driven him mad by maltreatment. It was reported that, among other things, they had been parading him naked through villages with a rope around his neck.

But the raid was cursed from the start. A rain squall broke when the armada neared the village, and due to the lack of visibility, ships carrying three groups of Nungs had to make three complete orbits before they could find their preselected landing zones. If there had been any element of surprise, it was lost then. When the men got to the hut where the American was supposed to have been held, they found it deserted. Nor was there any evidence that a prisoner had been kept there.

Worse still, a fourth group of nearly thirty Nungs and two Green Berets—the men whom Nutter had tried in vain to save—landed in the midst of several hundred VC with the eight .50-caliber machine guns. The VC seemed to be waiting for them. Thus it was suspected that the whole thing was a VC trick—that they had planted the story about the American prisoner to lure a rescue force to its doom.

Now, as Nutter was hiding under the lily pads, he was determined that he would never allow himself to be taken captive. A fierce instinct for survival asserted itself. "I'm going to be hard to kill," he told himself. *"I'm going to be hard to kill."*

A new danger suddenly arose. American gunships were blasting the mangrove thickets with rockets and machine-gun fire. Artillery shells from nearby Vietnamese Army bases came whistling in, and the ground trembled from exploding shells.

"Damn it, we've got to get out of here or we'll be killed by our own people," Nutter said.

The three men pushed through the mangroves for nearly an hour and a half. Several times the two enlisted men fell down and did not want to get up.

"Men, you have no choice—you'll die if you remain here," Nutter said.

The three Americans came to a deserted hut in a clearing. It appeared to be the Vietnamese equivalent of a country store, with jars of candy on the shelves. Nutter found a picture of Ho Chi Minh on the wall. He took it down and beamed at it. "You guys got a grease pencil?" he asked. He wanted to write an unprintable piece of impudence on it.

Swindler and Olson exploded in laughter. All of a sudden they were like schoolboys gleefully preparing to scribble an obscenity on the principal's picture. But their fun was spoiled: they could find no pencil and had to put Uncle Ho's picture back on the wall unblemished.

Coming out of the hut, the men saw a VC facing them

forty yards away. The VC raised a weapon, but Swindler beat him to the draw and shot him dead with his M-14 rifle.

The Americans ducked back into the mangroves and pushed through the thickets for half an hour. Suddenly Olson, who was carrying another M-14, came face to face with a second VC, who also was armed. The two men stared dumbly at each other.

"Olson—kill him," Nutter whispered.

Olson and the VC remained transfixed.

"Kill him!" Nutter hissed.

Olson darted forward and smashed the man's head in with his rifle butt. As the VC fell, Nutter plunged his survival knife into the VC's chest.

The Americans ran on through the mangroves. It became so thick that they were forced to wade neck-deep in a small canal, hanging onto mangrove roots along the bank. Then Nutter, who was in the lead, saw a third VC sitting on the bank in an inlet. The VC reached for a rifle that lay beside him. Nutter pointed his Thompson submachine gun and the VC withdrew his hand. The VC did not know it, but the Thompson was full of mud and probably could not have been fired.

When Nutter waded into shallower water, the VC saw the survival knife in Nutter's other hand. The VC tried to grab his rifle. Nutter grabbed the man first. The two men wrestled, trying to drown each other. Twice they plunged underwater. Nutter was much bigger than the VC, but he had lost a lot of blood from his wounds and injuries, and he was exhausted from the flight through the mangroves. As a result, the VC was getting the best of him.

The VC got a grip on the handle of Nutter's knife. Nutter felt his own fingers slipping from the handle. He knew that if he did not do something in a moment, he would be dead, with his own knife in his chest. In desperation, he let go of the handle—and grabbed the knife by the sharp blade. With a mighty wrench, he tore the knife from the VC's hand, cutting a large and deep gash in his own hand in the process.

Then he plunged the knife up to the hilt into the VC's chest.

Swindler, who had been some distance behind, got to the inlet, grabbed the VC, and held him underwater until he stopped struggling.

They hid the body under the mangrove roots.

They pushed on. They came to a little clearing and found two VC in foxholes, with only their heads showing. Nutter pointed the Thompson at them. The VC had weapons in the foxholes, but they offered no resistance; they came out with their palms pressed together in supplication.

"What in hell am I going to do with these guys?" Nutter said.

"Kill them," said Swindler.

"No, don't do it," said Olson.

Nutter agonized. He could not allow them to raise an alarm, but he did not want to kill prisoners in cold blood. He hit on a solution: tearing their shirts into strips, he bound and gagged them. After patting the two grateful VC on the head, Nutter and his men plunged back into the swamp.

They had gone only fifty yards when Swindler cried, "Damn it, another Charlie."

Swindler was wrestling with the VC. Nutter darted up and sank the knife, to the hilt, into the VC's chest.

Now it was dark. The Americans had been on the move for nearly five hours and had killed four VC. They came to a sampan tied in a canal. Swindler and Olson got in and started to cast it off.

"Get out of there—we're going to walk," Nutter ordered. "It's too dangerous to travel by sampan. If the VC don't get us, our own gunships will."

They came to another clearing. Looking across, they saw

what seemed to be a VC command post, with VC soldiers coming and going in a steady stream.

"Let's take it," Nutter said.

"We're too tired and we haven't got enough firepower," Swindler protested.

"Yeah, but we sure would raise hell with it," Nutter said, wistfully.

"And we'd all be dead in the morning," the sergeant replied. For once, a major was overruled by a sergeant. The men moved on.

They came to a small mound and crawled onto it to rest in a dry place. A moment later, they froze: they heard voices speaking in Vietnamese. Nutter peered cautiously over the front edge of the mound and saw weapons sticking out of a firing slit. They were on top of a VC bunker!

Moving hurriedly away in the darkness, the three Americans approached another bunker and heard a baby crying. Nutter peeked in and saw that it was full of women and children who were seeking shelter from the holocaust.

The Americans moved on. They reached yet another clearing and lay down at the treeline, too exhausted to continue. They saw VC moving all around them in the dark. Nutter's worries increased. He felt that they would surely be found if they remained there. But where to go? He saw a small dike covered with hip-high grass in the midst of the clearing. Perhaps, he thought, they could hide in the grass.

As the men moved out to the dike, a helicopter dropped a flare, illuminating the clearing to daytime brightness. The men groaned and stood motionless. But the VC did not see them and when the flare died out, the men ran to the dike and threw themselves face down in the grass.

It was the first time in nearly seven hours that they were able to rest on dry land.

But there was no respite. American jet planes came shrieking down out of the sky, dropping bombs on either side of them. The explosions were so close that the men were sprayed with water and dirt. Spent shrapnel, still hot to the touch, plopped down around them. Every few minutes an illuminating flare would light up the area so brightly that they could read their watch dials with ease.

Ten minutes after reaching the dike, the three Americans saw thirty to forty VC pass along the treeline where they had been hiding. If they had remained there, they would have been discovered—and would, in all likelihood, be dead by now.

A new enemy appeared—a very tiny and insistent one. Swarms of mosquitos attacked their faces and hands, driving them wild. The men decided to tear off parts of their T-shirts to cover their faces. But, with VC all around, they were afraid that the noise of ripping cloth would give them away. So they timed each rip to coincide with a bomb explosion.

At midnight Nutter was running a high fever: his leg wound had become infected. His face was so hot that he could not stand to have it covered; he removed the cloth and let the mosquitos chew up his face.

There was a lull in the bombing.

"Before we got shot down, I asked you guys if you wanted to try and rescue those men," Nutter whispered. "Would you do it again?"

"Yes, sir," said Swindler.

"Same goes for me, sir," said Olson.

"I'll get you out alive. I promise you I will," Nutter said. "The whole Arvin 21st Division and all of the gunships in the Delta will be here at daylight."

The Arvin 21st, the best division in the South Vietnamese Army, was operating in that area.

Nutter could not sleep because of fever and wounds. Swindler had a cigarette smoker's hack, but he suppressed each cough until a bomb landed, then, during the explosion, let loose with a mighty bark to clear his throat.

Both Swindler and Olson managed to doze fitfully during the night. But they were covered with bruises and cuts from the crash and the flight through the mangroves, and they moaned continually in their sleep.

From one A.M. onward, Nutter heard VC loading their wounded and dead onto sampans and moving out on a canal. Sometimes, after bomb and artillery bursts, there were screams and moans from the VC.

Dawn came at six-thirty. Miraculously, the Americans were still alive. Hundreds of bombs and shells had fallen around them, but they had not even been nicked. Now that the long night was over, their chances both of being rescued and of being killed by the VC had risen sharply. Helicopters would return to the area soon and, with luck, the men might attract one. But daylight also meant that it would be much easier for the VC to find them. The strings were being drawn ever tighter, and over and over Nutter kept asking himself, "How's it ever going to end?"

The helicopters showed up, as expected, and began orbiting the area. The three Americans could not stand up to signal the ships because some VC were still in the area, and so they lay on their backs, wiggling pieces of cloth across their chests. One helicopter came within a hundred yards, but the crew failed to spot the men on the ground.

Then their spirits rose. They saw twenty helicopters landing Arvin troops a mile away. These hopes, however, were soon dashed: at eight-thirty A.M. the men heard people speaking Vietnamese. They reckoned that these were VC, retreating from the Arvin.

The three men laid out their remaining ammunition. They would make a last stand. And they would save the last three rounds for themselves.

The men who were speaking Vietnamese came nearer, saw the Americans—and opened fire. Swindler stuck his head up and noticed that the men were wearing steel helmets, which the VC never wear. "They're Arvins!" he shouted with a whoop of glee. He ran out into the rice paddy, despite the hail of Arvin bullets, to welcome them—and sank to his waist in mud.

The Arvin troops saw that the men were Americans and not, as they had imagined, VC. An Arvin soldier ran up and pulled Swindler from the mud. Swindler embraced him and they did a little dance.

Nutter tried to get up, but his wounded leg gave way and he fell down. An Arvin officer came up to him on the run. "Where VC?" he said.

Nutter pointed to the treeline. The officer told one squad to stay with the Americans, then led the rest of the company in a headlong charge against the treeline, firing as they went.

An Arvin soldier gave the Americans cigarettes.

Moments later, four American gunships spotted the three men. They recognized Nutter and waved to him. Then they formed a tight circle, orbiting just above the ground, to keep the VC at bay.

"We're safe at last—no Charlies can get us now," Nutter said.

A dustoff chopper came in and Nutter was put aboard on a stretcher. He and Olson and Swindler were flown to Soc Trang Air Base, where a woman Nutter thought he had seen someplace before greeted him. Nutter was in a daze from shock, exhaustion, fever, and loss of blood. He knew he had seen the woman before, but where? Was it in the movies? The woman took his hand and smiled a famous wide-screen smile. "I've been waiting for you all night," said Martha Raye.

Miss Raye had come to Soc Trang to entertain the troops the day before. She had worked as a nurse at one time in her life, and when the battle erupted, she spent the night treating the wounded. She washed Nutter's wounds, put a stitch in one of Swindler's cuts, and brought the men soft drinks.

Swindler and Olson were cut and bruised, but otherwise in good shape. Nutter, however, had to be sent to a hospital in Japan for a series of skin grafts on his leg. Then he flew to

Kentucky to visit his wife and two children briefly. That done, he returned to duty in the Delta, four months after the raid.

The raid had been a disaster. The crazed American prisoner, if he had been in the area in the first place, had not been liberated. It might all have been a VC trick. An estimated one hundred VC had been killed, but the price was too great: forty Arvin soldiers, seventeen Nungs, and four Americans lay dead after the battle; twelve other Nungs were missing and presumed dead.

Out of it had come only one thing: an epic performance by three Americans who, when other men might have given up in despair, had simply refused to die.

Major Nutter was awarded the Distinguished Service Cross, the nation's second highest military combat award, and Sergeant Swindler and Spec. 5 Olson were awarded Silver Stars.

When the historian chronicles a battle, he organizes facts and provides order and a logic to conflict. But anyone who has gone through a firefight knows that it is the epitome of disorder and confusion. In this first person account, Stan Goff, winner of the Distinguished Service Cross, gives a grunt's-eye view of combat.

Stan Goff

The Big Battle

That day, as I remember, we started going real, real slow. We were riding along in a thick woody area, and all of a sudden, out of a clear blue sky, we heard a "boom bam . . . DIDIDIDIDI . . ." The APC stopped and we jumped off and got down beside the tanks. We were looking, trying to figure what was happening. It was way in the back. When you had thirty-five mechanized vehicles, you had to figure this entourage was a huge thing—like a wagon train, it was so damn long. Of course, they knew we were coming. What happened was that one of the carriers got hit. It wasn't a bad hit, but the five guys on top of it got blasted by a shell that hit the side of the carrier. So we had to stop and wait; my squad just stayed put. We didn't know whether we were going to get hit with another rush or not. We just stayed behind the thing. We sat there and waited until the medivac came in and carried the five guys away.

Slowly we found out what happened. One guy got his arm almost torn off; another guy got hit in the eye. Damn! So we said, "Well, this is the shit. This is what we've been riding so God damn long for." We were moving toward the major conflict. By this time, we were all ready for it. "Let's get it on. Fucking bastards." We were cussing them out, all of us, because it was mostly brothers that got it that day, guys we knew. "Eugene got it, man?" "Yeah, man, he got half his fucking arm torn off." "Anyway, he's going home?" "Yeah." "He got outa here . . ." Throughout the war, no matter how you got out, even if you got a leg blown off you, you got out alive. Your time was up. But it was *the way* you got out that was the significance. That was what the American people didn't realize, how tough it was. To be hit and have his arm torn off, that was like somebody giving him two hundred thousand dollars. That was how much his life was worth. His arm. To get out of the war, his contract was his arm.

I guess the caravan stopped about an hour. Then we started moving again. We knew we had to get the assault in the backs of our minds, because the next tank to get his could be us. So we rode along and I thought about what we were going to do if we got hit. If they came out of the bushes right now, what was I going to do? I had the pig in a ready position and I was going to sling it right down and start spraying. That was all I was thinking. The carriers were lined up at the edge of this one huge rice paddy. They started coming alongside each other, but we weren't told to dismount. So we still stayed on them while they were getting into position. Nobody told us that anything was over across the paddy at all. Nobody said, "OK, there's an NVA regiment over there. Go get 'em." All we knew was that there was a woodline over there.

I never will forget how we approached it, the tanks and APCs quietly lining up in parallel formation. The rice paddy was about two times the length of a football field and about a football field in width. I heard guys mumbling, but I was just listening for a command, which could come from anyone, like the driver. Everything was moving so fast. Within a fifteen-minute interval we stopped and lined up at the rice paddy. Then the word came, "All right, dismount and stay at the back of the carriers." So the men started to climb down the sides of the vehicles. All of a sudden, the carriers started reconning by fire. They just started firing at this woodline, "Boom, boom," with all these big tank guns, just tearing that fucking woodline all up. Man, the whole damn woodline opened up, "BOOM didididid wham WHAM . . ." Rockets. I heard guys getting hit from over to my left. I heard a tank get hit. I didn't know how bad.

Now my mind was jumping. By this time everybody was reconning by fire. I was firing back automatically even while this barrage was coming in. Everybody was standing up there doing nothing but firing like hell. Pretty soon we were told, "Back up, back up, back up, we're going to be backing up, pull back." So we started pulling back. I thought to myself, "God damn. Shit. Fuck it, it's hell over there . . ." This regiment probably had left a suicide battalion over there to knock shit out of us, so that the rest of the enemy could go on and do what they had to do. We pulled back into the opposite woodline.

While I pulled myself together, I was looking around for my men. They were really shaken up. I could see the shock in their faces—no blood at all in their faces. They said, "Hey, man, are we gonna go across to that woodline?" I said, "Yup, I think we are." "Oh, man, that's suicide." "Could possibly be, man." I didn't know what was going on toward the other end of the column. There was our whole fucking company here, 125 men; add the cav unit, and there were three hundred men, easily. Our company was beefed up and now I knew why. After we pulled back into the woodline, I made sure that my weapon was clean. That was what my squad saw me doing.

I never will forget Piper looking at me and shaking his head. It looked as if he was almost ready to cry, because he knew we might be looking at each other for the last time. And I guess there was a sort of unity between Piper and me, because politically he had tried to make every man see the full thing of what our country was doing. Here it was, just taking us to our death. We were nothing but bodies, that was all; out for a huge body count. And this was it; just setting us up for this race across that paddy. I saw the hurt in his face as he looked at me. Because I had the pig, I guess he thought his brother might get blown away. I took my eyes away from him, because I said to myself, "I'm not going to think about that, I don't want to think about that. I'm not going to get blown away." But I knew the look—he looked at me as though I was a dead man. I guess he figured he would stand a chance of surviving—but the pig—everybody was going to shoot at the pig.

Soon we heard a helicopter come in. They were medivacking guys. One of the tanks was blown away; it took a direct hit. I think we lost that tank and a carrier in the fighting, so they evacuated that team. Somebody asked, "When are they going to send in the planes?" A lot of guys thought they were going to send in planes.

And then we found out that we were actually going to assault that woodline. "Assault on the woodline?" a lot of guys were saying. I wasn't saying anything. "Oh, man, these motherfuckers—" guys were bitching. Then all of a sudden we heard the CO say, "SHUT UP, and that's an order! I mean it, God damn it. Now, we're going to assault this fucking woodline and that's that." An order. Other than the original recon by fire, there was no artillery on the woodline. The CO said the next man that opened his God damn mouth would be court-martialed. We got ready to assault the woodline.

I got my weapon all cleaned and made sure that all my
guys were around me, and I didn't do too much talking. I
said, "OK, men. Primarily what I want you to do is just stick
by me, OK? Emory, when I call for that ammo, I want you to
have your ass right here—you got it?" "I got it, Goff, OK."
"OK, fine, just keep your head down, man." "OK." And I
thought to myself, "This little fucker sure has a lot of balls." I
mean, never once, all the time he'd been in-country did I ever
see him blink. I sort of favored him over the rest of the guys,
even Carl, because I knew what Carl would do. Emory would
never have any type of fear or apprehension. I never did even
see him swallow hard. He'd only been in-country about six,
eight weeks. Here he was, about to see the biggest battle of his
whole life—and he was just sitting there, drinking in every
word I told him. He stared me right in the eyes, as I stared
him right back, and he just drank in every word I told him. I
don't know, I guess some of the other guys thought that I was
gung ho, and, to a certain degree, they were trying to stay
away from me. But he didn't. And then again, Carl and the
other three guys knew that I was vulnerable with the pig, too.
When I found out that Emory wasn't gun-shy like that, wasn't
so paranoid, I really took to him. He had most of my ammo.

You see, a gunner needed an ammo bearer that was not so
worried about his own head that he couldn't effectively feed
the gunner the ammo. I would be blowing lead out of that pig
so quick I'd go through a belt in ten seconds, needed a man to
be able to hand me the ammo. He didn't have to stick it in the
weapon. I did that. He just simply handed it to me, and I
flopped it in there. I could do it faster than he could, anyway.

As we got ready to go back up to the woodline, the NVA
stopped firing, waiting for us to charge. It was very quiet over
there. Then the tanks moved out and started firing as they
went, the NVA returning their fire. We all started moving out
too, walking at first, just walking behind the tanks, letting
them do all the firing. As the fire came in, I heard it hit on the
top of the tank that I was behind—ding, dang, ding. As the

tanks started going faster and faster, they cut us loose as they got ahead of us. Obviously, as that cover pulled out about ten feet ahead, we started lowering ourselves and we started firing. As they finally pulled away from us, we all hit the dirt, out in the middle of the rice paddy, and started inching our way toward the dike. Then we were all running toward the first dike with the tanks forty feet ahead. We couldn't fire too much because they were still too close to us. So we mostly kept our heads down and moved toward that first dike, about two feet high—high enough for protection. As infantry, our job was to take care of the NVA who might have moved on foot to attack the tanks and the personnel carriers from the rear.

As the tanks moved forward, they were shooting like hell, burning up the people in the woodline. My squad was to my immediate right. We were getting all kinds of pig firepower from that brush and all the way to the left. I couldn't see what was happening at the other end of the company; I only knew what was going on in the 2nd platoon.

Now, what were they going to do? The NVA were sitting back there and waiting for us to actually try and attack them head on. What were we going to do? The NVA's sole intent was to have us try to attack them, and they were going to circle us and cut us off from the rear. That was the whole trip.

I was at the dike, firing like hell with Emory right with me, just handing me that lead. He said, "Hey, Goff, I'm out of lead. What do you want to do?" "Don't worry, I got enough right down here," and I was still firing. "What I want you to do is go and get all the ammo from the other guys down at the other end of the company. Find anybody that's got ammo, just get it."

So this kid, on his hands and knees, crawled along in back of the dike, collecting ammo and bringing it back up to me, and I was firing like hell. I probably went through two thousand rounds. Everybody was depending on Goff right then; Goff was the firepower. And I knew I was quieting that area, because my firepower was very effective. As I was running I was steadily blowing out lead. I saw these guys moving around in the woodline. But primarily I wasn't looking at the guys; I was only looking at the angling of my weapon and where my firepower was going. That was the only thing I was worrying about. And as I was going, I was steadily laying down my firepower so effectively that I was just not getting hit myself. That's the only explanation I can come up with.

Emory and I were running up and down this rice paddy firing. The guys would tell me, "Hey, Goff, right here, right in there, man." I would sit down between two guys and blow out where they thought they were getting heavy concentration of fire. Then Emory and I would run into another area along the dike. When Sergeant Needham hollered, "Goff, Goff, over here man, I got thirty or forty of them, right there, right there," I'd fire right where he told me to fire. Those were the thirty or forty NVA I am accredited with in that area. Emory was not with me. I told him to stay while I ran over and was firing my ass off in this particular area, so he started firing his M-16, too.

We were in the middle of the paddy at the first dike, which we went over. We cut down that body of men so well, knocked out their firepower, that we could move now on toward the second dike at the end of the paddy firing steadily. After we got to the second dike, I went on firing for about fifteen more minutes, but then my pig fell apart. It just blew up in the air like it did earlier at the creek. This time the barrel did fine, but the pins came out of the side of the weapon. It just got too hot, and when it expanded, the pins and the locks and the keys that held it in place were no longer workable, and the pig just came apart. It came apart in my hands. The top of the tray popped up; it was sprung, and I couldn't keep it down. I couldn't fire without the tray being down. By that time there was hardly any activity. I was still staring at the woodline, and the guys saw how it was. "Goff, are you all right?" Emory said. "Are you all right, man?" "Yeah, I'm fine, man." Just exhausted as hell, I could hardly talk, my whole mouth was so dry. I was slumped on my knees at the second dike, just staring. The second dike was almost at the woodline. With us being at the woodline and me sitting there exhausted, and with the area completely quieted, a few of the other squads started to run into the woodline, crouched, searching, looking, weapons at the ready.

They started taking a body count. That was when the CO went into the woodline—to see if they could find any prisoners or whatever. But I'd done most of the work. The rest of the guys were sitting. I'd been doing all the running, so I was dead to the world. The guys just told me to sit there, because my pig was out of action. They got me Juju's pig; he was the other gunner. They told me to sit there while they went to take a body count, which they did. I just sat there with my men and held down the rest of the platoon.

So after that, the main body of men were told to pull out of the dike area and move on up to the grounds of this plantation. We were still firing, taking in rounds over on our right as we moved up. It was coming out of the woods on the right flank. I never will forget this area. Did you ever see grading crews on the road? That's how the whole area looked, obviously from the tanks that went into this area. I was on my knees sweating profusely.

Then we started moving toward another dike about two or three feet high. As I went, I sort of lost my head; I mean I wasn't thinking too clearly. My helmet had fallen off and I knew it was off, but I didn't try to stop and get it even though rounds were still coming in. I didn't see anything in front of me, but I heard the tanks yards and yards ahead of us, way down on the right flank. We were told to wait at the little wall, that the tanks were going to come back for us. Three tanks came back for us. During the battle they were way in front of us. They had gone into the woods only so far and decided to come back and pick up the company. We assumed that our orders were to move after the retreating NVA. That was why they came back and picked us up. We'd blown away their line, so we were going in after them.

I was groggy, but we had to move out; so what if I was groggy! I could hardly get up on top of the God damn tank, I was so weak. Sitting up there, I saw all these bodies, or parts of bodies—hands, arms—so much so that it was making me sick to see all these bodies lying on the ground. I realized that it could have been me down there. That was what I kept thinking. I'd just look off into the woods and see rows of bodies, NVA soldiers with backpacks on, T-shirts, parts of uniforms. Obviously, the NVA had tried to strip the bodies as much as they possibly could, to try to prevent us from knowing what rank they were. They'd take anything of value. There were all kinds of dirt marks dug into the ground. From where my tank was it was hard to tell the tank gashings in the dirt from streaks where bodies had been dragged away. But you knew they had dragged away as many bodies as they could. There were blood marks in the dirt. I got tired of looking. I thought to myself, "See, that's what we were doing."

We moved on the pursuit then. We drove about twenty minutes, traveled about a click down into this deep gully. Then the orders changed. I don't know why. We turned around and came back to the plantation house on the outskirts of the original rice paddy. We dismounted and I walked about ten or fifteen feet up to the porch and collapsed. "I can't move." It was no laughing matter then. I was conked out on the ground. And I stayed there. My sense at that time was that I had just been in a helluva battle, and that I had done nothing more than anybody else did; that I had done nothing outstanding, but that I was alive; I had survived. I hadn't even gotten hit. And at the same time, I was wondering how many people were hit, how many men had we lost? I was laying down there on this ground, and I was looking up at the sky. Finally I just closed my eyes and thought, man, if somebody came along right now and shot the shit out of me, he'd just have to do it, cause aside from the fact I was breathing, I was dead

anyway. I just had to lay there, just try to get myself rejuve-
nated. I was completely wasted. I was shaking, just out of it.

Then I heard the medic walk up. Doc took a look at me,
said, "Goff, are you all right?" I said, "Yeah, yeah, I'm all
right. I'm all right, Doc, just tired." "Yeah, we all are." He
walked away. Then I heard the sergeant and the CO come up.
I thought I heard them say something like, "This guy did a
hell of a job." I thought to myself, "CO says I did a hell of a
job." It made me feel good, like any compliment to somebody
for working hard. At that particular time I didn't care, except
that I did a good job according to the company commander.
That the company commander would notice you, out of a
hundred men, that would make you feel good. So after that,
the medivacs were coming in and carrying guys that had been
hit out of the field. I heard pros like Piper saying, "Oh, man,
another fucking Khe Sanh." I knew that I had survived a major battle.

Vietnam was a young man's war. The infantryman's daily grind—whether in the "hills" of the Central Highlands or the muck of the Delta—was extraordinarily punishing. Yet in every unit there were a few old men (over thirty-nine), usually senior NCOs, who managed to keep up with the kids and sometimes even taught them a trick or two. In his factual account, Ronald Glasser introduces us to First Sergeant Mayfield, a forty-three-year-old "lifer."

Ronald J. Glasser

Mayfield

Mayfield lay in the water, listening. He was tired. Not exhausted, just tired out. A single round cracked out from the tree line, but nobody bothered to fire back. Closing his eyes, he tried to relax.

"They're coming, Sarge."

"I know," he said wearily. A few moments later, the gunships swept in over the shore line.

"OK, Otsun. Get 'em ready, we're going home."

They waited, looking over their sights, while the gunships chewed up the tree line. Then, moving out, they began the long walk back to the boats. Mayfield waited until all his men were moving, and giving the smoking tree line one last look, he shouldered his weapon and followed his troopers. Someone else could count the bodies; today he was just too tired, and he wasn't about to lose any more men. The last gunship, cutting playfully low over the paddies, rose suddenly just as it passed over them in some kind of adolescent salute. Shaking his head, Mayfield watched it go.

An hour later they reached the shore and he stopped on a slight rise overlooking the bay. All around, the paddies in crazy checkerboard patterns of green and brown ran right down to the edge of the river. His men, spread out in front of him, were moving slowly through the mud and water, walking cautiously, like hunters moving through a corn field. He didn't know half of them. A first sergeant, and he couldn't keep up with the replacements. Five times in the last week he'd had to bend over the wounded and ask their names. Two had been hit in the head and had lost their tags; nobody even knew who they were, not even the troopers who carried them in. He couldn't keep a second lieutenant; they ran through his fingers like the mud they worked in. He'd lost three that month alone, one right after the other. Finally he'd had to take over the 1st Platoon himself while Clay, the Company Commander, took over the 3rd; that way, at least they'd be on opposite sides of a fire fight; if one got hit, the other might be able to hold the unit together. And they were getting hit. Whereas before they'd been running into VC squads, they were running into platoons now and NVA cadre. It was getting tougher all the time.

The tango boats were waiting, motors running, their gun crews nervously looking over their 50's, watching the water line. Thirty meters offshore a hydrofoil, twisted and broken, lay on its side. The troopers, without even bothering to look at it, climbed into the boats. A few, still standing in the water, were already lighting up some grass. Nearby, a Navy helmet was sloshing back and forth in the shallow water. Mayfield, waiting for everyone to get in, stared at it.

Everybody pays, he thought. There ain't no place that's safe.

Twenty meters down the shore, Clay, shielding his eyes from the sun, waved at him and climbed into his boat.

At least in Korea, he could walk off his hill and relax, Mayfield thought. Disgusted, he threw his M-16 to his RTO and climbed into the platoon's command boat. A few moments later, they were running down the center of the river.

No one talked. They had been out four days and they hadn't been dry once. They had taken twenty casualties in the same area, whereas just two weeks before they had taken fifteen. Stretching out, Mayfield took a cigarette out of his helmet band and looked at it. Forty-three years old, he thought, and I'm back living on cigarettes and water. His troops lay sprawled around him; two or three were already cleaning their weapons. Mayfield watched them, realizing without the least satisfaction that if they had to they'd go again and again. It wasn't because they wanted to or even believed in what they were doing, but because they were there and someone told them to do it.

Strange war. Going for something they didn't believe in or for that matter didn't care about, just to make it 365 days and be done with it. They'd go, though; even freaked out, they'd go. They'd do whatever he told them. Three mornings in a row after lying in the mud all night, they got up and pushed the gooks back so the choppers could get the wounded out. They charged, every time, just got up and went, right over the RPD's and the AK's. No flags, no noise, no abuse. They just got up and blew themselves to shit because it had to be done. The same with ambushes. They'd do it, and if led right, they'd do it well. But they always let him know somehow that they would rather be left alone; it would be OK if they caught the gooks, but if they didn't, that would be fine too. At first it had been disconcerting—troopers who didn't care but who'd fight anyway, sloppy soldiers smoking grass whenever they could, but who would do whatever was asked. Skeptical kids who made no friends outside their own company and sometimes only in their own squads, who'd go out and tear themselves apart to help another unit and then leave when it was over without asking a name or taking a thanks, if any were offered.

It had taken Mayfield a while to get used to it, but after a month in Nam he began to realize and then to understand that his troops weren't acting strangely at all, that, if anything, they were amazingly professional. They did what they were supposed to do, and it was enough. They had no illusions about why they were here. There was no need for propaganda, for flag waving. Even if there were, these kids wouldn't have bought it. Killing toughens you, and these kids were there to kill, and they knew it. They took their cues from the top, and all that mattered from USARV to the Battalion Commanders was body counts.

He was bewildered the first time he heard a Company Commander arguing with the S-2 that the four AK's they'd brought in, even though they hadn't found any bodies, meant four kills or at least three. "You can't shoot without a rifle, can you?" he said. "Now, can you?" The killing thing seeped down to every rifleman. Some units were given a quota for the week, and if they didn't get it, they were just sent out again. He'd heard about units of the 101st burying their kills on the way out and digging them up again to be recounted on the way in. Just killing made it all very simple, and the simplicity made it very professional. Everyone knew the job—even the dumbest kid. The time thing of 365 days just nailed it down; no matter what these kids did or how they acted, they knew they had only 365 days of it and not a second more. To the kids lying around him, Nam simply didn't count for anything in itself. It was something they did between this and that, and they did what they had to do to get through it—no more.

Mayfield took off his helmet and let it drop into his lap. Twenty-six years, and he was out fighting again; he should have been in a division operations, not running a leg company. Somebody had really fucked up. He consoled himself with the thought that only three first sergeants had been killed in Nam.

"Something wrong, Sarge?"

"Nothing," Mayfield said. "Just wondering what it would be like having a desk job in Saigon."

"Dry," someone commented from the front of the boat.

The tango boats moved in a straight line formation down the river. Turning his head, Mayfield looked out through the metal gun slits. The jungle, thick and green, ran right up to the water's edge. After four years of fighting in the Delta it was still all VC. Never again, he thought; not like this, not here. Even if he had to retire. Never again. That much he promised himself.

Their harbor was a number of APB's, APL's, and World War II LST's anchored out in the center of the Miaon River. It was the brigade's base camp. They lived on these boats and deployed from them. If the S-2 found the gooks far from the coast, the choppers took them in. If close, the tangos were used for insertion. It really didn't matter, though; any place in the Delta was wet.

The boat suddenly slowed, and with the engines easing into a heavy rumbling, the men began picking up their gear. A moment later, the boat bumped gently against the hulls of the harbor and, sliding along their sides, came to a stop. Hunched over, the men started moving for the hatches. It was a bright, hot Delta day; the sky, a crystal blue, was almost as difficult to look at as the sun itself. The men climbed out, walked over the metal roofing of the tango boats and up the ladders to the LST's and "apples."

There was no joking; indeed, there was little noise. On deck the company broke up into little groups of no more than four or five. Mayfield walked over to the railing, sat down, and began taking off his boots. While he was untying them, the adjutant came up and told him they'd gotten eleven replacements and he could have them all.

"Any lieutenants?" Mayfield asked, pulling off his soaking boots.

"No, just medics and grunts."

Mayfield began peeling off his socks. "Any ever been here before?"

"No, all cherries."

"OK," Mayfield said, carefully checking his feet. "Get 'em together." He would have liked replacements to get used to the Delta first, but they were short.

The new boys were in little groups toward the bow of the ship. Mayfield introduced himself and asked the married kids to raise their hands, then split them up so they wouldn't be in the same platoon; he didn't want all the married ones killed at once. After dismissing them, he went down to his bunk.

Usually, they were out three days and rested one. That was a grueling enough schedule. Now, with the pick-up in activity, Brigade was cutting that down. It was getting to be three and a half days out and half a day back.

Early the next morning, with only eight hours of rest, they were ordered to move out again. No one complained; as they got ready, a few of the troopers looked suspiciously at their peeling feet, but that was all. Mayfield wrote a quick letter home. He stuffed his usual six packs of cigarettes into his helmet and checked his ammunition clips. They took the things that would matter in a fire fight, nothing else. Nobody bothered with malaria pills; if it hit you malaria was good for six weeks out of the fighting. Nobody darkened his rifle barrel or carried charcoal to blacken his face. The land belonged to the VC. You couldn't kill them unless you found them, which for the most part meant they had to find you.

Only twice in the last four months had they surprised the gooks. The first time was on a sweep near Quang Tri; they were crossing some high ground. It was early in the morning, and they caught them sitting behind a hedgegrove, eating. They even had their weapons stacked. The Captain had waited until the whole company was on line, and then they had killed them all. Forty-seven, just like that.

The second time was a month later. Mayfield's platoon had tracked a VC squad for three days, keeping after them until they caught them in the middle of a paddy. Such things were good for morale, but they didn't happen often.

This morning they were inserted by chopper. The slicks

moved them inland, keeping above 1500 feet. Two kilometers from the LZ, they dipped down and came in right over the paddies. The pilot and the door gunners cleared their weapons, and two of the accompanying cobras moved out ahead and a little to the side. It was 100 degrees when they hit the LZ.

With the slicks in line, hovering a few inches above the paddy water, the troops jumped off, moving away in a crouch to keep the prop wash from blowing them over. During the insertion, the gunships and cobras circled in protective lazy spirals in and out over the landing zone. Finally the slicks pulled out, and the gunships gave the area one last look, then pulled out after them and followed them back to the boats. Regrouped and moving out, the men, already soaked with sweat, began walking through the filthy water, some for the hundredth time. After the roaring of the choppers, the tinkling of the men's gear sounded almost musical. A radio squawked and just as quickly was cut off.

"Otsun," Mayfield said matter-of-factly. The RTO turned around. "Tell the men that if I hear one more radio, I'll shoot the son of a bitch myself. Understand?"

The platoons separated so that there were at least 200 meters between each of them, in staggered columns: tiger scouts up ahead, points, and then the main body of almost a hundred men pushing through the muggy heat of the Delta. By noon they were passing little villages, no more than a few wooden huts, built behind mud dikes. Some of the villagers came out to watch them go by. Everyone looked alike, friends and enemies. The little old woman standing next to her hut could have just that morning changed the batteries on the land mines, which might that evening be blowing them to shit. It was hard to like them anyway; it was hard to like anything in that heat.

The whole time Mayfield had been in the Delta he hadn't gotten one piece of information out of these people. The only consolation was that they might be just as close-mouthed with the VC. Maybe, from what he'd been told, the VC they'd been helping, or at least not hindering, had really pushed them around at Tet and were still pushing them, killing chiefs and stealing kids. You couldn't be sure; the truth probably lay somewhere between, like the mud bunkers the villagers had built near their huts. They were there for protection against gunships as well as Charlie—whoever was around at the time. The only thing Mayfield was sure of in all that suffocating heat was that the Army wasn't winning these people for anything.

They had walked for almost five hours; the sun on an angle reflected blindingly off the shallow paddy water. Mayfield, halting on the edge of a hedgegrove—his troopers already moving out into the next paddy—stopped for a moment to put on his sunglasses.

The first mortar round hit fifty meters to his right. Even as he was diving off the hedgegrove, automatic fire was cracking into the mud around him. Mortars were going off all around; a string of bullets hit near the side of his face, slapping mud up into his eyes. Twisting, he began crawling as fast as he could away from the slapping sound of the bullets. He was crawling blindly, arms and legs digging frantically into the soft mud, when he felt a sharp blow against his upper arm, like a baseball bat hitting him across the shoulder. Changing direction, he quickly began rolling over and over, perpendicular to the way he'd been crawling. There was noise and confusion all around. Covered with mud, choking on it, he kept rolling to his left. A mortar round or rocket hit somewhere above his head, the concussion driving his helmet down onto the bridge of his nose. Stunned, he stopped his frantic rolling. When the pain cleared, he could hear the rattling of RPD's somewhere up ahead, the firing of AK's everywhere. They'd been caught out in the open. Rolling onto his stomach, he wiped the mud out of his eyes; NVA, he thought, pulling up his M-16 so he could fire it.

"Otsun!" he yelled.

An RPG sputtered across the paddy, exploding on a rise off the left.

"Over there, dammit, over there! There, goddammit!" he yelled, emptying his own weapon into the hedgegrove directly in front of them. It was about fifteen meters away. The fire from the boys in the paddy shifted into the grove. Suddenly the middle of the grove exploded, sending out streaks of burning frags and bushes in all directions. "Take it!" Mayfield yelled, and springing up, still screaming, he was charging toward the grove when a round hit his pack and spun him off his feet. But the platoon was moving, concentrating their fire even while he was struggling to get back to his feet. They were moving past him; they took the grove with less than twenty boys standing. They had some cover now, but the other sides of the contact were still pouring fire into the paddies.

Mayfield yelled for Otsun again. A corporal, covered with mud, a bandolier of filthy M-60 ammunition slung across his chest, pointed toward the front of the grove. Otsun was face down in the mud, the radio still strapped to his back. A mortar round hit behind the grove. A soldier broke for the radio. Slipping down the side of the grove he reached the RTO and was pulling off the radio when a round caught him in the head and pitched him backward. Another trooper rolled out of the tangle, reached Otsun, grabbed the radio, and yanking it free threw it into the grove. Mayfield crawled after it, checked it, and put it on its base. Hunched over, with rounds cracking through the grove, he switched the radio on to the command net. Nothing. He checked it quickly again to make sure it was working and twirled the dials. Suddenly he realized that all the RTO's could have been killed outright or their radios destroyed. It could have happened; a waving antenna is an inviting target. They might have been the first to go. It was a good enough ambush for that.

Mayfield pressed the button. A tracer rough spun off the

top of the grove. Someone behind him was screaming for a medic. Looking out through the bushes he checked the paddy. That early mortar round had saved them.

"River 6/River 18," he said into the microphone. "River 18/River 6. 6/18, we're taking heavy automatic fire; RPG's and mortars; probably NVA. Grid 185/334 heavy automatic fire. 18/6 leaving freq to air support freq, leaving your push now." Mayfield looked around; the gooks were in the groves in front of them, behind them, and to their flanks. "You!" he yelled, waving over one of the troopers. He sent the grenadiers to their flanks with orders to use shotgun rounds, and was giving orders for the placements of the M-60's when the radio crackled.

"18/6, four phantoms up at 40 right near you, switch to air-support freq code named Thunderchief."

Mayfield switched the dials. There was no SOP for the 4's; you just talked to them.

He pressed the horn button. "Thunderchief, 18."

"18, this is Thunderchief. Be over you in two minutes."

A VC moved out of the grove on their right. Mayfield was reaching for his weapon when one of his troopers stood up and emptied his M-16. The bushes around the gook were torn apart and, spinning around with the torn leaves, he tumbled into the mud. Mayfield pulled his gun closer to him, but left it on the ground.

"18, this is Thunderchief," the radio said. "Air currents too heavy. Diving . . . Now!"

Still holding the horn, Mayfield picked a smoke canister out of his webbs, pulled the pin, and threw it out in front of the grove. He took out another smoke grenade and threw it to the left. The thick smoke curled back over them.

"18," the radio crackled, "where the fuck are you? OK, see you, green smoke."

Mayfield picked up the microphone. "Roger, green, request first round W.P."

"Roger, 18. Coming in from the west. Get your heads down."

Mayfield dropped the horn. "Tac Air!" he yelled, "Tac Air!" The cry was carried up and down the grove. Taking off his helmet, he pushed himself flat on the ground and, burying his face in the dirt, covered his ears. Everyone was doing the same thing.

"18," the radio squawked, "see the smoke." A second later a phantom came roaring in over the grove, no more than fifty feet off the ground. The sound was deafening; even with his hands over his ears, the noise was painful. The earth vibrated, and then the air seemed to be sucked up from the ground. A moment later, the ground heaved up into his face, and with a dull shock the explosions, carrying dirt and rocks, passed over them. Without lifting his head, Mayfield picked up the horn.

"Thunder/18, Shell H and E; repeat, Shell H and E."

"18/Thunderchief," the voice answered. "Roger that."

The second phantom came in even lower. Pressed into the ground, Mayfield saw the shadow pass by, heard the same deafening roar, and this time the incredible explosions of H and E.

"Once more," the voice said lightly. "I still see something moving. Hang on, coming around again."

A dirty haze from the explosions rose up in front of the grove, blocking out the sun. All the firing had stopped. They came in together this time—six yards apart, four feet off the ground. Mayfield dug in even deeper. The tangle of the hedgegrove was blown apart by the jet's exhausts. Then, roaring over, shattering the air, the planes passed. A moment later the heat and concussions of the explosions seared past them, burning the tops of the grove. Mayfield looked up and, through the dirt, saw the two planes already a half mile away, still on the deck, beginning to bank to the right and left.

The hedgegroves in front and to the sides were flaming wrecks. To his left, he could hear the whooshing of incoming artillery. Mayfield switched to the command net. It was bursting now: Red Legs, Dust Offs, Tac Air—they were giving casualties out in the open. Mayfield couldn't recognize one voice; the Old Man in the C and C chopper was overhead, taking care of the whole thing. Behind them the firing was picking up again.

The medics had carried the wounded into a clear space toward the back of the grove. Mayfield, watching them stack the dead, was just getting up when a rocket hit right in the middle of the area, and the concussion knocked him over again. Numbed, he struggled back to his feet. Around the aid station the bodies were sprawled all over the place. He could hear the gunships whooping in off to his left. Still dazed, he pressed the button. He had been holding on to the horn the whole time.

"Priority one, this is River 18." He repeated it without waiting for an acknowledgment. "Need Dust Off, urgent."

The Old Man cut in, "River 18/6, switch to air-evac net."

Mayfield had trouble moving his arm. "Dust Off, this is River 18, urgent." While he was talking he stared at the shambles that had been the aid station. Some of the men had already left the perimeter to help; there were cries all around for medics. They must have all been hit, he thought. The VC were dropping rounds everywhere. He was counting slowly to himself, totaling up the casualties, trying to be accurate. He pressed the button: "Fifteen wounded; repeat, fifteen wounded—eight, ten, critical."

The radio crackled, "River 18, this is Dust Off 4. Is the area secure?"

"Negative." An M-60 opened up again on his flank.

"Roger, River 18, coming in. River 18, can you give me smoke?"

"Negative," Mayfield said. "I have you visual, will direct you in." He couldn't afford to give the gooks a better target than they already had. The mortar might have been luck; but it also might not have been. He stayed on the horn, directing them in. The first Dust Off came in, gliding in over the paddies. Just as he saw it breaking, he heard the 51 open up. The pilot ignored the bullets and took his chopper right through the stream of tracers. At the last moment, just as he was settling it in, the machine wavered and then, stricken, twisted over on its side and, rotating slowly about its center, cartwheeled gracefully out over the paddy. The tip of its main rotor hit the mud. A second later it exploded, burning up in a bright flash of igniting magnesium. Two gunships on the perimeter moved in and hit the area of the 51 with machine-gun fire, racking it apart. Another Dust Off bore in, this time at a steeper angle. Mayfield worked the horn, keeping the gunships close so that the Dust Off could get in. He could see more slicks crossing the horizon. The fighting seemed to be moving off to the east.

The second med evac made it in, and they loaded on the bodies. A loach circled protectively overhead and, higher up, a cobra circled in the opposite direction. While they were loading, Mayfield plotted out artillery targets—just in case—and sent in the coordinates. He didn't have enough men standing to stop anything. If anything happened, he would have to plaster the area with artillery and he wouldn't have time to call in the coordinates while he was doing it. He ordered the batteries to stand ready to fire on his command. Meanwhile, the company was sorting itself out. The air strikes had settled things down, and now only an occasional sniper round came through.

"Hey, Sarge."

"Yeah."

"Better take care of that arm."

Mayfield looked down at his shoulder. His fatigues were ripped, and his skin was caked black with dirt and blood. Testing his arm, he found he could still move it a bit. He waited by the horn until he was sure they'd be OK—they'd pull out. Getting up, he walked through the mud to what had been the aid station. The dead, partially covered with muddy ponchos, were again stacked in piles. The wounded, filthy and dirty, were laid out next to them, with blank, empty looks on their faces.

A trooper kneeling next to one of the wounded was trying to start an IV. The medic, the only corpsman alive, flack vest open, moved from patient to patient. Two soldiers, their weapons cradled exhaustedly in their arms, were just sitting near the wounded. Mayfield, dragging himself, plodded up through the mud that was strewn with broken bits of albumin cans.

"Sarge!"

A trooper, walking up to him, slipped and barely kept his balance, splattering mud all over him. "Sorry," he said apologetically. "The RTO from 3rd Platoon says the choppers are coming."

"I know," Mayfield said. He looked around him. As dirty as it was and as hot, he didn't want to go. Sweating and exhausted, he didn't want to leave—not right away, anyway. They'd fought for this mud, his men had died for it; he wanted something to show for it all. He didn't want to have to keep bringing them back to it again and again. He wanted to stay; they'd won it.

"Sarge."

"Yeah."

"The Old Man says to get ready; as soon as the wounded and dead are out, we're moving back to the boats."

Lest we forget, long before the U.S. engaged ground forces in Vietnam, a relatively small number of Americans was actively involved in an unsuccessful effort to "save" Vietnam's neighbor, Laos. This short story is a good reminder of our earlier adventure in Southeast Asia.

Asa Baber

Ambush:
Laos, 1960

Less we forget, long before [...]
[...] Ameri-
cans were actively involved [...] an insurrection) there in
"neutralist" kingdom of Laos. This short story is a
[...] speculation of our earlier adventure in Southeast Asia.

Here at Camp Pendleton it's summer even in winter and I dream of the grasshoppers. Here in sunny money land I listen to the singing and I wait to break, to crack like a cup and spill my soul. If I wasn't plunking my white-haired librarian it would be unbearable. She saves me as she straddles me.

Don't be too superior, brothers, because you haven't seen it all yet. Sometimes I think I've seen it all. Everything opens up and makes terrible sense and I want to die then.

Now out of Laos it has become a clean world again. The smell of my rotting feet is gone. The malaria has retreated to my gallbladder, there to sleep, and my brain is slowing down. They give me pills for that. I understand all the words spoken around me. There is no excuse for my sorrow except that I've seen the strange alliances of nations and I think we're all filled with bile. When the doctors talk to me I say all this but they don't understand me.

There are cypress trees outside my window, and across Vandergrift Boulevard there is an artificial lake. The Engineers use the lake to practice building water obstacles and bridges. At dawn the sun lifts over the avocado orchards beyond the obstacles and bridges and lights up the road. Then I can see the artillery trucks headed towards Roblar Road and the firing ranges. All day the choppers and OE's fly over the hospital. They're noisy but they can't stop the singing.

My room is in one of the white frame huts built at the beginning of World War II. It has Venetian blinds that make prison shadows and a white rail bed and a print of a Utrillo on the wall. I don't know how a print like that found its way into a Marine Corps hospital. I hope it came with the room because I'm sure many men have died in this room and it would be better to die looking at that street scene with the red splotch of paint than the naked wall. I don't plan to die here except on the bad days when the fever comes back and the dysentery hits again. When I can't eat anything and my bowels pass water and blood, I look at the Utrillo and think about dying.

They're very kind when they question me.

I tell them it's screwed up over there, but they only listen to what they want to hear, both the navy doctors and our own G-2. I try to tell them about the tangled things, that the French are strong with patrol leaders down to the platoon level, that Russian civilian pilots are flying the airlift Ilyushins, that the North Vietnamese run the Fire Direction Centers.

They listen to me and say yes yes we know all that. They know because they read reports. But it makes it a crazy war when you're over there.

Even Major Kline came by to see me. He lied to General Grider the night we were shipped out. Sutton and Devereux and I were lined up taking shots. They were pumping exotic vaccines into both my arms. Major Kline told the General we'd been on a twelve-hour alert. Yes sir they're ready sir the last shots of a series yes sir. Devereux got mad and said the last shots of a series like a one game World Series. The General knew somebody was lying but there was nothing he could do. So we flew to Wake Island and then Tokyo and then Okinawa without calling anyone or saying goodbye. I don't like Major Kline and he doesn't like me, but he owes me something and he knows it.

The grasshoppers come when I sleep. They have the heads of dolphins and they buzz like locusts. They come from left to right across my dreams and always chant we're coming to get you we're coming to get you. Then I try to wake up but I'm too heavy for myself and I have to keep on dreaming while the grasshoppers hurt me. Sometimes I wake up screaming when I see Sutton with his non-head or Devereux with his wet intestines or Buon Kong in his burning skin.

I met my librarian when I was screaming one morning. She'd brought books in a cart. She thought I was still asleep and bent over me saying there there, it's all right. I kept screaming so she wouldn't go away. She bent very close and I put my hands on her breasts. They felt like warm doves. She wasn't sure of me and backed away. She was angry when she realized I was awake; she wouldn't give me any books to read. Now she gives me all the books I want. She smells of quince and sharp things. She has blue eyes. She is only ten years older than I am but she has white hair.

What I want most is to have Matchko scrubbing me. She knew all my tight nerves and muscles. Sutton loved her like he loved all the Okinawa whores. He was very immature about sex. He was always buying little personal presents for Matchko. That last night at the baths he bought her a pearl and holly-leaf pin. He tried to bring it in to her while she was bathing me. She was pulling on me with the vibrator and oil and I was up in all my six-by-six glory.

Sutton couldn't believe she'd cheat on him. Not his "Matchko." His Matchko of the rabbit warren and rice fields. His gold-toothed contortionist who'd paid for her hut with

God knows how many copulations. He stood there frozen and fearful while she manipulated me and winked at him. He threw the pin at her and ran out. He went north of Kadena to the native whorehouse area where no American should go. He was caught and tied by his feet to the back bumper of a taxi and dragged for miles with his head bouncing on the road.

When they dumped his body on a street in Naha, there was nothing left of his head but pulp. I saw it the next morning after Devereux and I spent the night looking for him.

Sutton was good in his job but stupid in life. He was one of the oldest captains in the Marine Corps. They couldn't afford to get rid of him. He had all the languages they needed: French and Mandarin and Japanese. He even knew some of the Meo dialect. If he'd lived, he might have helped us.

One of the doctors asked me if Sutton was queer. I said he was no more queer than some of the others. He wanted us to go to the baths and get a rubdown from Matchko. He'd lost his wife because he could make love only with whores, but that didn't make him so different.

There's a myth that the military is a masculine profession, but I don't buy it. It's a profession where men dress for other men. Spit polish and web gear and linseed oil and bleach. For my white-haired librarian I'll clean and comb myself, but for a Commanding Officer I won't go to so much trouble. Sutton was sloppy at inspections too, but he dressed well when he went whoring. I don't think he was queer.

When Sutton was killed I was made C.O. of the Interrogation Team. We were attached to Task Force 116. We thought we were going into southern Laos. The panhandle area near Mahaxay and Tchepone covered Route Nationale 9. We had black and white lists and air recon maps.

We were sent to Vientiane instead.

My room is as white as noise. The sheets and bandages are white. I'd like to see a calendar. It's either the end of February or the beginning of March. February is a cheating month so I hope it's over. I do not think I'll die this year because it's an odd year, 1961. I'll die in an even year like my father and my grandfather.

The red-haired doctor asked me if I wanted to go back to Laos when I got better, but he wasn't serious.

I wanted to tell him how soft and fine a country it is with its rain forests dark and green all year. The tree trunks are branchless, topped with lianas that hold ferns and orchids and wild figs. Walking through those forests, you can't see the sun. Flying over, you can't see the forest floor. There are groves of small softwoods mixed with wild ginger, rhododendron, and bamboo. There are coconuts and areca palms and bananas. There are tigers, panthers, elephants, deer.

When there's a war, our newspapers call these forests "jungles."

I can't tell the doctor what's it like there because his spirit isn't with me. I often see the *phi,* the spirits, of Sutton and Devereux and Buon Kong. They're wandering the earth and they'll always be with me. They're back in Laos in Meo country harvesting the poppies now. They're lucky; *phi* can be in two places at once.

The plants are waist high now, in full bloom of rose or white or blue or mauve. I'd like to be back at the harvest before the pale-green stems are cut. The women go to the fields before the dew lifts. They collect the sap and wrap it in banana leaves. The brown blocks are sold for very little in Xieng Khouang Province and for a lot in Saigon.

The *phi* are strong spirits and must always be honored. They're in the trees and mountains and rivers. They're in every human being and every dead person.

I think it was Sutton's *phi* that came as a goat to warn us.

Go north of Vientiane on the Royal Road, Route Coloniale 13. For twenty miles there are flat paddies and thickets and the sky is open. Then climb to Ban Namone as the road circles and becomes covered with forest.

Here are the lowland people. They aren't good fighters. Pull them into combat and they'll shoot their rifles into the air. To teach them to shoot to kill, you have to set up targets, let them fire one shot at the target, walk them to the target and show them the bullet hole, go back and have them shoot again.

Their houses are on stilts. Pigs and chickens live underneath. The men sleep most of the day and the women grow enough rice to survive.

These lowland people will be the last people to fight for anything.

After Ban Namone comes the valley of the Vang Vieng. Here the road starts to climb steeply through Ban Pha Tang, Ban Thieng, Muong Kassy. At Sala Phou Khoun the road to the Plain of Jars goes east, Route Nationale 7.

All of these roads were built under the supervision of the French. The French also collected taxes and rice and salt and women under their "protectorate," which lasted a number of generations. The French set the image for the white man.

A white man is a Frenchman, diseased, the way anything white in Asia must be diseased, whether it is spoiled buffalo meat or moldy fruit or human flesh.

In the mountains near the Plain of Jars live the fighters, the Meo. They build their houses on the ground. They are great hunters and riflemen and horsemen. They live off the land. They eat corn, cabbage, eggplant, onions. They live long lives doctored by the gall of bear and python, marrow of tiger, deer's soft horn.

Devereux had worked with the Meo before Dien Bien Phu when he was attached to the French. He wanted to get back to them and he got permission for the two of us to go. We had to travel in civvies and an unmarked quarter-ton and we had to take a government driver named Buon Kong who drank *choum*, a rice wine, while he drove. He strapped a transistor radio to the emergency brake and gave us a bumpy concert.

After the turn at Sala Phou Khoun we were in no-man's

land. We shared the wine. Devereux even stopped calling me Lieutenant. I think it was the last happy time of my life.

When Buon Kong saw the goat, he stopped the jeep. He was drunk and he tried to back the jeep while staring at the goat. It was a very dignified goat and it walked slowly across the road without looking at us.

Devereux yelled *allons allons* and Buon Kong backed the jeep even farther saying *c'est impossible c'est impossible c'est la morte.*

Devereux stood up in the back seat and slapped Buon Kong on the ears. I jumped out and ran at the goat. That's when they hit us. They probably thought I'd seen them.

There was a great horrible compression of air, dust, and noise. I don't think they were using launchers or grenades because they wanted the jeep. They had .50's and their own Chinese weapons and aimed high to spare the chassis.

We hadn't come all the way into their set-up. They hadn't gotten behind us. They opened up a little too early.

Everything hit Devereux's belly. He folded and fell out.

I ran into the brush. I'm ashamed I ran, but there wasn't anything I could do. Sometimes the doctors push me on this. They think I wanted to be a hero.

Buon Kong tried to be a hero. I guess he wanted to throw the extra jerry-can of gas at them. It bounced against his leg as he carried it a few steps down the road. The bullets were cracking and spitting around him.

I rolled down the slope and heard an explosion.

Then there was that deep silence after battle when your eardrums vibrate and your sense of balance slowly returns.

I kept my head down. I could hear one of them sweeping through the grass. I raised my head and he looked at me. He was a white man, maybe French or Russian. He fired a few shots down the gully and climbed back to his platoon of gooks.

They wanted the jeep and they took it.

I crawled back to the road. Buon Kong was still burning.

Devereux's guts were in his hands. He had died looking surprised. I went into the brush. I didn't start walking back until that night. It took me three days before I reached the road north of Vientiane.

Here in Camp Pendleton the blinds are raised each day and the sunlight comes into my bleached vanilla room. There are deer running through the sage in the canyons near San Clemente. You can walk the firebreaks on the ridgeline and hunt them. I won't ever be a good hunter again because my hands shake. The doctors give me pills and say I'll get over it, but I don't think so.

My hands shake because I have to fight the grasshoppers and listen to the singing. That makes me tired.

The singing is always in the back of my head. I don't know what song they're singing, but it's a march of some kind with a steady rhythm and stamping feet and many voices.

It's not pleasant, and sometimes they stop singing and they shout.

After a long, tiring, and sweaty day, nothing gave a grunt more joy than finding out he was leaving the relative comfort of his night fighting position to participate in an ambush patrol.

Tim O'Brien

Ambush

"Tonight," Mad Mark said quietly, "we are sending out an ambush."

It was near dusk, and the lieutenant had his map out, spread on the dirt in front of a foxhole. His squad leaders were grouped in a circle around him, watching where he drew X's and taking notes. Mad Mark pointed at a spot on the map, circled it, and said, "We'll be bushing this trail junction. Headquarters has some pretty good intelligence that Charlie's in the neighborhood. Maybe we'll get him this time."

He drew two red lines on the map. "First Squad will set up along this paddy dike. Make sure the grenade launchers and machine guns aren't bunched together. Okay, Second Squad lines up along this hedgerow. That way we form an L. We get Charlie coming either way. Third and Fourth squads stay here tonight. I'll lead the ambush myself." He asked if there were questions, but the squad leaders were all experienced, and no one said anything.

"Okay, good enough. We'll move out at midnight or a little after. Make sure you bring enough Claymores. And for Christ's sake don't forget the firing devices. Also, tell every man to carry a couple of grenades. No freeloading. Let's get some kills."

The night turned into the purest earthly black, no stars and no moon. We sat around our foxholes in small groups, some of us muttering that it was bad luck to send out ambushes on nights as dark as this one. Often we had simply faked the whole thing, calling in the ambush coordinates to headquarters and then forgetting it. But Mad Mark apparently wanted to give it a try this time, and there was nothing to do about it. At midnight the squad leaders began moving from foxhole to foxhole, rousing men out. We hung grenades around our belts. We threw our helmets into foxholes—they were a hindrance at night, distorting hearing, too heavy, and, if it came to a fire fight, they made it hard to shoot straight. Instead we put on bush hats or went bareheaded. Every third man picked up a Claymore mine. We wiped dirt off our rifles, took a drink of water, urinated in the weeds, then lay on our backs to wait.

"The wait," Chip murmured. "I hate the wait, seeing it get dark, knowing I got to go out. Don't want to get killed in the dark."

When Mad Mark moved us out of the perimeter and into the darkness, the air was heavy. There were none of the sounds of nature. No birds, no wind, no rain, no grass rustling, no crickets. We moved through the quiet. Metal clanging, canteens bouncing, twigs splintering and hollering out our names, water sloshing, we stepped like giants through the night. Mad Mark stopped us. He spoke to two or three men at a time, and when it was my turn he whispered that we must hold the noise down, that he, at least, didn't want to die that night. It did no good.

Mad Mark led us across a rice paddy and onto a narrow,

winding dirt road. The road circled a village. A dog barked. Voices spoke urgently inside the huts, perhaps parents warning children to stay down, sensing the same certain danger which numbed all twenty of us, the intruders. We circled the village and left it. The dog's barking lasted for twenty minutes, echoing out over the paddies and following us as we closed in on the trail junction.

One of the most persistent and appalling thoughts which lumbers through your mind as you walk through Vietnam at night is the fear of getting lost, of becoming detached from the others, of spending the night alone in that frightening and haunted countryside. It was dark. We walked in a single file, perhaps three yards apart. Mad Mark took us along a crazy, wavering course. We veered off the road, through clumps of trees, through tangles of bamboo and grass, zigzagging through graveyards of dead Vietnamese who lay there under conical mounds of dirt and clay. The man to the front and the man to the rear were the only holds on security and sanity. We followed the man in front like a blind man after his dog, like Dante following Vergil through the Inferno, and we prayed that the man had not lost his way, that he hadn't lost contact with the man to his front. We tensed the muscles around our eyeballs and peered straight ahead. We hurt ourselves staring at the man's back. We strained. We dared not look away for fear the man might fade and dissipate and turn into absent shadow. Sometimes, when the jungle closed in, we reached out to him, touched his shirt.

The man to the front is civilization. He is the United States of America and every friend you have ever known; he is Erik and blond girls and a mother and a father. He is your life, and he is your altar and God combined. And, for the man stumbling along behind you, you alone are his torch.

The pace was leisurely, and the march brought back thoughts of basic training. I thought of the song about the Viet Cong: "Vietnam, Vietnam, every night while your sleepin' Charlie Cong comes a-creepin' all around." I thought of the

Legend of Sleepy Hollow, of imminent violence and impotent, gentle Ichabod Crane wondering which turn of the road, which threatening shadow of a tree, held his nightmare in hiding. I remembered a dream I'd had as a kid, a fourteen-year-old sleeping in southern Minnesota. It was the only dream I have ever remembered in detail. I was in prison. It was somewhere in a very black and evil land. The prison was a hole in a mountain. During the days, swarthy-faced, moustached captors worked us like slaves in coal mines. At night they locked us behind rocks, every prisoner utterly alone. They had whips and guns, and they used them on us at pleasure. The mountain dungeon was musty. Suddenly we were free, escaping, scrambling out of the cave. Searchlights and sirens and machine-gun fire pierced the night, cutting us down. Men were bellowing. It rained. It was a medium drizzle, bringing out a musty smell of sedge and salamanders. I raced through the night, my heart bloated and aching. I fell. Behind me there were torches blazing and the shouts of the swarthy-faced pursuers. I plunged into a forest. I ran and finally came out of the trees and made my way to the top of a mountain. I lay there. The torches and noise and gunfire were gone. I looked into the valley below me, and a carnival was there. A beautiful woman, covered with feathers and tan skin, was charming snakes. With her stick she prodded the creatures, making them dance and writhe and perform. I hollered down to her, "Which way to freedom? Which way home?" She was a mile away, but she lifted her stick and pointed the way down a road. I loved the woman, snakes and stick and tanned skin. I followed the road, the rain became heavier, I whistled and felt happy and in love. The rain stopped. The road opened to a clearing in a dark forest. The woman was there, beads of water scattered on her arms and brown thighs. Her arm was around a swarthy, moustached captor, and she was laughing and pointing her stick at me. The captor embraced her, and together they took me away. Back to prison. That was the dream. I was thinking of that dream as we walked along, finally coming on the trail junction.

Mad Mark dispersed us along the two trails, setting us up in the L-shaped formation he'd mapped out back at camp.

He gave me a Claymore and pointed at a spot along the east-west trail. I felt brave and silly walking out onto the dark road. The deadly device worked just as it had during training. I inserted the blasting cap in a hole on top of the mine. I opened up the mine's little metal legs and plugged them into the dirt, aiming the concave face out toward the middle of the junction. I crept back to the hedgerow, unwinding the wire behind me; then I plugged the wire into its firing device, put the thing on safety, and waited to blow the head off a slinking Asian communist. It would be Ichabod's revenge.

We were paired into ten teams of two men each. One man in each team slept while the other watched the road. An hour on and an hour off until daybreak. My partner was a kid named Reno; that was what everyone called him. His real name was Jim or something. He probably gave himself the name when he came to Nam. He probably chose Reno over such names as Ringo, the Sunset Kid, and Flash. He was a squad leader, and I didn't like him much. He liked his job too well. He gave me his watch, and he rolled onto his back. He pulled his hat down and was asleep. He slept quietly, and that was in his favor, I thought.

Watching the road was not an easy thing. The hedgerow was thick. I tried it on my knees, but that didn't give enough elevation. I tried standing, but there is a certain horrible sensation that comes from standing on your feet on an ambush. Finally I stooped and squatted down. It hurt the thighs, but the road was visible, and it would be difficult to fall asleep that way.

I took hold of the Claymore's firing device, testing its feel. It fit my hand well. I flicked the safety back and forth, making certain it wouldn't jam. I held the thing in my hand for the next hour.

I toyed with my M-16, patting the magazine, rubbing the trigger. There was the fear that none of the machines would work when the moment came. I pictured myself desperately yanking at that trigger, over and over, and nothing would happen except a staccato, metallic clicking sound.

Other thoughts stirred. I peered out at the road, my eyes frozen there but my brain dredging up all sorts of memories and fantasies. I imagined that the twenty of us had suddenly become the objects of this night's hunt, that we were fooling ourselves to think that we remained the hunters, in control of the war and our destinies. There we lay, twenty lonely GI's without our foxholes, without our barbed wire, without a perimeter for protection. All the enemy need do was steal up on our rear. Ten of us were sleeping. The others gazed stupidly in one direction, out at the trail junction, as if the war gods had it arranged that the Viet Cong should trot down before our gunsights like drugged turkeys. I remembered an old Daffy Duck cartoon. A well-equipped hunter—red cap, ten-gauge shotgun, sacked lunch—lies in wait behind an elaborate blind, chortling at the cleverness of his concealment. And all the while ol' Daffy is prancing up from behind the doomed fellow, sledgehammer and sticks of red dynamite at the ready. A whole theater full of preadolescent sadists ripped into piercing, shrill laughter when Daffy sent the incompetent, gaping hunter to Never-Never Land aboard a gratifying, deafening shock wave. I led the laughter. I'd always favored the quarry over the hunter. It seemed only fair.

I glanced backward. Only trees and shadows.

I nudged Reno, gave him the wristwatch, and curled up around my rifle. It was cold. The ground was wet. Reno slapped a mosquito and sat cross-legged, staring dead into a clump of bushes. He was a veteran, I thought. He knew what he was doing. I was thinking about the impossibility of sleeping, thinking that maybe I should have let Reno take more sleep, when I fell into peaceful, heavy rest.

Reno awakened me. My fatigues were drenched, a soggy web of green cloth. It was drizzling and it was cold. I asked Reno for the wristwatch. It was three-ten. Reno had cheated by a few minutes. My sleep should have ended at three-twenty, but he was a squad leader, and there wasn't anything to say about it. He grinned. "Don't get too wet, New Guy," he said, not bothering to whisper. "You catch pneumonia, and we'll have to ship you to the rear. I'll bet you'd hate that." He lit a cigarette, cupping it in his palm. That was stupid and against the rules, but I couldn't decide if it were more cowardly to tell him to put it out, which would have made him chuckle at my jumpiness, or to keep quiet and hope he'd die of lung cancer, which would make me wonder about my courage to act properly. The rain finally put the smoke out, and Reno rolled around on the ground until he was asleep.

I passed the hour counting up the number of days I had left in Vietnam. I figured it out by months, weeks, and hours. I thought about a girl. It was hopeless, of course, but I tried to visualize her face. Only words would come in my mind. One word was "smile," and I tacked on the adjective "intriguing" to make it more personal. I thought of the word "hair," and modified it with the words "thick" and "sandy," not sure if they were very accurate anymore, and then a whole string of words popped in—"mysterious," "Magdalen," "Eternal" as a modifier. I tried fitting the words together into a picture, and I tried closing my eyes, first taking a long look down the road. I tried forcing out the memory of the girl, tried placing her in situations, tried reciting the Auden poem in a very brave whisper. For all this, I could not see her. When I muttered the word "hair," I could see her hair plainly enough. When I said "eyes," I would be looking smack into a set of smiling blue irises, and they were hers, no doubt. But if I uttered the word "face" or tried to squeeze out a picture of the girl herself, all there was to see was the word "face" or the word "eye," printed out before me. It was like asking a computer to see for me. And I was learning that no weight of letters and remembering and wishing and hoping is the same as a touch on temporary, mortgaged lands.

I spent some time thinking about the things I would do after Vietnam and after the first sergeants and rifles were out of my life. I made a long list. I would write about the army. Expose the brutality and injustice and stupidity and arrogance of wars and men who fight in them. Get even with some people. Mark out the evil in my drill sergeants so vividly that they would go to hell lamenting the day they tangled with Private O'Brien. I would expose the carelessness with which people like Reno played with my life. I would crusade against this war, and if, when I was released, I would find other wars, I would work to discover whether they were just and necessary, and if I found they were not, I would have another crusade. I wondered how writers such as Hemingway and Pyle and Jack London could write so accurately and movingly about war without also writing about the rightness of their wars. I remembered one of Hemingway's stories. It was about a battle in World War I, about the hideous deaths of tides of human beings, swarming into the fight, engaging under the sun, and ebbing away again into two piles, friend and foe. I wondered why he did not care to talk about the thoughts those men must have had. Certainly those suffering and scared human beings must have wondered if their cause were worthy. The men in war novels and stories and reportage seem to come off the typewriter as men resigned to bullets and brawn. Hemingway's soldiers especially. They are cynics. Not quite nihilists, of course, for that would doom them in the reader's eye. But what about the people who are persuaded that their battle is not only futile but also dead wrong? What about the conscripted Nazi?

I made plans to travel. I thought of buying or renting a secondhand boat and with six or seven friends sailing the seas

from Australia to Lisbon, then to the Côte d'Azur, Sicily, and
to an island called Paros in the Aegean. Perhaps I might rent a
cottage in Austria, perhaps near a town called Freistadt just
across the Czechoslovakian border. Freistadt would be the
ideal place. The mountains were formidable, the air was clean,
the town had a dry moat around it, the beer was the best in the
world, the girls were not communists, and they had blue eyes
and blond hair and big bosoms. There would be skiing in the
winter and hiking and swimming during the summer. I would
sleep alone when I wanted to, not in a barracks and not along a
trail junction with nineteen GI's.

The thought of Freistadt, Austria, turned me to thinking
about Prague, Czechoslovakia, where I'd spent a summer trying to study. I remembered an evening in July. Drinking beer
with a young Czech student, an economics specialist. Walking
back from the *hostinec,* the fellow pointed out a poster that
covered three square feet on a cement wall. The poster depicted
three terrified Vietnamese girls. They were running from the
bombs of an American B-52 bomber. In the background, a
North Vietnamese antiaircraft gun was spewing the planes with
lines of red fire. A clenched fist in the foreground.

The Czech asked what I thought of it. I told him I was
ambivalent. I didn't know. Perhaps the bombs were falling for
good reason.

He smiled. "I have an invitation to extend, a proposition for
you. If you find it distasteful, just say so, but as an interested
bystander I hope you'll accept. You see, my roommate is from
North Vietnam. He studies economics here at the university. I
wonder if you'd like to talk with him tonight." He chuckled.
"Perhaps you two can negotiate a settlement, who knows."

It was a three-hour conversation. With my Czech friend
helping with the translation, we carried on in French, Czech,
German, and English. The fellow was cordial, a short and reserved man who told me his name was Li and offered me a
seat on his bed. I asked if he thought Americans were evil, and
he thought awhile before he said no. He asked me the same

question and I said no, quickly. I asked if the North Vietnamese were not the aggressors in the war. He laughed and
stated that of course the opposite was the case. They were defending Vietnam from American aggression. I asked if the
North Vietnamese were not sending troops to the South in
order to establish a communist regime in Saigon, and he
laughed again, nervously, and informed me that to speak of a
divided Vietnam was historically and politically incorrect. I
asked Li if he believed that President Johnson was an evil man,
another Hitler. Personally, he said, he didn't believe so.
Johnson was misguided and wrong. But he added that most
North Vietnamese were not so lenient.

"What else can they think when they see your airplanes
killing people? They put the blame on the man who orders the
flights."

We talked about democracy and totalitarianism, and the
fellow argued that the government in Hanoi could be considered a wartime democracy. Stability, he said, was essential.
We argued some about that, and my Czech friend joined in,
taking my side.

When I left him, Li shook my hand and told me he was a
lieutenant in the North Vietnamese Army. He hoped we
would not meet again. That was in 1967.

I roused Reno out for the final watch. It was four-thirty,
and the sky was lighting up and the worst was over. Reno lay
on his back. His eyes were barely slit, and there was no way to
be sure he was awake. I nudged him again, and he told me to
relax and go to sleep. I put the Claymore firing device beside
him, brushed his foot a little as I lay down, and closed my
eyes. I was nearly asleep when I remembered the wristwatch. I
sat up and handed it out toward him. He was wheezing, sound
asleep. I kicked him, and he sat up, lit a cigarette, took the
wristwatch, and sat there in a daze, rocking on his haunches
and staring at his clump of bushes.

An hour later, when Mad Mark hollered at us to saddle up
and move out, Reno was on his stomach and wheezing. He

was a seasoned American soldier, a combat veteran, a squad leader.

Not every ambush was so uneventful. Sometimes we found Charlie, sometimes it was the other way.

In the month of May, we broke camp at three in the morning. Captain Johansen leading three platoons on a ghostly, moonlit march to a village in the vicinity of the My Lai's. Johansen deployed the platoons in a broad circle around the village, forming a loose cordon. The idea was to gun down the Viet Cong as they left the ville before daybreak—intelligence had it that some sort of VC meeting was in progress. If no one exited by daybreak, the Third Platoon would sweep the village, driving the enemy into the rest of us.

Alpha Company pulled it off like professionals.

We were quiet, the cordon was drawn quickly, securely. I carried Captain Johansen's radio, and along with him, an artillery forward observer, and three other RTO's, we grouped along a paddy dike outside the village. Captain Johansen directed things by radio.

In less than an hour the Second Platoon opened up on four VC leaving by a north-south trail. Seconds later, more gunfire. Third Platoon was engaged.

Second Platoon called in again, confirming a kill. The stars were out. The Southern Cross was up there, smiling down on Alpha Company.

The artillery officer got busy, calling back to the rear, preparing the big guns for a turkey shoot, rapidly reading off grid coordinates, excited that we'd finally found the enemy.

Johansen was happy. He'd lost many men to the Forty-eighth Viet Cong Battalion. He was getting his revenge.

Rodríguez, one of the RTO's, suddenly uttered something in Spanish, changed it to English, and pointed out to our front. Three silhouettes were tiptoeing out of the hamlet. They were twenty yards away, crouched over, their shoulders hunched forward.

It was the first and only time I would ever see the living enemy, the men intent on killing me. Johansen whispered, "Aim low—when you miss, it's because you're shooting over the target."

We stood straight up, in a row, as if it were a contest.

I confronted the profile of a human being through my sight. It did not occur to me that a man would die when I pulled the trigger of that rifle.

I neither hated the man nor wanted him dead, but I feared him.

Johansen fired. I fired.

The figures disappeared in the flash of my muzzle. Johansen hollered at us to put our M-16's on automatic, and we sent hundreds of bullets out across the paddy. Someone threw a grenade out at them.

With daybreak, Captain Johansen and the artillery lieutenant walked over and found a man with a bullet hole in his head. There were no weapons. The dead man carried a pouch of papers, some rice, tobacco, canned fish, and he wore a blue-green uniform. That, at least, was Johansen's report. I would not look. I wondered what the other two men, the lucky two, had done after our volley. I wondered if they'd stopped to help the dead man, if they had been angry at his death, or only frightened that they might die. I wondered if the dead man were a relative of the others and, if so, what it must have been to leave him lying in the rice. I hoped the man was not named Li.

Johansen and the lieutenant talked about the mechanics of the ambush. They agreed it had been perfectly executed. They were mildly upset that with such large and well-defined targets we had not done better than one in three. No matter. The platoons had registered other kills. They were talking these matters over, the officers pleased with their success and the rest of us relieved it was over, when my friend Chip and a squad leader named Tom were blown to pieces as they swept the village with the Third Platoon.

That was Alpha Company's most successful ambush.

ODD JOBS

Kent Anderson's excellent novella focuses on the men who had some of the most extravagant, if least known, combat adventures. Those men served in the special-operations group that carried out secret missions into North Vietnam, Cambodia, and Laos. Typically, special-ops types had two or more tours in Vietnam and more than their share of Purple Hearts and valor decorations. Anderson's character sketches may seem overdrawn . . . but they are not.

Kent Anderson

Sympathy for the Devil

A sheet of paper was tacked to the wall over Hanson's bunk:

EVERY DAY IN THE WORLD
100,000 PEOPLE DIE
A HUMAN LIFE MEANS NOTHING

—General Vo Nguyen Giap
Commander in Chief
North Vietnamese Army

IN ORDER TO DESPISE SUFFERING, TO BE AL-
WAYS CONTENT AND NEVER ASTONISHED AT
ANYTHING, ONE MUST REACH SUCH A STATE
AS THIS—AND IVAN DMITRICH INDICATED
THE OBESE PEASANT, BLOATED WITH FAT—

OR ELSE ONE MUST HARDEN ONE'S SELF
THROUGH SUFFERINGS TO SUCH A DEGREE AS
TO LOSE ALL SENSITIVITY TO THEM: THAT IS,
IN OTHER WORDS, CEASE TO LIVE.
                                    —Anton Chekhov

1

Hanson stood just inside the heavy-timbered door of his concrete bunker, looking out. There was no moon yet. The teamhouse was a squat shadow, bigger and darker than the others. The only sound was the steady sobbing of the big diesel generators, but Hanson heard nothing. If the generators ever stopped, he would have heard the silence—a silence that would have bolted him wide awake, armed and out of his bunk.

He stepped from the doorway and began walking across the inner perimeter toward the teamhouse. His web gear, heavy with ammunition and grenades, swung from one shoulder like easy, thoughtful breathing. The folding-stock AK-47 in his right hand was loaded with a gracefully curving 30-round magazine. It looked like a huge science fiction pistol.

As he got closer to the teamhouse he could feel the drums and steel-stringed bass guitar on the back of his sunburned forearms and on the tender broken hump on his nose. Then he could hear it.

Hanson smiled. "Stones," he said softly. He didn't have enough to pick out the song, but the bass and drums were pure Stones.

He slid the heavy lightproof door open, and stepped into the bright teamhouse. Jagger was raving from the big Japanese speakers, "Under my thumb, under my thumb's the squirming dog who's just had her day, under my thumb . . ."

Quinn was pouting and strutting to the music: one hand hooked in his pistol belt, the other hand thrust out, thumb down, like Caesar at the Roman games sending the pike into another crippled loser. His small blue eyes were close-set, cold and flat as the weekly casualty announcement.

Hanson shrugged his web gear to the floor, shouted, "Let me guess," and pressed his hand to his freckled forehead. He pointed at Quinn and shouted, "Mick Jagger, right?" When he raised his arm the snub-nosed combat magnum glinted from its shoulder holster.

Quinn ignored him, pounding the floor like a clog dancer.

The refrigerator looked like a battered white bomb. It was turned up to HIGH in the damp heat, and gouts of frost dropped to the floor when Hanson opened it to get a *Black Label* beer. The seams and lip of the black and red can were rusty from the years it had been stockpiled on the Da Nang docks. Years of raw monsoon and swelling summer heat had turned the American beer bitter. But it was cold, it made his fillings ache when he drank it.

On top of the refrigerator was a flesh-colored quart jar. Hanson screwed off the top and took out two of the green and white amphetamine capsules. He knocked them back with the icy beer.

"Beats coffee for starting your day," he thought, smiling, recalling the double-time marching chant back at Fort Bragg, "Airborne Ranger Green Beret, this is the way we *start our day*," running the sandhills before dawn. Rumor had it that one team had run over a PFC from a supply unit who had been drunkenly crossing the road in front of them. The team had trampled him and left him behind, never falling out of step, chanting each time their left jump boots hit the ground, "*Pray* for war, *pray* for war, *pray* for war."

He sat down on one of the footlockers and began paging through the *Time* magazine that had come in on the last mail chopper.

The Stones finished "Under My Thumb," paused, and began "Mother's Little Helper." Quinn turned the volume down and walked over to Hanson. Quinn moved with an ominous deliberation, like a man carrying nitroglycerin. People got uncomfortable when he moved too close or too quickly.

"Keepin' up with current events, my man?" he asked Hanson. "How's the war going?"

"This magazine says we're kicking shit out of 'em," Hanson said, tapping the open magazine. "But now, what about the home front. Here's this young man, a 'Cornell Senior' it says here. 'I'm nervous as hell. I finally decided on a field—economics—and then I find out I'm number 59 on the draft lottery.' Huh now? Just when he decided on economics."

Hanson kept thumbing through the magazine, singing softly, "Mah candy man, he's come an' gone. Mah candy man, he's come an' gone. An' I love ever' thing in this godomighty worl', GOD knows I do . . ."

To the west a heavy machine gun was firing, the distant pounding as monotonous as an assembly-line machine. Artillery was going in up north. Three guns working out. They were good, the rounds going in one on top of the other, each explosion like a quick violent wind, the sound your fire starter makes when you touch off the backyard charcoal grill. Normal night sounds.

Hanson read the ads outloud. "'There's a Ford in your *future*.' 'Tired of diet plans that don't work? . . .'"

Quinn interrupted, "Then come to Vietnam, you fat fuck, and get twenty pounds blown off your ass."

A short, wiry man came into the teamhouse. He wore round wire-rimmed glasses and looked like Wally Cox.

"Silver," Hanson yelled to him. He almost said, "How much weight did you lose on the Vietnam Diet Plan," but changed his mind. Silver had lost half his team and his partner was in Japan with no legs. Instead, Hanson asked him, "How's the hole in your ass?"

Silver couldn't talk without moving, gesturing, ducking and jabbing like a boxer. He talked fast and when he laughed it was a grunt, like he'd just taken a jab in the chest. "I like it a lot," he said. "Thinking about getting one on the other side, asshole. Symmetry, you know? Dimples. A more coordinated limp."

"How much longer you gonna be on stand-down, you skinny little gimp?" Quinn asked him.

"Couple weeks. I'll fake it a little longer if I have to. Captain says he's gonna try and get Anadon up here from the C team for my partner. I don't want to go out with some new guy."

"Candy man, he been gone. Well I wish I was down in New Orleans, God knows I do. An' look here," Hanson said, holding up the magazine. "President visiting the troops."

Silver limped slightly as he walked over. He looked at the two-page color spread. "Shit," he said, then laughed. "I was there. After they fixed me up but before they said I could come back here. The *troops* down there. Spent three weeks building wooden catwalks around the guns so the Prez wouldn't get his feet muddy. 'Course they weren't able to use the guns for fire missions all that time. They issued the troops brand new starched fatigues an hour before he was due, and made 'em stand around like at parade rest so they wouldn't get wrinkled.

"So the Prez gets there . . ."

Silver went over to the icebox and got a Coke and put a mark next to his name on the beer and pop tab on the wall. He pulled the poptop off, put it on his little finger like a ring, and took a long drink.

"The Prez gets there, and they start processing the troops past him, and he like asks 'em: 'Hi, son, and where are you from?'

"The troop says, 'Uh . . . Waseca. Minnesota, sir.'

"The Prez says, 'Beautiful state, Minnesota. They've got a fine football team at the University there, too.'

"I'm hearing all this on the P.A. system they got. They'd kind of put me and some of the other people out of sight. I wasn't looking too good."

Silver glanced down at his baggy fatigues, "You know, at

best I don't look like a model soldier. Anyway, the Prez gives the guy a big handshake and says, 'I just wanted to personally let you know, private uh . . .'

"'Private schmuck, Sir,' this fuckin' cannon loader says and turns so the Prez can see his name tag but there ain't no name tag 'cause somebody forgot to put out the word that name tags had to be sewn on the new fatigues. Some supply officer's military career is *over*.

"So the Prez says, 'I'm here, Private Schmuck, because I wanted to let you boys know . . .'"

Silver laughed his tight laugh. "Huh. Bunch of brothers standing near me. Go into the routine."

He pulled himself up tight and began strutting and jabbing his finger at the floor, talking angrily to himself. "Boy? You *Boys*? Fool up there best not be talkin' 'bout *boys*, one of the brothers up there. That's the motherfuckin' truth, that ain't no boolshit. *Say*. Gimme some of that power now."

Silver took a sip of Coke and went on in his normal voice, "The brothers started doing the power handshake and all the white boys started moving away. So the Prez shakes some more hands, gives out a few medals, and says what a fine job we're doing, and that he, *your President*, was doing everything he could to get us boys home. Then he climbs in his chopper and flies away, all the officers up there kind of crouching at attention, trying to hold their hats on in the rotor blast."

"And you sat through the whole thing," Quinn said. "You enjoy the show that much?"

"I was afraid to leave. I was afraid to *move*. I'm glad I didn't have to shake hands with that fucker. I didn't want to get within 100 feet of him. That was Mr. *Death* standing up there shaking hands. They had gunships flying patterns I couldn't fuckin' believe. Then you got MPs all over, trying to look sharp, nervous and trigger-happy as hell. And then these *guys*. All around the Prez. Skin-head haircuts, mirror shades so you can't see their eyes. They didn't look . . . rational, you know? And they were all packing Uzis on assault slings under their coats. Anything move too fast or the wrong way, it would've got shot 800 times. Half the camp would've got wiped out. Like a bunch of ARVNs in a fire fight, shooting at everything."

Silver looked at the wristwatch hanging through the buttonhole of his breast pocket. "Better get down and take the radio watch," he said. "End of the month. Gonna be clearing artillery grids all night. They gotta blow up what's left of the old monthly allotment or next month's allotment will be smaller. That's logical, right. The US Army is logical. It's a logical war.

"Hey, you want anything blown up? Fifth Mech's set up a new firebase. 'Firebase Flora' in honor of the commander's wife. Got everything, 155s, 175s, eight inch. Want me to have them plow the ground for you?"

"How about that ridge?" Hanson said.

Quinn nodded.

"You know the one," Hanson said, "'bout eight clicks north."

"The one where Charles ate up that company of dumbass 5th Mech?"

"Yeah. Might as well put a little shit on that. South side, kinda walk it from the valley halfway up the side. We'll probably be over that way in the morning."

"OK," Silver said, "you fuckers watch your ass over there. Charles has got you by the balls when he gets you in Cambodia. I fuckin' know."

Silver went down into the underground, concrete-reinforced radio bunker and relieved Vyers. He sat at a small desk surrounded on three sides by banks of radios, some of them as big as filing cabinets. They all hummed slightly, each at a different pitch, radiating heat like a closed oven door.

Silver spent his first few minutes studying call signs, code names for different units, and firebases. The call signs were composed by computer each month and changed in an attempt to confuse the enemy about what name a unit went by. Call signs were two words, such as "inside packs," "formal granite," or "recent voice." At times the random combinations sounded ominous and units were glad when they were changed.

His glasses flashing in the dim yellow and blue dial lights, Silver looked demonic, his face the color of someone already dead.

Mr. Minh walked into the teamhouse, smiling. All his teeth had been filed to points, as was the custom of the Rhade Montagnard tribes, but his were capped in gold with jade inlays the shapes of stars and crescent moons. He was the Montagnard team leader. The gold and jade caps were a sign of wealth and respect. And they were part of his magic. He had high cheekbones and quick black eyes bright with pride and courage. His shoulder-length black hair was tied back with a piece of green parachute nylon. He was wearing striped tiger fatigues, and his web gear was hung with grenades and ammo pouches.

Mr. Minh wore a small amulet, a *Katha,* around his neck. Chicken man had made it for him. It protected his body from bullets. Once Hanson had asked him, "Mr. Minh, I have seen Rhade KIA and they were wearing Kathas, how could that be?"

Mr. Minh thought a moment, shrugged, and said, "Bad Katha." Mr. Minh knew that he would die some day, and he had no fear of death. If he lived well and fought bravely, he would be reborn as a hawk, or a hill spirit, or a tiger. All life was the same. Death meant nothing.

"We are ready, Sar," Mr. Minh said to Hanson in his soft hill tribesman's voice.

"OK, Mr. Minh. Maybe ten minutes."

When he went back out the door, Hanson could see the shadows of the three other stocky "Yards." Their foreheads and weapons flickered in the starlight like a school of piranha in the dark river.

Quinn was checking his gear. Hanson began a last-minute equipment check, more a confidence ritual than anything else. He'd gone through his AK-47 the day before, checking for worn or broken parts while cleaning it, then test-fired one clip. He carried the Communist weapon instead of the standard American M-16 because the sound of the AK-47 would not give away his position, and the NVA could not be sure he was an American. The M-16 fired red tracer rounds while the AK-47 fired green, and if they made contact at night the tracer rounds would pinpoint him. On the illegal-cross border operations all equipment was "sanitized." No insignia was worn and all weapons and equipment were of foreign manufacture, most of it acquired from the big CIA warehouse in Da Nang. If they were killed on the wrong side of the border, the North Vietnamese could not "prove" they were Americans.

Their web gear looked much like a parachute harness. Wide suspenders hooked into a heavy brass-grommeted pistol belt. Two pieces of nylon webbing ran from the front of the pistol belt through the inside of the thighs to the back of the pistol belt. Thirty pounds of weapons and equipment were hung and taped to the web gear.

Two snap links were attached to the suspenders at the shoulders. A helicopter could hover 120 feet in the air, drop nylon lines to attach to the snap links and pull you out, leaving your hands free to fire or drop grenades. They could pull you out even if you were wounded and unconscious. Even if you were dead.

The ammo clips were jammed in the pouches with the bullets facing away from the body in case an enemy bullet detonated them. At the bottom of each pouch there was a plastic-covered pressure bandage. Printed in red on the plastic, a cartoon sequence showed how to unwrap the bandage and apply it. When unfolded the bandage was the size and thickness of a paperback book. The words OTHER SIDE AGAINST WOUND were printed in large red letters, like a title, on the back.

Hanson wore a small survival compass around his neck like

a crucifix. In one thigh pocket, wrapped in plastic, having curved to the shape of his thigh, was a 30-year-old copy of *The Oxford Book of English Verse.*

Hanson pulled a small tin whistle out of his pack, and played a verse of "Molly McGee." He put the whistle to his eye and sighted down it, aiming at Quinn.

"Do you know," he said, "that they have whole tin whistle*bands* in Ireland, whole grade schools all playing tin whistles. Maybe I'll go to Ireland when they decide to stop the war."

Quinn threw on his pack. "I'm going back to Iowa. One of these days they're gonna decide they've had enough and some General is gonna say, 'Well, looks like we've won. Let's go home.'"

Quinn carried a crude-looking weapon that seemed to be made of sheet metal and steel tubing. In his huge hand it looked like a cheap child's toy. It was a Swedish submachine gun with a built-in silencer. Quinn had glued felt to the face of the bolt to muffle the clicking of the firing mechanism. It could kill at 100 yards, the bursts of fire sounding like someone absently thumbing a deck of cards.

Hanson threw on his forty-pound pack, picked up the AK and tromped to the refrigerator. He dropped another cap of speed in his breast pocket and stuck a Coke in his pack.

As they went out the door Jagger was singing "Paint It Black."

The five dark forms crossed through the outer perimeter and headed west. Another heavy machine gun opened up in the distance, and the big red tracers floated gracefully, like glowing golf balls, across the sky. Scores of them hit a hillside and rebounded in random patterns.

Artillery rounds blinked silver and yellow and bluish-white against the mountains.

Hanson watched them, his eyes slightly dilated. "God *damn,* Quinn," he said, "it's always springtime in Vietnam."

Before dawn, they would be across the border.

Most of the NCO clubs in Vietnam had plywood walls and a sheet-metal roof that kept out the rain, but not the heat or the stink of the piss-tubes out back.

The Special Forces NCO club looked like one wing of an exclusive mountain resort. The walls were stone. The bar was stone and hand-carved mahogany, and the big mirror was tinted a pleasant cool green. A huge green beret was set in the flagstone floor in thick glass bricks, the Special Forces crest was inset in chrome and brass. The club was air-conditioned, the Vietnamese barmaids were pretty, and Chivas was 30¢ a shot.

The SKS mounted over the bar had been captured by Quinn and Hanson and traded for two pallets of beer for the camp. The SKS had belonged to a survivor of an ambush, a ragged straggler who wasn't in the killing zone when the ambush was sprung. Hanson and Quinn went after him. Hanson threw himself onto his stomach, braced his weapon and fired two bursts. One round from the first burst tore the straggler's calf and he stumbled. Hanson walked the second burst diagonally from hip to shoulder, and the soldier slammed into the ground face first, bucking like a stunned carp. Hanson ripped another burst across his back to make sure that he was dead, then kicked him over like a rotten log that might have thousands of blind white bugs under it. There was an SKS under him, an obsolete and rare rifle worth 400 dollars as a trophy.

"Food on the *table*," Hanson said.

"Yeah," Quinn said, "and you almost fucked it up."

"What?"

"That's right. Shootin' him up like that. Look."

The last burst of brass-jacketed bullets had gone through the body and torn a furrow through bloody gray-green grass and sunbaked clay that lay in little piles like bleeding chips of flint.

"A little lower," Quinn said, "and you'd have hit the SKS. Shoulda shot him in the head."

"You're right," Hanson said, "you're right. They always give the SKS to the fuckups like him. Anybody worth a damn would have an AK. You're right. It's like Asian wood lore."

Hanson put a fresh clip in his weapon. He slung the SKS over his shoulder and started to walk off. He stopped and looked in the dead man's face. Already he was starting to look like all the others. His eyes were gluey and flat, the tiny wrinkles and lines that had made his face different from everyone else's were beginning to soften and fade.

"All you dead people look alike," Hanson said to the body, "but you don't have to worry about being slow or fucking up anymore." He smiled, shook his head, and walked off.

Hanson and Quinn often went after trophies when they weren't on recon. They'd take half the combat recon platoon, all Montagnards and Nungs, the best soldiers in the hatchet team, on ambushes and sweeps. The sweeps through enemy-controlled areas—everything outside the camp wire—were officially called "search and destroy" operations in the beginning. But when the American public began seeing nightly TV film footage of dead Asians and Americans they began to consider the implications of words like "destroy."

The army changed the name of the operations to "search and *clear*." Most search and clear operations took place in free-fire zones, large areas of countryside where every living thing was considered an enemy (enemy soldier), enemy supporter (enemy farmer), or enemy asset (enemy buffalo, enemy rice). It was OK to kill anything that moved in a free-fire zone. Hanson and Quinn didn't like to kill the water buffalo; it took them so long to die and they moaned so, but the Nungs liked to and it was good to keep the Nungs happy and mean. Everyone was afraid of the Nungs.

In a free-fire zone you didn't have to wait a fatal second deciding if it was a farmer, buffalo, or armed enemy breaking through the bush.

As TV coverage of the war increased, the army changed the name of free-fire zones to "*safe* zones."

One day while stripping ambush victims of trophies Hanson remembered his Asian wood lore, the SKS rule. There was a single shot, and Quinn felt a chubby hand pat his foot. He looked down at the flap of brain stuck to his boot, then thrust his foot out and studied it like the ugliest girl in Iowa coyly looking at her new party shoe. With a scholarly frown he said, "Humm. I wonder what he's thinking about right now."

"That's a Nine-O . . . Nine O. At *least*. Very nice. Performance *and* degree of difficulty," Hanson said.

Quinn beamed.

While the recon platoon set up a defensive perimeter, Hanson, Quinn, and Silver would go among the dead, rolling the bodies over, cursing some and praising others for their clothes and equipment.

An officer's pith helmet with an enameled red star was a 50-dollar item. An officer's belt buckle, recycled aluminum from American bombs with an enameled red star, would go for 75 dollars. A buckle without the star was worth half that. They had to fill in with Montagnard crossbows, plain pith helmets, jungle hats, and the NVA battle flags that Co Ba and her daughter made.

There were occasional novelty items. Hanson once found a Red Chinese copy of a Scripto fountain pen on a dead lieutenant. It had the word SCRIPTO on the nib. The engraving on the side exhorted the dead 2d Lt. to STEADFASTLY ATTACK AND DESTROY ALL AMERICAN IMPERIALISTS.

Hanson studied the engraving and pictured the engraver working on the pen, worrying that he would not have room to get the last word on the pen that was to be a gift to the young officer from his parents, thinking how wrong and terribly important even little things often seemed.

Cheaper items like plain pith helmets brought *much* more money if you shot a hole in them and sprinkled them with some chicken blood, but it wasn't wise to do that too often. Not that it mattered so much that the buyer might suspect that it wasn't human blood—an authentic result of a soldier having his head blown open—it was simply a matter of economics. Too many of them on the market would lower the price.

It was almost five and the bar was filling up. Janis Joplin was wailing from the jukebox, "So comeoncomeonCOMEON-COMEON an' TAKE IT, YEOW! if it makesyoufeelgood . . ."

Only two soldiers in the bar were wearing camouflage fatigues. They had gotten off a chopper from the north only ten minutes before. Standing together at the slate-topped bar they looked like two reflections of the same soldier. The baggy jungle fatigues were mottled and striped to blend with the jungle, the dead browns and greens of healing bruises or of a body left too long in the sun. The backs of their hands were crosshatched with small scars and blood-crusted welts. The fine blond hair on the backs of their hands and wrists had been burned to brown stubble over hurried cookfires. They both had an easy, tireless concentration.

But they were not at all alike.

Quinn was much bigger than Hanson. He was bigger than anyone else in the bar. His features were as small and blunt as his eyes. It was a face that could take a lot of damage and still function. He rarely smiled. When he did smile it was not a comforting expression.

He'd been a linebacker in college until he'd gotten into a fight. During the fight the crowd that had gathered, laughing, shouting, and making bets, slowly quieted as Quinn worked with the same cold rage that filled him when he chopped wood, or stacked bales of hay on his father's farm, that drove him to study the textbooks full of useless facts that got him off the farm and into college where five afternoons a week and every Saturday he would trade blow for blow with others like himself for the entertainment of the same people who were silently watching him outside the bar.

Quinn had stepped back, letting the semiconscious man fall

to the ground, kicked him once, viciously, in the ribs, and walked away.

"That was the night," Quinn had told Hanson, "I realized I'd been doing shit I hated all my life. I hated the farm, I hated those goddamn books, and I hated football. I didn't want to tackle those motherfuckers, I wanted to kill 'em. Of course, three months later, three months after I stopped hurting quarterbacks and ends as bad as I could—blindsiding running backs right out of the game, while those college wimps up in the stands held their weenies, and their beer, and their date's tit— three months later the army had my ass."

Quinn smiled when he told that story.

Quinn finished his Budweiser and looked at Hanson in the big bar mirror. "You'll be back . . .," he began.

"Do me a favor. Shoot me in the head when I step off the plane, OK? Save me the trouble of humpin' waiting for Charles to do it."

"You'll be back. You know those killer guard-dogs the zoomies use to guard their airplanes 'cause the dogs are smarter and meaner than their handlers? They don't let those dogs go back to the States, they just blow 'em away when they're through with them 'cause they're just too . . ."

"Not bad, Quinn. A nice little analogy there. You have the makings of a poet. I don't read much poetry. It's mostly written by women and queers, and doesn't make much sense. I think *you've* got what it takes."

Hanson smiled a lot. He often seemed to be debating something with himself, nodding his head, narrowing his eyes, smiling. At a glance, his eyes seemed full of humor, and they were. But with a depth of humor that went on and on and got blacker and darker until after that glance it was like peering down into an abandoned well and feeling the edge begin to crumble beneath your feet.

Hanson wasn't quite average height. He wasn't exceptionally strong or fast with his hands, but he adapted quickly and learned fast—as some animals do, while others die out in a world where there are people who will hurt you and kill you for no reason at all.

One night in Fayetteville a good ole boy threw Hanson into a jukebox. He had 60 pounds on Hanson and threw him *into* it. Hanson was wedged into the chrome, plastic, and shattered glass, and for just a second he almost laughed, thinking that it was like being in a traffic accident—the Dolly Parton that silenced Dolly in mid-song.

Then he pulled himself out of the wreckage, stacks of C&W 45s clattering behind him, wheeling away across the dance floor. Hanson started for the good old boy, trailing shards of red and blue plastic like sparklers.

The good old boy lost the fight right then. Not when Hanson, head down, was pumping quick lefts and rights into his belly and kidneys leftrightleft like a machine. Not when he hit the floor like a bag of brixment. It wasn't even when Hanson started putting the boots to him, playing a tune on his ribs.

It was when he saw Hanson pry himself out of the jukebox. When he realized that the only way he could stop that little som-bitch was to kill him, and that that little fucker didn't care about a thing in the world except kicking his 210 pound peckerwood ass. It was then that his guts went flabby, and he just gave up and waited for it to happen and get it over with.

The way Hanson walked, a cross between a bounce and a swagger, made him look cocky. He wasn't able to change the way he walked, and he discovered in basic training that he couldn't march.

His drill sergeant would scream, "HANSON, QUIT BOUNCIN' AN' MARCH. YOU FUCKIN' UP MY MILITARY FORMATION." Then he'd come up close to Hanson, who continued to march and stare straight ahead, and ask him in a gentle, fatherly voice, "Don't you like me, Hanson? Is that it? Is that why you messin' up my military formation? Sergeant Collins told me that my formation looks ragged and poor. It hurts my feelings when he says that. Is that why, Hanson? Don't you *like* me?

"I ASKED YOU A QUESTION, HANSON. DO YOU LIKE ME?"

"YES, DRILL SERGEANT. I'M VERY FOND OF YOU. I LIKE EVERYTHING ABOUT THE ARMY."

"YOU LIKE ME? YOU SOME KIND OF FAGGOT? YOU WANTA SMOKE MY POLE?"

"NO, DRILL SERGEANT."

"NO?" the drill sergeant would scream, double-timing next to Hanson, his face close to Hanson's. "NO? I DON'T LIKE YOU, HANSON. I DON'T LIKE COLLEGE BOYS. THEY SO SMART THEY CAN'T DO ANYTHING. WHAT CAN YOU DO, HANSON?"

Hanson smiled. "PUSH-UPS, DRILL SERGEANT."

"THAT'S RIGHT. THAT'S EXACTLY RIGHT. GET YOUR ASS OUT HERE AND DROP FOR FIFTY AN' I WANTA HEAR YOU SOUND OFF LIKE YOU GOT A PAIR."

Hanson would drop out of the formation and do fifty push-ups, sounding off like he had a pair with each one, "ONE THOUSAND, TWO THOUSAND, THREE THOUSAND . . ."

If Hanson smiled when the drill sergeant screamed at him, he'd be accused of thinking it was funny to fuck up the formation, and do 50 push-ups. If he tried not to bounce, he looked worse and the drill sergeant would say that he looked like a monkey trying to fuck a football, or that he marched like he had a Baby Ruth bar up his ass, and he'd do 50 push-ups.

For eight weeks he did at least 100 push-ups a day. At the end of the eight weeks he was the only man in the company who was given PFC stripes. When he was getting on the bus for infantry training, the drill sergeant told him, "Don't get your ass blown away, Hanson."

Hanson smiled. "OK, Drill Sergeant."

After infantry training, airborne training, and Special Forces School, he'd spent 18 months in Northern I-corps pulling long-range and cross-border recon missions without getting his ass blown away. He still smiled a lot at things that didn't seem funny to most people. He was still alive. In two days he would be on his way home.

Sergeant Major Crews ignored the air policeman posted at the hurricane fence. The AP's job was to demand that you produce ID, that you state your business, then write it down in a log book before he motioned you through with his M-16. He was supposed to challenge everyone who entered the air base, even people who worked there, people he knew, even generals. Especially generals, who would demote him and probably put him in the stockade for not challenging the shiny Cadillac with the red stars on the bumper.

The AP didn't know Sergeant Major, and he didn't challenge him. He looked away and pretended not to see him, like someone who has wandered into a tough neighborhood pretends not to notice the stares or hear the insults, walking stiffly, eyes straight ahead.

Sergeant Major Crews was not really a sergeant major, E-9. He was an E-7. People called him Sergeant Major because that had been his rank before they busted him down to buck sergeant. The reason for his demotion was officially recorded as "conduct unbecoming a senior NCO." The real reason was classified. The real reason was never recorded. A number of ranking army officers had wanted to bust him out of the army and put him in Leavenworth, but the CIA had told them that a court martial would be "embarrassing" for everyone, and that it would be best just to "let it alone." Sergeant Major had agreed to accept the demotion quietly. It was a formality that cut his pay check but not his power. His status as Sergeant Major was affected very little. He knew too much.

Sergeant Major had done three tours in S.E. Asia that were recorded in his Army 201 file. He had done two other Asian tours that were not recorded in any army files. His 201 file showed that he had been in Okinawa during those periods.

He had a slight southern accent that was very pleasant. No

one had ever heard him raise his voice above the level of polite conversation, even in a fire fight. In combat he used hand signals to direct his Chinese Nung squad leaders.

There was a knotted rope of scar around Sergeant Major's ankles, like someone who has worn leg irons for years on a chain gang. All the old S.E. Asia hands had the ankle scars. They were from the leeches.

Inside the air force base was the headquarters of the NCO in charge of routing supplies from the giant Da Nang warehouse complex to smaller camps in I-corps. The NCO saw that food and supplies were loaded on the cargo planes, inventoried, and balanced out in the books. The officers and enlisted men who worked with him stayed only one year, then were replaced by others interested only in doing *their* year and going home.

The Senior Supply NCO was big and smart and ruthless. He had been in Vietnam for four years in charge of supply. Each year's new batch of supply personnel knew only what the Senior NCO wanted them to know. As long as they cooperated with him, they had a pleasant year away from the fighting. But if anyone began checking manifests too closely, or asking too many questions, life became difficult for them; their inventory began coming up short, their civilian labor force began breaking or misrouting things, or not showing up for work. As a result, they were not promoted, and they were sent home with bad efficiency reports.

The Senior Supply NCO had highly placed Vietnamese friends who owed him favors. He had large bank accounts in several states back home.

His office was an olive drab mobile home. Inside, it looked like that office tucked way back on the two-acre lot of gleaming single-wides and wood-grain and chrome double-wides, the office where you take the wife to close the deal. It was air-conditioned, carpeted, and richly furnished. The handsome walnut liquor cabinet had been manifested for a major general in 1966, but had been misrouted, along with the sectional sofa.

The Supply NCO had a pretty Vietnamese secretary. She was more than pretty, she was perfect. Like a doll. He had paid for the operation that had removed the Oriental eye-folds so she would look more American, a "round eye." He had sent her to Japan to get the silicone injections in her breasts. She was wearing a mini-skirt and spike heels that had been ordered from Los Angeles.

"Sergeant Major," the Supply NCO said, with the warmth of a successful businessman, "welcome to my hootch. Come on in," he said as Sergeant Major walked on in.

"Thought I'd stop by to settle our account and see if the beer is ready to go. I'm going up north in the morning and I won't get back down this way for a while."

Sergeant Major had ordered two pallets of beer for the launch site. Two pallets was roughly 30 times the amount authorized for the camp, but the beer had been "diverted from normal channels" and on one of the thousands of yellowing supply records the number 897 had been changed to 895. The two pallets of beer no longer existed.

"On the dock and loaded up," the Supply Sergeant said, "I got a pilot who's gonna make a 'detour' on his way to Quang Tri. Hell of a detour," he laughed, "but I've got his flight time and fuel records covered."

"Real fine," Sergeant Major said. He pulled an envelope out of the fatigue pocket that had the master parachutist wings and the combat infantryman's badge with two stars sewn on it. "That was two-forty, American," he said, counting out the bills.

"I believe we were looking at two seventy-five, Sergeant Major."

"No, it was two-forty," he said without looking up, still counting out tens and twenties.

"Why don't we check the books. Sugar . . ." he called to his secretary.

"I don't have to look at the books. I know what the *books* will show."

"What is it you're trying to say . . . Crews?"

"I'm not *trying* to say anything," he smiled, "I can usually get my meaning across without too much effort. I'm saying that it's two-forty."

The roar of cargo planes, helicopters, and Phantom jets surrounded the mobile home like rush hour traffic on a freeway.

"Sergeant *Major.* Thirty-five dollars. We've done a lot of business together. I wouldn't care one way or the other, but it's gonna throw my books off."

"It isn't much money, is it? Thirty-five dollars." He pushed a stack of money across the table. "Here's the two-forty, and," he said, counting off a smaller stack of bills, "here's the thirty-five. Now if I pay you what *you* think is the fair and honest price, is that beer going to be at my camp *tomorrow?* I wouldn't want to have to come back down here to see you."

"It'll be there."

"Good." Sergeant Major smiled. He tapped the smaller stack of bills. "Now if you think that that money belongs to you, just pick it up."

Sergeant Major's eyes seemed to be focused at some middle distance, as though he was mildly interested in something terrible that was about to happen at the far end of a city block.

The Supply Sergeant had begun to reach for the money when he saw whatever it was at the end of that block. His hand stopped, and he pulled it back very slowly, like he'd made a mistake and had reached into the wrong cage, the one where they keep the mean little animal with all the teeth.

"In any event," Sergeant Major continued, "I'll see you next time I'm in Da Nang, and we can do business as we always have, can't we."

"Of course, Sergeant Major."

"Fine. Why, look at the money still here. It must be mine."

He picked the money up. "See you next time then. *Chao Co,*" he said to the secretary.

Besides being big and smart and ruthless like the Supply Sergeant, Sergeant Major had the reputation of being a little crazy. He didn't mind that at all. He even did things to keep the rumor alive, like the time he'd cut the liver out of an NVA captain he'd killed, cut it in five pieces and shared it with his five Nungs, eating it raw, the blood dripping down their chins.

"It's all theater," he'd told Hanson. "It's good to have people think you're crazy. Even if they've heard you *might* be crazy, that's enough. They're going to be afraid of you, because crazy people aren't predictable. It's dangerous to try and second-guess them, because you can never tell which way they might jump. Or how hard."

Sergeant Major liked Hanson. He'd taught him a lot about staying alive in 18 months. Hanson loved him like a father. And Sergeant Major wasn't *really* crazy. As long as there was a war.

There was a screech behind Hanson and Quinn. They spun around, Hanson going for the shoulder holster.

Sergeant Siebert's monkey was drunk. He was strutting on top of Sergeant Siebert's table in the bar, his arms raised like a furry little acid-rock singer, shouting, "Awright! Tha'sright! Le's get it *on* now, *one time!*"

In one of his delicate monkey fists he clutched a french fried potato, in the other a rubbery red Penrose hot sausage. He was wearing diapers. It was a club rule that monkeys had to be diapered or they would not be admitted. The club had few rules and they were all reasonable.

"Hey, Sergeant Siebert," Hanson asked, "how's the new monkey working out? We heard that the other one crashed and burned."

"Yeah, too bad. Furry little fucker just couldn't get the hang of maintaining altitude. Kept a glide angle of just about dead vertical all the way down."

Sergeant Siebert's other monkey masturbated whenever it got excited, whenever it got mad, or hungry, or frightened. All the time. Sergeant Siebert's "A" team wouldn't have minded an occasional hand job, but the monkey did it all the time. It was like having a pervert in camp.

The monkey would grab something solid with his left hand—a chair leg or an engineer stake—and jerk against it like a straphanger on a lurching bus, while he pounded away with the other hand, shrieking tirelessly. The "A" team built a wire cage where they could give him a chicken to fuck once a week, like some of the other camps, but he ignored the chicken, grabbed the wire, and began to rock and shriek. It was not considered manly for a Special Forces mascot monkey to jack off when he had chicken pussy available. It was considered even less manly to pull its pud out of fear, but the pleasant flutter of incoming mortar rounds always aroused him.

Sergeant Siebert had the monkey with him one day in a C-130 full of supplies for the camp. He was in the cargo plane's tail section with the supply bundles that were draped with huge blue and green cargo chutes. He was the "bundle kicker" and wore earphones so the pilot could tell him when they were close to the drop zone.

The four big engines were roaring as the plane went into a steep dive to avoid ground fire, and then leveled off at 400 feet to hit the small DZ. The slanted tail of the plane cracked, then slowly opened downward with hydraulic whines and groans, filling with dark green jungle.

Sergeant Siebert knelt by the shining caster tracks watching the small red light, waiting for it to blink out and for the one next to it to flash green. He didn't see the monkey above him jerking wildly at a piece of nylon strapping, his little monkey eyes full of fear, looking out the wind-roaring open tail.

The light flashed green, the plane went into a steep climb,

and Sergeant Siebert started rolling out the food pallets and rope-handled ammo crates, static lines snapping past where they caught, and snatched each chute open.

Then, as he later phrased it in his southern accent, "It felt just like somebody had hawked him up a big goober and spit it on my neck."

Without missing a bundle, he grabbed a handful of fur and side-armed the convulsive monkey out the tail.

"Last I saw of him, the little sombitch was still whackin' it, getting smaller and smaller."

The new monkey was sitting on the table looking mournfully between his knees like a drunken little king, holding the french fry and sausage like scepters of his authority. He pitched forward and the sausage skittered across the table.

"God damn," Sergeant Siebert said sadly, "an' this little dude can't hold his liquor."

He sat back in his chair and looked at his drink. "I think we're gonna have to have a team meeting back at camp and decide on a new kind of animal for a mascot."

Sergeant Major strode into the club. He was wearing what he called his "fancy fatigues," the ones with all the patches. He wore them because headquarters regulations required that "all unit and award insignia *will* be properly displayed on the class uniform appropriate for them." Sergeant Major and the other old hands referred to the patches, and wings, and insignia as "trash" because they all had them. He was uncomfortable wearing them off the Special Forces compound because they attracted attention, and Sergeant Major had spent 25 years learning not to attract attention. At the launch site he wore camouflage fatigues without any insignia. All equipment at the launch site was "sterile," it could not be officially traced back to the U.S.

"Sergeant Major," Quinn called, "step on over and let young Sergeant Hanson buy you a drink. He's buyin' for all of us today."

"Well, now, I'll do that. Make mine a Bushmill."

They took their drinks to a table, and Sergeant Major said, "Ah, trooper Hanson, you wouldn't listen. Giving up the military for a world of slack-jawed out-of-step civilians who have absolutely *no* supervision. They're going to be everywhere, and they can't even cross a street without having a light flash on telling them to 'walk.'"

He took a sip of Bushmill, looked at Hanson, and said, "And here I had plans to mold you in my own image."

They sipped their drinks for a moment, then Quinn slapped his hand against the back of Hanson's chair and said, "And who's gonna be the camp intellectual when you're gone?"

Hanson grinned. "Lieutenant Farr. He outranks me, and he has superior intellectual credentials as well. The man has a master's degree, Quinn."

Quinn laughed. "Farr pulled rank on him once because he was losing an argument in front of the captain. They were arguing about Farr's—what's that fuckin' thing, my man?"

"Thesis," Hanson said.

"Yeah. Thesis. Farr's own specialty. He was goin' down the tube in front of the captain, and he had to pull rank to keep from lookin' like the dud he is. What was that argument about, anyway?"

"I don't know," Hanson said. "I didn't know what he was talking about. Some kind of Sociology, I think. *One* of them 'Ology's.' Psychology, Criminology, one of those. It's a good deal, you get to be an expert on something without ever having to do it. The Ology field is wide open—Warology, an exciting old field of scholarship combined with stimulating new methodology. Peaceology can be taken before *or* after warology in the intensive humanities interdisciplinary program. A lot of specialties there. Bulletology, gunology, computer body-count readout. Dead-gookology—there is a language requirement there—but dead *grunt*ology is a similarly structured program and requires only a minimum GRE score plus three letters of introduction and a sincere interest in the field."

"That dipshit Farr," Quinn snarled, "he ain't never gonna make 1st Lieutenant, he's gonna die in grade. He can't talk and think at the same time. That saying 'he don't know whether to shit or go blind,' that's Farr."

"I told you, Quinn, he's an Ologist. They gotta be like that. They spend years learning to transform life into theory, then apply their theory to life. It's hard, Quinn, it's very difficult to do that because things start getting self-contradictory and incomplete; your statistics don't check out and you gotta keep throwing them back into the computer. It's *hard*. So the best way to keep from going crazy—getting rashes and pimples, swollen glands, limp dick—you gotta keep from paying too much attention to what's going on, from the raw scores."

"My man," Quinn said proudly, "you're *really* full of shit."

Sergeant Major smiled his pleasant fatherly smile. Hanson and Quinn were his best recon team leaders. When he'd first seen them at the launch site he'd thought it would work out that way. He could usually tell; he'd processed enough of them through, and done enough paperwork on the dead ones. He could usually tell now.

Quinn was tough, good, and mean, but he'd never have been more than just competent on recon if Sergeant Major hadn't put him with Hanson. Some of Hanson's craziness rubbed off on Quinn, and that was what had made the team so good.

More often than not, Sergeant Major thought, the crazy ones lived through it, even though they took chances that made you think they were trying to get killed. The crazy ones like Hanson killed a lot of Communists, and brought back a lot of good intelligence. And they were always the ones who knew, just as well as Sergeant Major did, that none of it mattered at all.

The heavy web gear slung over Quinn's left shoulder swung up, then back as he walked. He carried the Swedish "K" in his right hand, the fat silencer a dull black. He was wearing his camouflage fatigues and a floppy brown jungle hat he had taken off a dead NVA. They were better than the American-issue hats; they had a plastic insert that kept the rain out, but they were dangerous to wear if gunships were working the area.

Hanson looked like a child next to him in Levis and a green T-shirt. He was singing softly, trying to sound like Dylan, "John *Wesley* Hardin' was a friend to the poor, well he ta-raveled with a gun in ev*ree* hand . . ."

"Charlie McCoy," Hanson thought, "damn it, that's right. That's who plays bass on that. Those tight little drum riffs are nice, too."

The PFC radio repairman didn't notice Quinn and Hanson approaching. He was watching his baby ducks. He'd bought them from a woman in Da Nang City, paying her 20 times what they were worth, smiling and telling her, "Thank you, mama-san." She'd smiled back with her black teeth, hating him, and that had made the PFC happy for the rest of the day.

He didn't know he'd been cheated, but it wouldn't have mattered if he had known. He was used to being fucked over. He was big, pudgy, and awkward. He was very pale and his stiff black hair grew out in tufts. At a glance there seemed to be something "wrong" about him, the kind of oversize boy who always wore a slide rule on his belt in high school, and had no friends.

The five yellow ducklings were swimming in the Rubbermaid dishpan he'd bought at the PX.

"The only part *I* like," Quinn slapped the "K" into his left hand, crouched like a bowler as he swept a duckling from the water, and rose gracefully without breaking stride, "is the head."

He bit down, pulled with a twist—the delicate, grinding crack like a precision machine under an enormous overload—

and the body came away. He threw it carelessly over his shoulder, and the fuzzy wings twitched madly as though the ruined, bloody little bird refused to believe it was dead.

The PFC had the same bewildered look they always have in the newspaper photo under the headline: MASS KILLER SURRENDERS: FORMER TEACHER SAYS HE WAS BRILLIANT STUDENT.

Hanson listened to the erratic little brush and thump of the bird as they walked casually on.

When they were out of sight of the PFC's hootch, Hanson said, "The timing. The *pathos* of it. I think we have a nine-five, maybe a nine-seven here . . . as soon as you *swallow* it."

Quinn spit out the wide-eyed yellow head and laughed. "You'll be back. You won't get along with those people, my man. They have no appreciation for that kind of talent." He turned and began to walk away. "Well, I got a chopper to catch."

"Hey," Hanson said.

"Yeah?"

Hanson grabbed Quinn by the sleeves of his fatigues and began to shake him the way you'd shake a child you were angry with. Quinn's web gear rattled, grenades clacking against each other like pool balls.

"You son of a bitch," Hanson said, "you bastard. Watch your *ass*. You go out there and let some fool get you blown away, I'll kill you."

"No sweat, my man. I plan to skate till you get back. Have a nice airplane ride, sport."

Quinn turned and walked on.

Hanson walked down to the wide white beach. It was growing dawn. The black hills across the bay were going to be green soon. Dead gray waves began to flush pink and gold, rising endlessly and patiently, crashing back into the surf.

Hanson heard a faint steady drumming. There was a black dot over the mouth of the bay, the perimeter gunship.

★   ★   ★

The door gunner in the perimeter ship was bored. It was like sitting in a windy open wall-locker a thousand feet in the air. The fat Huey helicopter had been circling the huge military complex for four hours. For four hours he had been watching the dark beach. The other door gunner had been watching the dark ocean. The door gunners wore helmets with tinted bubble-faced shields that covered everything but their mouths. They wore thick, rigid ceramic flak vests that curved around their neck and chest. They looked like giant insects. The dead weight of the vest pulled and jerked on its shoulder straps each time the Huey banked around the perimeter.

In front of the door gunner, the M-60 machine gun hung barrel down, rocking slightly like an oar in an oarlock. The belted bullets draped down from the gun, folding into a box by the gunner's foot.

He leaned out, into his seat harness, and looked down the beach. There was a single speck against the white sand. He pushed the chrome nubbin down into the black plastic handle, and spoke to the pilot through his helmet mike, "Hey, sir. Let's put her down on the deck. Wake that stud up."

The pilot was bored, too. He was a Cobra gunship pilot who had come back to Vietnam for a second tour. They had assigned him to the perimeter ship until his orders for a Cobra unit came through. The Cobra is a fast attack helicopter; flying a Cobra was like driving a Corvette. The fat Huey was like a delivery van.

The paddle rotor blades that held the Huey in the air tilted alternately up and down as they spun, stabilizing the helicopter. When a pilot changes the angle of the blades, it is called "pulling pitch," and causes the chopper to go up, or down.

The Huey was a mass of plastic and alloy steel held in the air by a precise balance and counterbalance of turbine and rotor blades. It is almost impossible for a Huey to maintain an exact altitude when it is moving forward.

The pilot pulled pitch hard, and the Huey dropped like

dead weight. He eased back and held it four feet above the sand, bringing his speed to 85 knots. He smiled. He could feel it all: the flutter of the rotors, the staggered interacting gears, and the shriek of the jet turbine.

The pilot was flying too fast and too low. He knew that. He hadn't felt so good since his last Cobra mission.

His right ear lobe was ragged, as though it had been eaten by some disease. It had been torn away on his last Cobra mission by a 7.62 bullet that had smashed through the canopy of the Cobra, meeting him as he dove directly at the RPD machine gun. The pilot had killed 12 people in less than a minute that day.

The pilot was holding the Huey at four feet by instinct, by feel. It was almost as though he was not involved, as though he was watching himself fly. He knew that if he even began to think about making a mistake, to interfere with his instincts, the Huey would twitch, dig a skid in the sand, and go into flaming cartwheels.

Hanson watched the Huey grow, slowly at first, then faster. The larger it was, the faster it grew until it was all he could see. It hung there in front of him, the skids at shoulder height, the rotors driving empty air into wedges of sound, jet turbine screaming like pure white light.

Hanson looked up and met the pilot's eyes. The pilot nodded and smiled. But the Huey was moving at almost 100 miles an hour.

The Huey was moving, and then a huge insect was looking at Hanson. It smiled beneath its dark bubble eye and held human fingers in a "peace" sign.

The Huey was half a mile down the beach and getting smaller.

The ocean was a deep blue now. Hanson watched an aircraft carrier and two destroyers out on the horizon slowly altering their positions. It was as though they were trying to spell something out to him in sign language.

2

The padded seat tipped back and pulled him down into it. A shudder ran through the 707, Hanson's arms lifted slightly from the arm rests, and all the GIs cheered as it rose from the runway at Tan Son Nhut. Hanson looked up at the ventilation nozzle hissing air like a tiny ball-turret gun. In a seat near the rear of the plane, one GI was wearing handcuffs and crying softly.

Later, Hanson got out his *Oxford Book of English Verse*. It was mildewed, sweat stained, and bloodstained even though he had kept it wrapped in a plastic bag. He turned to Yeats's poem, *Cuchulain's Fight with the Sea*. He skipped to the ending where the warrior-king Cuchulain kills his own son, having been at the wars so long that he did not know him. Afterwards, the Druids chanted while he slept, making him believe that the sea was his enemy:

> *Cuchulain stirred,*
> *Stared on the horses of the sea, and heard*
> *The cars of battle and his own name cried,*
> *And fought with the invulnerable tide.*

Hanson always pictured him cursing and tirelessly slashing with his sword at wave after wave as they rolled in at him.

Hanson looked out the dark porthole window at the huge wing of the plane outlined by the blue-yellow glow of the jet pods.

"So," he thought, "well."

The Tokarev was in the carry-on bag between his feet—a heavy Russian automatic about the size of an army .45. A red star was set in the center of the black plastic grips. Much of the bluing had been worn down to bare metal by the stiff military holster, and there was some rust-pitting on the slide, but for many years it had been well-cared for.

The pistol had a yellow tag attached to the trigger guard

with a metal seal, authorizing him to take it on the plane. Like everyone's, Hanson's luggage had been searched, and he had been frisked before boarding the plane. The search was for narcotics and weapons, explosives and ammunition. A Specialist-4 glanced at the Tokarev, then stared Hanson in the eyes and barked, "You got any rounds for this weapon, troop?"

For an instant Hanson wanted to kill him. That quick. He was not accustomed to that tone of voice, especially from someone who was drawing combat pay for searching suitcases. But he only shook his head and said, "No."

Hanson's eyes were dangerously mild and attentive when the Spec.-4 glared at him and said, "If you do have any, troop, you're in big trouble."

Hanson shrugged, smiling slightly, and said, "Don't have any."

The Spec.-4 gave him one last hard look and said, "OK, troop," and jerked his thumb toward the door. As Hanson walked out he heard the Spec.-4 say, "Come on, let's move it. Next."

Outside, Hanson said to himself, "Big trouble." He smiled. He said the two words again, and again, changing inflection, "*Big* trouble. Big *trouble*." His smile grew wider, "Big *trouble*." Halfway across the tarmac he was laughing. "Got some *big trouble* here, Spec.-4. Deep shit, my man." Then he began to get angry, but stopped himself, saying, "No need. No need." He began to sing to himself as he walked toward the 707, "Somewhere in the black minin' hills o' Dakota there lived a young boy name o' Rocky Raccooon. One day his woman ran off . . . *Oh big trouble* . . . with another guy, hit young Rocky in the eye-hii . . ."

The NVA captain was propped in a sitting position against a bamboo grove, badly wounded in the legs. His men were gone.

The hatchet team had been after them all morning: a reinforced platoon. But the captain had led them well; the hatchet team had taken casualties.

It had been a nice morning, not so hot; a slight breeze made the bamboo grove clatter softly. The brown stalks were the size of a man's leg, the smaller stalks were green.

The captain got off one shot with the Tokarev. It blew Hanson's canteen up, snatching him to one side as if someone had pulled at his pistol belt. For a moment Hanson thought that he'd been hit, that the canteen water was blood.

He met the captain's eyes and saw no fear in them.

He put two six-round bursts into the captain's chest.

Hanson stripped the body of its pistol belt and picked up the Tokarev. The body had a letter in its pocket, and a picture of a woman and child, wrapped in a plastic bag. Hanson put the letter and picture back in the shirt, wrapping it well because the shirt was soaking through with blood.

He looked at the body and said, "Well . . ." but there really wasn't anything to say. It was the best ones who died, he thought. That did seem wrong.

Hanson reached down into the carry-on bag and popped the clip out of the pistol. He made his way down the narrow aisle past the rows of sleeping GIs, some of them softly spotlighted by reading lights, their cheeks and eyes hollow. The plane hit a pocket of turbulence, and all the green-clad GIs leaned to one side, rose slightly, then sank back down into their seats.

When he reached the tail of the plane, a pretty blond stewardess wearing a blue cap looked up. He smiled at her, and she looked back down at the paperback book she was reading.

Inside the lurching little bathroom—glaring light and stainless steel—he loosened the web belt. There was a wide strip of white adhesive tape across the inside of his thigh. He slowly pulled the tape away and the bright bottle-necked bullets dropped one by one into his hand. He threw the tape away, tightened the belt, and pulled the clip from his pocket. Each round made a solid "click" as he thumbed it into the clip.

He loaded the rounds the way a man might deposit dimes in a pay phone.

Back in his seat, he slid the loaded clip into the butt of the pistol and stuck the pistol between the arm rest and the side of the plane. For 18 months not a minute had passed when he did not have a weapon in his hand or within easy reach.

Outside the porthole the silver and black wing shuddered slightly. The muffled jets sounded like a waterfall.

"Well," Hanson thought. He smiled slightly, then had to squint to keep his eyes from watering. He leaned his head against the roaring wall, and was asleep in seconds. He dreamed about the skull.

It had been a year and a half since Hanson had reported for duty at CCN. The gate into the compound was a narrow path cutting through the wire: triplestrand and engineer stakes, coils of concertina piled shoulder-high and head-high, two-layered webs of tanglefoot with trip-flares hung like beer cans littering the ground cover along a highway. Triplestrand, concertina, tanglefoot all the way in like jagged steel hedges and lawns.

Claymore antipersonnel mines perched on little folding legs facing the gate—almost jolly looking, like fat little "keep off the grass" signs. Across their faces were the words FRONT TOWARDS ENEMY.

There was no grass in the wire. It had been burned away with Mo-gas so often that the fired red clay smelled like over-heated machinery.

Two sandbagged towers inside the compound could rake away the gate and sweep the entire perimeter with interlocking heavy machine gun fire.

But it would not be the wire, or the Claymores, or the gun towers that Hanson would remember about that day; they would soon be as familiar and comforting and welcome as the outskirts of your home town after a tiring business trip to the city.

Hanson would remember the skull.

There was nothing crude or clumsy about the skull: it had been skillfully cut out and painted. A huge grinning death's-head wearing a green beret. Taller than a man, it looked down from a heavy cross-timber above the entrance to the compound. It was the black-socket eyes that stopped Hanson—the way they pulled wryly down toward the jagged nose hole. The skull seemed amused at itself. Below the skull, painted in large block letters, were the words: WE KILL FOR PEACE.

Hanson managed to get himself processed through the Fort Ord replacement center in a matter of hours. In a windowless, concrete building the planeload of GIs stripped out of their jungle fatigues and exchanged them for baggy dress uniforms. On the other side of a low wall another planeload of soldiers was reversing the process, leaving their dress uniforms in a pile and putting on stiff, new fatigues for their flight to Vietnam. Hanson imagined the two groups lining up on the runway and simply trading uniforms.

The wall was just high enough so that neither group could see or talk to the other.

O'Hare approach control had been tracking Hanson's 727 since it crossed the imaginary jurisdiction line that cut across western Nebraska. The plane became a green blip on the number six radarscope in the windowless, climate-controlled GCA room.

The copilot of Hanson's plane changed radio frequency. The FASTEN SEATBELTS sign blinked on.

Hanson was thinking about Barker, "the Kahuna." Drunk or sober, he would stride into the NCO club or the teamhouse and declare, "I *am* the Kahuna." Then he would demand, "Who is the Kahuna?"

Quinn, Silver, and Hanson would shout, "You are. You are the true Kahuna."

"Fuckin' A, troops, Fuckin' A, and the Kahuna is buying the first round."

Back at the base at Da Nang the four of them would walk along until Barker would pick out a headquarters or supply soldier, walk over to him, and ask in a confidential voice, "Hey. Do you know who the Kahuna is?"

He would usually pick out a big soldier. Barker was the smallest man on the team.

"Whathu fuck you talkin' about?"

"The Kahuna, man," Barker would whisper, looking furtively around, "who *is* the Kahuna?"

"I don't fuckin' know any Kahuna."

Barker would grab him by the shirt and begin shaking him, yelling, "*I* am the Kahuna, you stupid shit. I *am* the Kahuna. Don't forget it."

The other three would step out from where they had been hiding and surround the soldier.

"You fuckin' with the Kahuna?"

"Nobody fucks with him."

"He's the man. The true Kahuna."

"You best beat feet outta here, troop, 'cause we're *all* crazy."

They would stand glaring at the soldier until he was out of sight and walk on to the club, laughing, muttering, "Who is the Kahuna?"

The plane taxied to the terminal, and rocked slightly as the exit ramp locked onto the door. People began to stand up and get their carry-on luggage.

They found Barker the morning after the NVA batallion had tried to overrun the camp. He was draped over the big four-deuce mortar tube. He'd never gotten his first round off. The NVA were good. They had all the mortar pits bracketed before the attack.

The RPG rocket had hit Barker in the back of the head. There wasn't much blood. The explosion had cauterized most of the veins and arteries. There was nothing left of his head except the lower jaw hanging from his neck like a huge lip. When they carried him to the teamhouse to zip him up in the talcum-and-rubber-smelling body bag, the jaw flapped like he was trying to say something.

"Well . . ." Hanson thought.

"Sir."

Hanson looked up. It was the stewardess. The plane was empty.

He smiled and shook his head, "Sorry," picked up his bag and walked to the exit.

It was foggy, and the air smelled of Mo-gas and hot metal. Beyond the far runway, refinery burn-off tubes flared dirty yellow in the dark sky. Hanson thought he could hear a faint roar each time the flame pulsed. White smoke boiled under hundreds of floodlights.

A red fan of light swept through the fog like a rotor blade. Hanson could hear it hiss each time it passed over him, and he couldn't keep from ducking his head.

He hurried toward the terminal. Over the entrance a banner said:

WELCOME HOME GIS—CHICAGO IS PROUD OF YOU

The first thing he saw after pushing through the glass doors was a car. A gleaming metallic-blue Ford LTD. It turned slowly round with a mechanical groan. The headlights and bumpers winked, windows flashed as they turned through blue spotlight beams. Glossy color posters showed elegant men and women gazing at each other across the hoods of automobiles. Muzak droned from hidden speakers.

He turned and began to walk down the concourse following the arrows. It smelled of sweat, perfume, and cigarette urns. He passed men in suits carrying briefcases; angry-looking women in tailored dresses, bracelets, and bright lipstick, exhaling smoke; security guards with pistols on their hips;

black men pushing brooms or shining shoes. He felt that they were staring at him, but they looked quickly away.

Gift shops, snack shops, Avis, bars, all cut into the side of the corridor like bunkers. Arrow-shaped signs saying R-11 or Gifts/books, posters of beautiful women smoking cigarettes or running along white beaches. A loudspeaker boomed asking someone to "report to the Eastern ticket counter *please*." He passed a door that had a bull's-eye painted on it with the silhouette of a man spread-eagled in its center.

Hanson felt like an immigrant or refugee in his baggy uniform. Everyone he saw looked healthy and rich, but no one smiled. The last time he'd seen anyone laugh was at Fort Ord.

He saw a young soldier, and could tell by the insignia on his uniform that he was on his way to Vietnam. He stepped into one of the little bars to avoid him. The bartender was Hanson's age. He was wearing a loose-fitting silk shirt and a gold link necklace. When Hanson ordered a scotch and water the bartender frowned at him and said, "Eye dee."

"What?"

"ID. I've gotta see some ID."

"Oh yeah. Right. I've been on airplanes so long I don't even know who I am."

The bartender didn't change expression.

Hanson handed him his army ID card. The bartender looked at it, laid it on the bar, and walked away.

Hanson looked at the picture on the card. It had been taken three years before in basic training. The person in the picture had a shaved head and was staring dully somewhere beyond the camera.

The bartender set a drink in front of Hanson and said, "One fifty." Hanson laid some bills on the bar. The bartender took two and walked away. Hanson sipped his drink and thought about what had happened in the last three years. He was thinking about the skull when the young soldier walked in.

"OK if I sit down, Sarge?"

He was wearing crossed rifles on his collar. Infantry, 11-bravo, grunt, 16 weeks of training. The kind of kid who gets killed in the first two months, before he learns what to be afraid of, what to look out for—before he realizes that there are people out there who are *really* trying to kill him. It would probably happen in the first or second operation. In the regular line units they don't worry about new guys. The troops who have survived a few months look out for themselves and their buddies.

Hanson had over a year's training before he was shipped to Vietnam. He'd had two weeks of training patrols when he got there. New people were taken care of in Special Forces units; it was like a fraternity within the army.

"Sure," Hanson said.

"I don't want to bother you . . ."

"Sit on down."

The kid laid a thick manila folder on the bar. His 201 file, a record of his life for the last 16 weeks, medical history, uniforms and insignia issued, inoculations, pay vouchers, unit clearance forms, next of kin insurance forms, rifle qualification, Geneva convention training certificate, and right on top his travel orders for Military Command Republic of Vietnam.

Hanson looked at him in the dim light. He saw the basic Army-issue-dead-18-year-old. They all looked alike when they were dead. When Hanson looked at him he saw him as he would look when he was dead.

"Hey, look," Hanson said, "I gotta catch a plane, but lemme give you some quick, free advice."

"Sure, Sarge," he said, trusting Hanson because of the green beret and the ribbons on his coat.

"OK. When you get to your unit you look around for someone who's been there six or eight months. The reason he's still alive is because he knows what he's doing. Try and stay close to him. Don't piss him off with too many questions, just watch what he does and listen to what he says.

"Try and stay in the middle of the column. The middle is

good. And don't be afraid of being scared. That'll get you killed. People start shooting, you get down on the *ground,* OK? You make the first two months, and you got it dicked."

Hanson stood up and said, "Don't sweat it, you'll be OK. I can tell." He pushed the bills lying on the bar over in front of the kid. "Lemme buy you a drink. When you get back a year from now, you can buy somebody else one. Take care now."

As he walked out of the bar, Hanson heard the kid say, "Thanks a lot, Sarge."

"Thanks a lot, Sarge," Hanson muttered to himself as he walked quickly away, "thanks a lot for lying to me, for not telling me I'll be dead in six weeks, thanks for the *drink,* Sarge."

Hanson wanted to kill somebody. He wanted to kill everybody. He wanted somebody to pay.

As he walked toward his boarding gate, Hanson passed a bank of TV screens set into the wall. They were all turned to different channels, mostly game shows and soap operas. The sound was turned off and the whole wall flickered and blinked like a huge computer screen as the camera angles jumped and cut from scene to scene. On the game shows people were laughing and jumping up and down, hugging TVs and ovens.

One screen stood out like a blind eye. It was black and white. It kept showing the time, temperature, humidity, and wind speed, one fact indifferently replacing the next.

It was raining when Hanson's plane began to taxi down the runway. The tiny raindrops pulled across the round window, lurching sideways toward the tail. The domes and spires of the refinery gleamed under thousands of floodlights. They floated in the boiling white smoke and bursts of yellow flame. It looked like a city in the act of destroying itself. Hanson couldn't hear any explosions. He wondered what it would be like if he were deaf. But you can *feel* the explosions that come close enough to hurt you.

The brakes squealed as the plane stopped. It sat back and

shuddered as the engines began to rev. Hanson touched the window lightly with the back of his hand, and felt the pitch of the engines.

They began to move. A black and white sign flashed past that said: K-4 RUD CLOSED. Then the blue lights were snapping past like bursts of memory or foreknowledge of events you can't prevent, and the plane was in the clouds.

It was black outside the window. Hanson watched the raindrops drag across the glass. He wondered if it was the jet exhaust or the wind speed that made them act that way.

The pilot announced that it was 72 degrees below zero outside the plane.

In the seat behind him a child began to cry. A woman's voice said, "Jason, if you don't stop that, I'm really going to give it to you when we get home."

He kept crying.

Hanson couldn't remember ever seeing any children cry in Vietnam, not even the ones who were wounded, who had flies crawling on their wounds and faces. He tried to think of at least one, but he couldn't.

As he thought back, recalling face after face, he met the same listless stare each time. They didn't seem to blame him for whatever had happened to them, but they expected him to *do* something. Most of the time all he could do was wait for the medivac and watch them die.

He was still trying to recall seeing a child cry when his plane became a green blip on the GCA scope at his home town airport.

3

When Hanson reached up to pull a handful of razor-grass down for shade, his canteens and grenades shifted and tugged at him. He had been thinking about time. He glanced at his watch, and saw a green fly licking blood from a cut on the back of his hand. The sun whined and chirped in his ears. His crotch and armpits were wet, and the grass cuts on his hands stung. He killed the fly, and tried to recall what he had read about how the half-life of carbon was used to establish the age of prehistoric tools.

He squinted into the sun again, and the earth began to shudder against his chest and thighs. In the valley beyond the first ridgeline, greasy smoke rose and spread like thunderheads.

Far above, and to the west, three B-52s winked in the pale sky, but Hanson didn't see them. He stood up and watched the rest of the team rise from the tall brown grass: Quinn, Troc, Rau, and Mr. Minh.

It was quiet in the valley. Sound did not carry in the damp heat, but seemed to fall dead to the ground. They moved slowly. Any piece of equipment that might rattle had been taped down or removed. The only sounds were their boots on the baked earth and the rustle of canvas web gear. Dressed for speed and fire-power, they carried only water, ammunition, freeze-dried food, and explosives.

Hanson kept losing sight of the rest of the team in the acrid fog—dust, smoke, and the ammonia stink of high explosive. He could taste it on the back of his throat. The jungle floor was torn into steaming furrows. Lengths of vine and tiger thorns were tangled like concertina wire. The craters were as big as bedrooms, smelling of sulfur and freshly turned earth, fog clinging to their sides like dirty snow. Scorched bamboo groves hissed, and patches of brush and grass burned noiselessly.

Hanson watched a fired-mud clinker roll slowly down the side of a crater and disappear in the fog. His eyes burned, but he didn't rub them. The yellow dust had turned to paste on his face and hands.

"Anybody who isn't dead," he thought, "is going to be pissed off." He inhaled the smoke and dust, and suddenly had to bite his lip to keep from laughing. He thought about the simple pain in his lip that kept him silent and safe, and he considered the importance of pain in human life.

"Pain is like another language," Sergeant Major had once told him; "people usually understand it better than words. You can get right to the point. Pain works much better than words if you want to persuade someone to do something they don't want to do."

Hanson stepped around an uprooted tree, and saw the soldier, an NVA regular with a carbine. He was caked with the same yellow paste that covered Hanson's face and arms. Only his eyes seemed alive. He seemed to be staring at something far away, or thinking about something puzzling and important. A fine web of bright blood ran from his ears and nose, collected on his chin, and fell to his chest with soft *pops*. The blood puddled and slid down his arm through the dust to his elbow, then to his hand where it dropped from his fingers to the ground.

His eyes moved slowly until they met Hanson's. Then his feet got tangled up and he sat down like a character in a slapstick comedy who has his chair pulled out from under him. His eyes had a look of total surprise. His head dropped between his knees, and he toppled to one side.

Rau kicked him twice, once in the ribs and once in the head. When they left him behind his eyes were dead, and his broken jaw sagged with astonishment.

They found five more in the first collapsed bunker. It looked like a mining disaster, the bodies and sandbags shapeless and caked with dirt. Gouts of cooked rice were stuck to timbers, and there was a heavy smell of fish sauce. Another body was a few meters from the bunker. He must have been running for cover when the bombs fell. One gray foot was twisted up against the ankle. His toenails were yellow and torn. The face beneath the stiff black bangs was a patchwork of black and purple and shading blues, like farmland seen from an airliner. Fat green blowflies rose and settled nervously, lap-ping at the face like a veil. Something of the face was still there, like those puzzles in children's picture books, clouds and gnarled trees that suddenly take focus and reveal a hidden face.

The team continued silently on, finding several more broken bunkers. The only really funny thing that happened was when Quinn spun and threw his rifle to his shoulder. He had glanced up and seen a body hanging from the crotch of a tree. The rest of the team grinned. Troc whispered, "Same bird," and smiled.

At the edge of the impact area they turned north. The heat seemed like part of the terrain, as solid as the earth beneath Hanson's feet. The air was so humid that breathing was difficult; it was like drowning. Hanson touched the compass hanging at his chest and thought, "Good old North." He imagined going north, and north until the jungle changed to tundra, and mountains and solid ice.

A tiny deer broke from the underbrush, barking like a dog. Hanson and the rest of the team dropped into a crouch. The barking deer wheeled and went back the way it had come.

The sun was below the rolling hills when they started across the sluggish brown river. The water was warm and oily and, they found out, full of leeches.

They crawled into a peninsula of brush and bamboo to wait for darkness before sprinting across the valley to the first of the foothills where they would wait out the night.

Hanson pulled down his fatigue pants. Three gray leeches with pointed tails hung from the inside of his thigh. He squirted insect repellent on them and they dropped off, leaving bright little dots of blood. He found a bigger one on his ankle, the size of his little finger, gray as the slime in a sink drain. He flicked it off, hissing, "Shitshitshit."

Hanson soaked the leech with repellent and touched a match to it. The leech rose and writhed like a cobra in the colorless flame, a faint orange nimbus around its body. Hanson could feel the flame's heat on his cheek, and smell the sweetness in the heat and in his own sweat. The leech suddenly turned black and fell in the patch of charred grass. Hanson realized that he had been holding his breath.

Just before dusk became darkness, they doubled back and set up a night location by a bombed-out family temple. The temple was on a small clearing awash in the jungle.

Hanson pulled a plug of C-4 explosive from the end of a two-pound brick, and pressed it into a ball. He set his canteen cup over a chink in the temple floor, and rolled the C-4 beneath the cup. He touched a match to it and watched the rich orange flame spread around and envelop the little white ball. Patches of gold and bright blue glowed on the flaking gray walls. The C-4 consumed itself evenly, from the outside in, the surface liquefying, then blistering and burning away with a faint hiss, disappearing like a marshmallow held in a campfire. He dropped in another piece, and another, until the water began to steam, nervous little bubbles beginning to break on the dull gray bottom of the cup. If he were to heat it any more, the cup would have been too hot to drink from. Hanson lifted the cup and the bubbles stopped. He poured in a packet of instant coffee that floated on the water like dust.

Out beyond the ornate and shattered temple gate, jungle and sky were turning gray. Hanson stirred his coffee with a plastic spoon and considered the idea that color was only reflected sunlight, but it seemed just as reasonable that, at a given time every day, a part of the world simply turned black.

The countryside had begun to grumble with artillery and heavy machine gun fire. Hanson sipped his coffee and smiled. The guns control the land at night. The firebases cough and take over. They pull their men back inside their perimeter and flail the jungle with ordinance.

The coffee was hot and good.

Hanson and Quinn slung their hammocks near an artillery crater down the slope from the temple. Quinn's hammock swung gently as he whispered the chant, "Airborne ranger, green buh-*ray,* this is the way we end the day." Then he laughed, so softly that it sounded evil.

"I don't like these fuckin' arc light sweeps," he said, "body counters, one potato, two potato. That fuckin' *guy* in the tree. Scared the shit out of me. And that first guy. Just standing there. I don't know what he was lookin' at, but I don't think it's something *I* ever want to see. And that God damn little deer. The Yards got some kind of thing about them? Even Mr. Minh acted funny after we saw that deer. Seems like the Yards been acting funny ever since we started this sweep."

"Yeah," Hanson said, "that barking deer's kind of like a black cat. If you start on a trip and it crosses your path, you're supposed to back up and start over."

Quinn's hammock strings grated against the tree they were tied to.

"You really believe a lot of that Montagnard stuff, don't you? The omens and spirits," Quinn said.

"Shit, so do you. Mr. Minh believes it, and he ain't dumb. It makes as much sense as God with a big white beard up in heaven. Remember those fucking pictures in Sunday school. Like the one of Jesus, long blond hair, *sensitive* blue eyes, knocking at the door of the rustic little cottage, knock, knock, knock."

Hanson began to speak in a southern drawl, "An' that's all you have to do, children, when you hear Him knockin'. That is Lord Jeezus knockin' at yore heart, an' you need only to open up the door to receive His blessed love."

It had been the year Hanson's father was in Korea, and he was living at his grandmother's. After Sunday school he would go to church, and in the summer they handed out the cardboard fans with the flat wooden handle like a tongue depressor. There was always a funeral home ad on one side, and a gaudy color picture on the other: a pair of grim, blond angels hauling a portly man in a business suit into the sky, or a worried middle-aged man standing at a huge podium with a jury of thick-winged angels staring grimly at him. Beneath the pictures was a short paragraph that told how the artist had been a hopeless alcoholic until he found Jesus and accepted him as his per-

sonal Lord and Savior, and was now using his talents for the greater glory of God.

After the service everyone would stand in small groups in front of the church, the men smoking and talking, the women just talking. Up the street there was a green concrete building, a hospital for crazy people and alcoholics. One Sunday, just as Hanson was getting in the car to go home, a wild-eyed man in blue pajamas had come running barefoot from the hospital. Two huge men in white coats and heavy black shoes were chasing him. The man looked directly at Hanson as he ran past, and said, "They won't ever let you finish, will they?" and ran on into the littered little park that smelled like sewage.

One of Hanson's aunts had pulled him into the car and rolled up the windows, but he could hear the man scream when the other men caught him.

"What's wrong with them?" Hanson asked as the car pulled away.

"Why nothing, honey. We're just goin' to Grandma's for chicken. Like we always do."

Every Sunday they had cold chicken, biscuits, and mashed potatoes. Then everyone would drive to the cemetery—six to a car—to look at Grandpa's grave. Each of Hanson's aunts and uncles had a picture of themselves standing next to the tombstone, like sportsmen with a trophy kill.

Sometimes Hanson talked his way out of going to the cemetery; he hated riding in the hot crowded car, the windows rolled up to keep out the dust. It was one of those times that he became a born-again Christian.

He was alone in his grandmother's parlor that Sunday. A big picture of a kneeling Christ caught the afternoon light and seemed to move. His grandfather's open coffin had been put on display in the parlor. One of his aunts had lifted him up so he could see, saying to him, "Look at Grandpa, honey, he's going to heaven. This is the last time you'll see him till we're all up there together"

His grandfather's face and hands were powdered, and he looked very small.

Hanson's grandfather was the only corpse he'd ever seen before he went to Vietnam.

On that Sunday when he was born-again, Hanson turned on the TV in the parlor so he would feel a little less alone in the house. The Billy Graham Crusade for Christ was on. Hanson had expected the "Good Samaritan" Show, where contestants would tell their problems and cry, and the grimly smiling host would ask people watching the show to send in donations. The more he smiled and comforted the contestants, the more they sobbed.

But that Sunday it was Billy Graham. Just when it started to get dark, the music swelled and Billy told the crowd to come down from the stands and give their lives to Christ.

"Come down, come down," he said, "just look, my friends, hundreds of people are coming down to give their lives to Jesus Christ," he said, throwing his arms up, "and you people out there who are watching from your television screens, get up, get UP from your chairs and sofas, get UP and walk to your television sets.

"Stand up and witness for Christ there in your living rooms with us. Lay your hands on your television sets and pray with us."

And Hanson had gotten up, terrified, and pressed his hands down on the TV. The metal was warm and the tubes glowed through the grillwork in the back.

Hanson looked at the glowing face of his watch. He called the camp and waited.

No answer.

He pulled off the whip antenna and touched the copper contact points inside the base with the tip of his tongue, then jammed and screwed the antenna back down on the radio set. It swished back and forth in the dark dead air.

He called again. No answer. The radio hissed. A pink flare popped east of the river, dripping sparks and leaving a jagged trail of smoke.

Hanson looked over at Quinn, then called again, "Formal Granite, Formal Granite, this is five-four, over . . ."

Silver's voice crackled through the static, "This is Granite, it's your dime."

"It's a comfort, you know, this instant commo . . ."

"Yeah, yeah. All I get is complaints. Just like the phone company. You're comin' in weak, better change your battery. Anyway, you got a message for me?"

Hanson sent in the body count, and two night artillery grids. One grid was H&I fire, a corridor of high explosive to be fired throughout the night around their location. The other grid was plotted directly on the temple, to be fired in the event that they were attacked and had to run.

"I get any mail?"

"Yeah. Last mail chopper. Three letters from Linda and one from that broad in Canada who married the deserter. And one of those commie newspapers from New York."

"Tampering with mail is a federal crime."

"It's all commo. Part of the job. Your partner there got one of those 'GI Paks' from his church in Iowa. Lotta good stuff. 'What every soldier in the field needs,' it says. Toothbrush, shoestrings, deck of cards—you doin' any gambling out there?—pair of white socks, little box of raisins, and a plastic packet of Heinz catsup, about enough for one hot dog if you got one, and some Bugs Bunny Kool-Aid. Card says the ladies' auxiliary is behind us 'all the way.' Yep."

Over the radio Silver's laugh sounded like a weak battery trying to start a car.

"Any movies?"

"Yeah, Clint Eastwood flick. The Yards loved it. So, that's all I got on this end."

"OK. Look, things don't *feel* too good here. Have that stuff ready to shoot if we call for it, 'cause we're gonna have to be steppin' right along."

"You got it. Any more traffic? I gotta make radio check with Da Nang."

"Negative."

"OK. Granite out. Catch you later. Hey, how does this grab you?" A hysterical mechanical laugh came from the radio—the accordion-like laugh-box Silver carried around.

The radio hissed like a TV after sign-off.

Hanson lay in the hammock listening to the big guns. They fired in pairs or groups of three, and sounded like distant boxcars slamming to a stop. Moments later he could hear the big shells coursing over, and past. Some of the explosions sent shudders through the hammock strings. It was strangely comforting.

A voice broke static on the radio, grinding like a gearbox, "Granite, five-four, this is Night Bird, over . . ."

Hanson looked at Quinn. Quinn shrugged.

"This is five-four . . ."

"Uh, roger . . . Ah just wanted to verify your location an' advise you that ah *will* be workin' the area for a while . . ."

Somewhere to the south there was a drone of engines.

"Gunship," Quinn hissed, "night-vision gunship."

"Uh, roger that," Hanson said into the handset, "five-four copies."

"Uh, roger. Ah'll be doin' some huntin' then. This is the Night Bird, out . . ."

The engine noise grew louder and passed overhead. Hanson could see the glow from four engines flickering through the propellors, and a dark shape that blotted out the stars.

The engines faded, and the mini-gun opened up. A solid shaft of red tracers flashed silently from sky to ground like a neon light suddenly switched on, and a moment later they could hear the drone, the sound of a low-speed electric drill boring into stone. Then the red shaft died, burning itself out slowly from sky to ground, eating its tail, and when the sky was black again, the drone stopped. The engine noise was gone. They watched, staring into the dark, and there it was again, the red streak flickering like a child's sparkler.

★   ★   ★

The moon had set. Mr. Minh squatted by the temple wall facing toward the impact zone. He had arranged the contents of his Katha in a semicircle: a pinch of rice, a clinker, *excrement of fire,* the tip of a buffalo's penis, a tiny piece of quartz, a tiger's tooth, and the bill of a sparrow hawk.

He looked into the darkness and clucked three times deep in his throat, then three more. All he heard in return were footsteps behind him. They were the steps of Hanson, the one he called *Kep An.* He was different than the other Americans: he could sometimes read the omens; he even seemed to know that the spirits could not be controlled, but only coaxed. Still, Hanson was too full of anger and confusion.

As the footsteps came closer, Mr. Minh said, "I had a bad dream, Kep An. I dreamed that the sky struck us.

"I know this place. There was once a village where the bombs fell. There were big trees near the village, very strong spirits. It was the year we ate the forest of the Stone Spirit *Goo.* That was a long time ago.

"So. All I do is fight now, fighting is my work.

"We must be very careful, tomorrow and the day after tomorrow. The tree spirits are angry. I have tried to call them, to talk, but they do not answer. You must leave me now while I try again."

Hanson lay in his hammock and watched the stars disappear. A rain squall was moving in. The wind picked up and the rain slanted down like thread on a loom. The artillery reports were muted, grainy, like a blown-up photograph. A flare popped across the river, swung up and down with the wind, making a fuzzy peach-colored arc.

Rain always benefits the attackers: it covers the sound they make as they move into position. When it rains at night in the jungle, you are rendered deaf and blind. There is nothing to do but wait.

Whenever a flare popped, the split-leaf palm fronds overhead blinked and raged in the wind, the slits like eyes and mouths squinting and gnashing.

The radio hissed softly.

One summer, long before he had ever thought of the war, Hanson had been hiking near the edge of a large swamp. It was a hot day and the scrub pines gave little shade. He came upon a clearing that seemed to be studded with fleshy thorns. They were like Easter lilies, but they had no stem or stalk. Each plant rose from the ground like a funnel. No part of them was green.

The plants were a soiled white and seemed to be covered with bruises, though Hanson might have imagined that. The inside of the plants bristled with stiff black hairs. The hairs grew inward and down toward the narrow throat of the funnel. They were covered with thick syrup.

The overall effect was that of hundreds of huge nostrils snorting from the ground.

There were insects inside all the funnels, stuck fast to the sweet syrup, unable to climb through the bristles of hair. As they struggled they slipped deeper into the neck of the plant—flies, bees, beetles, and butterflies. For a moment Hanson thought about using his pocketknife to free some of the insects, or cut the plants off at the ground, but realized there was nothing he could do. There were too many. And anyway, that was just the way things worked. Inside one of the plants he saw what looked like a tiny animal with brown fur, just visible deep in the neck. The sweet smell of the syrup and of rotting meat hung over the field.

They collected their booby traps and moved out at first light, as the faint pinks filtered through dark green mountains. It was still cool, but the heat was already seeping in like an undertow. It was going to be hot. Hanson felt uneasy, like a runner waiting for the starter's gun. The sun rose slowly at first, ponderous, the color of rotten fruit. Then it climbed and got smaller and tighter and bore down on them.

*   *   *

The grave was fresh, probably someone who had survived the air strike only to die of his wounds. A heavy sweet smell rode the heat from the circular mound of earth. They should have dug it up to check for documents and insignia, but they moved on.

Hanson's cheek itched, but he didn't scratch it. He had that metallic taste on his tongue, and the backs of his hands tingled. He looked at Quinn and Mr. Minh. A patch of split-leaf palm fronds was the wrong color. It was something about the quality of the sunlight. The way the trail curved up ahead. He recalled some odd phrase in his last letter from home.

Someone back in the jungle coughed. There was the soft *pop* of a grenade fuse, and the grenade was floating through the air at him. It was a grayish-green cylinder with cloth streamers. Bullets snapped as they went blindly past him. Quinn fired a magazine and began to run. The grenade went off. Something pulled at Hanson's pant leg. The team was down in a low crouch, facing alternate sides of the jungle. Quinn ran past Hanson and said, "Shit." Troc emptied a magazine and ran. The firing coming from the jungle was ragged. The ambush had been sprung too soon, before they were in the killing zone. Because of the cough. Hanson smelled burned powder, fish sauce, and gun oil as Troc ran past him. Mr. Minh emptied his weapon and wheeled around. Rau began to fire. Mr. Minh was putting a new magazine in his weapon as he ran past Hanson who was pulling the fat White Phosphorous grenade from his shoulder harness. The brass from Rau's weapon glittered as it arced out of the chamber. Hanson had to tear the grenade loose with his teeth and his left hand. The electrical tape holding it tasted salty. Hanson fired toward the sound of the cough as Rau ran past. He pulled the pin from the pastel green and yellow striped W.P. grenade and threw it over the palm fronds. And he ran. He pulled the quick release on his pack-straps and ran. Shrugging off the heavy pack, he ran and tried to keep sight of Rau.

4

The night before the ground attack, five of the air force enlisted men had come to the teamhouse. The one with the chipped tooth looked in the door and caught Hanson's eye.

"Uh, hi," he said, "we were wondering if we could buy a few beers from you guys." He had a nasal, New England accent.

Quinn was working over his web gear. He looked up and glared at the airman. "Zoomies," he muttered, and went back to his web gear. "You guys. You guys," he said, imitating the accent.

"Oh, pardon me," Hanson said, "is it all right with you, Sergeant Quinn, sir, to sell these young servicemen a beer?"

Quinn ignored him.

Hanson turned to the airmen. "Yeah, come on in, ignore that bully, that mean person over there. Belly up, laddies," Hanson said, looking at Quinn and smiling. "First beer is on Sergeant Quinn."

Quinn didn't look up. "I hear you," he said. "You're feeling real froggy tonight. But I ain't gonna let you get me going. Yet."

Hanson got five beers out of the battered refrigerator and set them on the bar. "Allow me to open them for you, a courtesy. A small gesture of inter-service fraternity."

He opened one for himself. "A toast, to the men who dare the wild blue yonder."

"Yes, just ignore mean Sergeant Quinn there, I'm more representative of the young NCO you'll find in the elite corps of Green Berets, the 'fighting soldiers from the sky.'"

Someone laughed.

"Easy derision, racist laughter," Hanson said, "pay him no mind. That is Dawson, our Afro-American staff sergeant. We keep him around so if somebody fucks up, he can scream 'discrimination.'"

"Han-sun, I believe you had yourself a little taste of speed for dessert tonight, you so froggy."

"No, that's not it, Staff Sergeant. I never touch that dangerous drug. What it is," Hanson said, creeping around the bar, walking in a crouch toward the big black staff sergeant, "is that I'm worried that Charles is sneakin' around out there, sneakin' sneakin' to get you before you leave. GOTCHA," Hanson yelled and leaped for Dawson.

Dawson grabbed him and twisted his arm up behind his back.

Hanson started laughing. "I give, I give," he said.

Dawson let him go. "You weird little fucker," he said, "how come I ain't broke your back, all this time. Shee-it."

"See," Hanson said to the air force guys, "Dawson's going back home tomorrow, 'back to the world,' as they say in military circles, gonna DEROS after two tours. I bet him a case of beer that the camp was gonna get hit before he left. Shit, what time is it?"

One of the air force guys said, "9:30."

"That's close enough to midnight," Dawson said. "Break it out."

Hanson spoke to the one with the chipped tooth, "How'd you chip your tooth?"

"Playing cricket."

"Aw, don't be an asshole. I just was curious, OK?"

"Really. I lived in England and Ireland for almost five years."

"No shit?"

"I shit you not, yer grace. Was in England. I'm a rich kid. Cricket. Guy threw the ball at the 'stumps,' and hit me. Stupid game."

"So," Hanson asked, "how much longer till you get all the right lights to blink over there in that green mobile home?"

"Couple days. Couple weeks. Christ. Fuckin' humidity here. They designed the God damn thing in a lab somewhere—controlled atmospheric conditions and they expect it to work over here. They say it's 'air droppable.' A good kick against the door blows circuits."

The "green mobile home" was a highly classified, air-conditioned, humidity-controlled radio room that had been shipped as a single unit. It was part of a complex airborne and ground electronic network to be used to locate enemy troop concentrations. Recon teams, like Hanson's, would be inserted nearby the suspected enemy location to pinpoint the unit, then direct air strikes—if the enemy didn't pinpoint the team first. Quinn referred to the concept as "stomping through the bushes till you step in shit." Like many of the machines that had been designed to win the war scientifically, it didn't work.

"You guys got any officers over there?"

"No. That's one of the good things about the job. Being an officer doesn't mean you know anything about electronics, so no officers."

"Who's in charge?"

"Oh, me, I guess, and Pierce. Pierce knows what he's doing."

"Standard question," Hanson said. "What you doin' over here?"

"Like I said, I'm a rich kid. I fucked around over in England and Ireland when I should have been in school. I got a draft notice and, being a bright lad, I figured four years in the air force beats two in the infantry, so I enlisted."

"No. I mean *here*, in 'Nam. How bad did you have to fuck up to get sent over here?"

"I volunteered. See, you never been an electronics NCO at Brandenburg AFB, so you can't know. I had to sit in this room all day. There was a neon light over my desk that made this tiny little drone all day long. Nothing to do really. I used to sit under that God damn light trying to look busy. I was doing dialectics, you know, spending hours debating things with an imaginary opponent. You know, discussing the relative merits of two different kinds of radarscope image-configuration. I was going nuts. Thought pretty soon I'd end up like Nietzsche, throw my arms around a horse's neck and cry,

'Oh, my brother.' So . . . I decided to come and take a look at Vietnam. Is it really like the 6:30 news?"

"Cook's tour of the war," Hanson said. "OK."

They drank in silence for a few minutes, then Hanson looked up at the ceiling and said in a monotone, "Uh, this is Defcon, Bodycount."

Quinn was polishing the bolt of his Swedish K.

"Bodycount, this is Defcon, do you copy, over."

Still polishing the bolt, Quinn said, "Uh, roger-roger, Defcon, I copy five by five, over."

"What is our situation here, Bodycount? Do we have Max H&I concentrations this location? Please affirm."

"That is most affirmed. Max H&I. Firebase Bruise and Peggylee on call with selected ordinance to include Willy Pete, HE, Uh, Photoflash, flare, BLU-10 Bravo Firecracker, and nonpersistent CN nausea, and smoke. One oh fives, one five fives, and eight inch."

"Uh, roger Bodycount. Have you made contact with Colonel Fang's Phantom battalion and, if so, have you deployed as planned, Op-plan C73-Tango?"

"That is most affirmed, Defcon."

"Real fine, Bodycount. We have the Zoomie mobile home here, calibrated to the X-oh-A system for VHF and UHF capabilities. You may anticipate Max saturation, your location."

"Roger that, Defcon."

"Uh, roger-roger. We have the ordinance, the technology, and, Bodycount, we have the motivation. Good fortune surrounds us, Bodycount. Defcon out."

Hanson hissed through his teeth like a dead radio channel, then finished his beer.

Hanson walked to his footlocker and took the tin whistle out of his pack. He sat down on a rope-handled ammo crate that had black words stenciled on the raw wood: PROJECTILES/HE/105—LOT 177321.

Hanson bent his head, paused, then began to play. A slow,

frail piping, that seemed to reject yet confirm happiness. Sad and slightly eerie. Quinn stopped polishing the machine gun bolt.

When Hanson finished no one spoke for a minute. Then the air force guy said, "Banish Misfortune." Then, in an Irish brogue, went on, "And I haven't heard it played since the military called me from the pubs of Dublin. Stay where you are, lad, I'll be back."

He was back in a few minutes.

"Now," he said in the brogue, "sure the beer is fine, but I happen to have this bottle of Irish," and he set a green bottle on the bar, "and I happen to have this," he said, and pulled a dulcimer from under his arm.

"Now," he said, holding up one finger, "first, a taste of the Irish."

They drank from the bottle and passed it around.

"And now, sir, would you happen to know a little air, a favorite of mine, 'Sir John Fenwick was the flower of them all'?"

Hanson smiled, nodded his head, and they began to play.

And they played together—the dulcimer, and the tin whistle, and the song about a knight who was brave, and thoughtful and honest, and gentle and kind enough to be remembered as "the flower of them all."

The teamhouse was silent except for the song. Quinn looked up from his work, his cold little eyes almost thoughtful, or puzzled. He smiled.

When they finished the song, Hanson said softly, "Oh shit. God damn. Now wasn't that fine?"

They passed the bottle around until it was gone, and the air force guys got up to leave.

"Thanks for the hospitality," the air force guy said.

"Not at all," Hanson said, "see you tomorrow."

When they'd gone, Hanson realized that he did not even know the air force guy's name.

It was almost 2 A.M. when the rain started. The sappers, wearing only loincloths so as not to get tangled in the wire, began pushing the bamboo tubes through the wire. The bamboo was full of explosive that would blow paths through the wire for the assault troops. The sappers were brave. They were not drugged, or fanatic, and most of them did not believe in words like "liberation." They were good soldiers, men who had found themselves in a job they could do well. An elbow or ankle could pop a trip-flare and ruin the attack.

Once the sappers had pulled the bamboo tubes through the wire, they began throwing satchel charges into bunkers. When the explosions began, the assault troops blew the bamboo tubes and began to mortar the camp. Some of the sappers died in the explosions of the mortars, but that was a risk they took.

The assault troops moved through the paths in the wire and many of them died in the explosions of their own mortars.

Dawson had been on radio watch, monitoring the artillery units, headquarters in Da Nang, and listening to a football game in the States on a transistor radio. It was Saturday afternoon in the States. The announcer's voice was tiny and tinny as he screamed "And it's the 25, the 20, the 15, and Parker is *down* on their own 14. Yessir, folks, it's that kind of ball game." And Dawson could hear the crowd cheer, a tiny, tiny wail, the sound an insect might make as it burned to death. Then the B-40 rocket came through the teamhouse door and a tiny piece of shrapnel drove into the back of Dawson's head, and he fell across the bank of radios. He was not dead, but he couldn't move. He could still hear the radio, "and it looks like Nebraska is really going to have to get their defense machine moving against the Missouri Tigers . . ."

By the time Hanson was out of his bunker, the camp had begun to fire illumination rounds from the mortar tubes. The rounds burst like fireworks, hurtled earthward like meteors, and then were pulled up short by their parachutes, pink stars swinging with the wind, dripping sparks, and throwing black-green shadows.

A red fan of machine gun tracers swept in from the west, a wedge of heavy rounds popping as they passed overhead. The rain dripped down Hanson's face, through his moustache, and he tasted salt.

On top of the TOC bunker, Silver had taken the cover off the M-60 and was looking for a target. He found one and began firing six-round bursts. The muzzle flash blinked against his glasses. He was wearing a bandanna. The recoil of the M-60 pulled at his T-shirt like a heavy wind, puffing it out at the small of his back, plastering it against his ribs.

Hanson yelled, "Get some, Silver," and without turning his head, Silver pumped his fist up and down.

Way out on the southwest corner of the wire a trip-flare burst silver glare and dense white smoke. Hanson thought he could hear it burning with a wet sputter, but of course it was too far away to hear. Then, at the point of the camp nearest the trip-flare, he could make out the hesitant popping of a small gasoline engine being started. The popping rose and steadied into a cheerful little popping like a lawn mower on Saturday afternoon. The small gasoline engine is the power source for the quad-fifty machine gun. Hanson paused, staring through the dark and rain toward the sound.

The gun suddenly showed itself like a moving picture flashing on a dark screen, the sound turned all the way up. The linked brass rounds flickered in the muzzle flash, snaking toward the gray slab of the breech block. The gun crew moved in the strobe light of the four barrels like silent comedy stars trying to do something hilarious and impossible while there was still time. The crew kept feeding cans of ammo to the gun as the four barrels wove tracers smoothly crossing and recrossing the perimeter. One of the barrels burned out and raveled the pattern with a mad counterpoint of plunging rounds.

And Hanson crossed toward the four-deuce mortar position where he knew he would find Quinn, moving in a clumsy lope, heavy web gear shifting and pulling at him, weapon down in a low port arms. He saw a thin, naked man in the wire and fired at him. Pink flares, red and green tracers reflected in puddles and across tin roofs.

At dawn it was like the morning after a bad fire, everything burned and sodden. The time when people sort through the debris for whatever might be left.

They found Sergeant Major first. In the ditch. Hanson looked and realized that all the wounds were AK rounds. No frags or mortars. What that meant was that while Sergeant Major was walking—and he *had* to have known it—the other people were firing aimed rounds at him. It wasn't a chance frag, it was walking back and forth like walking in front of a firing squad. He remembered a line from an old song, "An' ever step you take, you walkin' in De Lions blood."

Quinn and Hanson carried him to the ammo shed. Whenever he carried a body, Hanson thought about how the man at the head and the man holding the feet had to pull against each other, so the body wouldn't sag and drag in the mud.

They laid him under the tin roof of the ammo shed and covered him with a poncho, very carefully, so the rain wouldn't drip on him.

Quinn tucked the poncho under Sergeant Major's feet like you'd tuck a child in bed. "Ah, shit," he said.

Dawson was in the teamhouse waiting for a medivac. Silver told Hanson that Dawson was alive, but couldn't move.

Hanson walked into the teamhouse and looked down at Dawson. Dawson stared up at him.

"Hey brother, you *al*most lost that bet, didn't you?"

Dawson just stared at him.

"Hey," Hanson said, "hey, can you hear me?"

"Blink your eyes if you can hear me, OK?"

Dawson blinked his eyes.

"OK. There you go. You gonna be OK. Right?"

Dawson stared at him.

"Please. It's true. Blink your eyes 'cause you know it's

true. Three times. Blink 'em three times. You know that B-40 frag ain't shit."

Dawson blinked his eyes, and tears began to roll from them.

Dawson had a bloody bandage across his black head, so Hanson held his arm instead of his head. "Hey, *hey,* it's gonna be OK." But Hanson knew he was doing more harm than good, and he walked out of the teamhouse.

He walked outside and heard Silver say something ". . . every one." "Got every one of those fucking zoomies. Poor dumb stupid fuckers."

All the air force guys were sprawled in the mud, maybe five meters apart. None of them had boots on, none of them had a weapon. They had all run out of the bunker in a panic, and Charlie had burned 'em down, one by one.

Hanson found the one who played the dulcimer. No boots, no weapon, no shirt. His pallid skin was covered with ugly purple holes. His face was covered with mud.

Hanson looked down at him and whispered, "You dumb fucker." And then he started talking to him as though he were still alive. "You *stupid* shit. What did you come over here for? To 'see the war,' right. You ever learn how to shoot that silly ass M-16? They ever take time to teach you that? They ever tell you that there's a lot of people over here who are trying to *kill* you for no good God damn reason at all? You and that dumbass electric mobile home that doesn't work anyway.

"Aw, man. Aw, man," Hanson was sobbing now, "just when I think I got things figured out, some shit like this has to happen.

"Banish Misfortune, what a crock of shit."

Quinn had walked up behind Hanson. Hanson spun on him. "Fuck off, Quinn. Just fuck off. I don't want to know you any more. You ain't my friend no more. I don't want any more friends. Fuck 'em. All they do is die. Just get the fuck away from me, OK?"

Quinn looked at Hanson and said, "Yeah," and walked off.

Hanson almost threw his rifle into the mud, but he was too well-trained to do that. "Fuckin' air force," he said.

By then the 5th Mech tanks had gotten there and were setting up around the perimeter. Naked sappers still hung in the wire like dead fish. One of the tankers had put a cigarette in the mouth of a dead sapper, and had his arm around the body. Another tanker was taking his picture with an Instamatic. Hanson knocked him down and stomped on the camera. Hanson turned his rifle on the other tanker and said, "I'll kill you, man. You ain't got the right to do that. You ain't got the *right*." The tears had made lines through the mud and sweat on Hanson's cheeks.

Hanson walked past a tank. The crew members looked at him funny. Hanson still didn't realize that he was crying. One of them said, "Guess it must have been rough, huh?"

Hanson looked at him. The tanker was just trying to say something to *help*.

Hanson nodded his head, "Yeah," and for most of the day, he denied the King of the Red Branch Kings, and Cuchulain, and that Sir John Fenwick was the flower of them all.

He heard the medivac come thudding in for Dawson.

A few hours later he walked into the teamhouse. Quinn was cleaning his rifle. He looked up, then back down at his rifle.

"Hey," Hanson said, "Quinn, buy you a beer?"

Quinn looked up and smiled. "Never turned down a free beer, have I?"

The tunnel rat was the grunt—usually a volunteer—who crawled in Charlie's burrows, flashlight and pistol in hand, seeking out the enemy. While many of the tunnel rats had their quirks, we never met one who was quite as unusual as Sgt. Bobo.

Lee K. Abbott

The Viet Cong Love of Sgt. Donnie T. Bobo

T he way it worked in MR 2, up around Ban Me Thuot, near National Highway 14, was the usual:

I found the hole first, it being dug near the base of a wretched looking Cay-dai tree and not well-camouflaged at all; and then Donnie T. came over, took a quick looksee and squatted down, his face the picture of cunning and eagerness. You could tell this was his favorite part.

"Here's the truth of it," he began, doffing his steel pot and shooing mosquitoes. "Up here, in the sunshine and fresh air, feeling good about himself and his job, which is tunnel-ratting, is me, Sgt. Donald Theodore Bobo of Prairie Grove, Arkansas, U.S. of A. and home of the Fighting Squirrels. And down there in that stinky spider hole full of snakes and corruption and other foulness is you, Mr. Charles Cong."

In the nine months we were there, he always started this

way, praising Mr. Charles as a worthy adversary and a gentleman, then introducing me, PFC Leon Busby, also a Fighting Squirrel, and saying that we were the Batman and Robin of tunnel rats, unlickable and mighty. It was a dandy speech, and an impressive history. Donnie T. would say that we were an Unvanquished Team, having gone to the same elementary and Junior High, having played in the same backfield (Donnie T. as the QB, me as a wingback), and having come within an "I do" of marrying twin sisters named Bonnie and Connie Suggs before coming to our senses and enlisting on January 18 of nineteen and sixty-seven. Sometimes, he'd even recite a poem, his favorite being the specialty of the Light Crust Dough Boys and Senator Bud "Pappy" O'Dell. This went: "I have a mother. I had to have. I love her whether she's good or bad. I love her whether she's live or dead. Whether she's an angel or an old dope head."

Then he'd relax while our translator, an ARVN cowboy named Duc Lap, chittered into that hole like a frightened monkey.

"War's a rotten thing," Donnie T.'d say, going on about how much him and me were enjoying our stay in Vietnam, and how we truly appreciated the hospitality of the friendly Yellow People, and how we'd been to all the good places like the White Rat, and how we particularly enjoyed seeing Mr. Bob Hope every year, but that if he, meaning Mr. Cong, didn't come out of his hole pretty soon, we'd be forced to blow his rice-sucking face off, etc. It was positively lyrical.

And then, likely as not, we'd sit a while, Donnie T. slurping at a can of C-ration cling peaches, me doing fanny bump exercises, and Duc Lap looking to us for guidance and compliments. Oh, these were lovely times—the heat heavy and lazy-feeling, the jungle steaming, bugs buzzing, and us at the apex of our youth, so to speak. Maybe an hour would pass before you'd hear Mister Charles.

"Eat bees, Soldier Boy," he'd say. (You got to take my word for it; I never cottoned on to the lingo.) Anyway, Duc

Lap would go stiff with fright (and usually faint dead away), and I'd roll into my mean-ass Combat Position and Donnie T.'d glow with smugness and self-esteem. It was, you can be sure, a joyous moment in the annals of war.

"You come on outta there," Donnie T.'d yell in Congtalk. And more: "Chung ting bubba rubba dam doo," which didn't mean a thing but was intended to convey fear and extreme seriousness.

Sure, there'd be some whining and such from Mr. Charles, maybe a burst of Commie automatic fire. But soon enough there he'd be, flushed by guilt and defeat and doom, his face a glaze of sweat and grime, and not a shot fired by yours truly.

But this was all before Donnie T. fell in love.

It was up in Hua Nghia Province, July 1968. By this time we had achieved a lofty reputation, having been responsible for the capture and confinement of forty-one sapsucking Commies and the destruction of approximately three tons of warmaking matériel (including a bike repair shop and two Vespa motor scooters and a volume of nasty French literature); so two mucky-mucks from MACV were trucked in to watch us do our stuff on this local Charles (named the Prince of Darkness on account of his ability to make evil out of our good intentions). You can imagine our shock when Charles turned out to be a girl.

The day was a scorcher, I remember, so we were dressed accordingly—Bermuda shorts, cotton polo shirts with the teeny alligator on the chest, and ventilated golf hats like Hubie Green uses. (Because of our fame, you see, we were extended certain courtesies like being able to go down to China Beach to raid the skivvy houses.) Anyway, after the Brass got settled on their specially built viewing platform, Donnie T. went to work at this black hole dug into the side of a hill, sweet talking and bullying.

But it was no good, and after an hour you could see the panic set in, etc. We were dry-mouthed. We tried it all that day—the appeal to Charles' vanity, the tug at the heartstrings, threats against his physical well-being, insulting his pedigree. I threw in some comments about the Catholics, letting him know I was sympathetic to the religious argument. Even Duc Lap stomped around a bit, yapping at some length about the Angry Mountain Gods, reunification of the Homeland, and blood-letting of every kind, finally giving up in a huff of outrage and sitting under a scrawny tree, sulking. Mortified, Donnie T. addressed the grumbling officers, apologizing for the delay. His body was a column of grief and confusion.

"What now?" I said. Duc Lap was sniveling openly, his shirt wet with slobber. "We don't get this bugger, somebody gonna fry our ass."

"Gut shot." His lips were white and pulpy. "No more Mr. Nice Guy."

In a second, Donnie T. had our ditty bag open and was hurling contraband into the hole, proven items of VC lure like dirty pictures of Idaho girls with remarkable bosoms, and PX goodies like tape decks and Otis Redding records.

No effect. I was devastated. The Brass were like stone.

So, as a last resort, Donnie T. began revealing his personal history. It was a humiliating two hours.

"I have stolen," Donnie T. screeched into that hole. He was a desperate man, all right, his face puffy and sweating like a wheel of cheese. "I have dressed up in girl's panties and had lewd thoughts about my mother. I have masturbated and picked my nose and lit my farts with kitchen matches. I have been covetous and deceitful and petty with my betters."

On and on he went, telling how him and me swam naked in the flumes and how we broke and entered Old Lady Sweem's house and how we lost our cherries to the same girl (Betty Lou Greathouse), even telling about the time we skipped school and drove down to Little Rock, got a room at the Motel Six, and paid twenty dollars each for some State Avenue white trash to go round the world and the thrill of it.

"I am a broke man," Donnie T. said by the end, his spirit

gone. Duc Lap was up a tree, praying. Naturally, the Brass were impatient and bugged out before the climax.

"Come out," Donnie T. was blubbering. "Take your prize. You have whupped the best."

At this point, he was on his knees, bare-chested, limp with woe. For a second, there was nothing, only a jungle silence of heartbreak; then this weird ha-ha voice comes echoing out of the hole: "G.I. Joe, what a schmoe!"

It was here that Donnie T. lost his poise.

The next few minutes were a blur. All I remember is Donnie T. diving into the hole with a roar, his legs disappearing and the awfulest rumble of a fight.

"Git some!" I was hollering. "Take it to him, D.T. You're the one. Whip up, whip up!"

Then, there he was, dragging this Charles out—this girl—his face lit like a lamp with love.

For a month Donnie T. was useless, only laying in his cot weary and unrecovered. He had the morning and afternoon terrors, his mind on one thing: love. Duc Lap would come in with a sackful of Hamlet Reports, each polka-dotted with the sites of fresh Charles holes, including some of the most famous like the Tay Ninh Trigger and the three Leos from Cheo Reo.

"Upsy-daysie," Duc Lap would say. "You zap Cong today?"

"Aaarrrgghh," Donnie T.'d moan, doubling up, cramped with love pains; and I'd swab his brow with a wet T-shirt.

Her name was Ting Nuh, but by the second week at Saigon Detention Center the spies were calling her Lucy. She was 18, an utter bombshell. The pictures started arriving almost immediately. There she was, in all her frail china doll beauty, in a snow-white interrogation room. Donnie T. perked up some when he saw those. "I'm dying, Leon," he told me one night, "just wasting into everlasting nothingness."

Then the rumors hit: She was the daughter of one of the Eleven Old Men of the Hanoi Politburo; she was the niece of a French Sex Queen. It was the silliest stuff. The spooks weren't getting anywhere with her. They were battling Cong pride and centuries of distrust. Then, at last, came the word: the debriefing of Lucy would be done by Sgt. Donnie T. Bobo. They'd give him a whack at her, only fair.

"Hot shit!" Donnie T. hollered when he heard that, rising resurrected out of his funk.

A spade spy named Jackson flew us down incognito in Air America. We called him James Bond on account of his keen interest in disguise and backstabbing. James put us up at the Continental Hotel, later making us pretty at a dummy beauty parlor on Tu Do Street. Next day we went downtown—me as a correspondent, Duc Lap as a Jap Teenage Idol, and Donnie T. as a USIA missionary which allowed him to look crazy and driven and jittery (which he was).

For a long time, we just stood and watched through the one-way glass, Donnie T. wheezing with lust.

"Love is squeezing my heart," he kept saying over and over.

She was his type all right—skin like fine paper, and big eyes, not to mention a body like a poem. It was a wicked fifteen minutes.

Duc Lap wanted to lop off her humpers, make burger meat or some such. "I make her talk," he insisted. "Go boom in face, plenty true. Girl no match for number one evil killer. Jap Idol angry for chance. Time no impediment." You could tell he was a true patriot.

I was thinking about Betty Lou Greathouse and how in the 10th grade me and Donnie T. went over to her trailer. Her folks were out of town and she was hot for Donnie T., not me. I was just a tag along, good company and so forth. But Donnie T. wasn't having none of that. "You want me, you got to take Leon," he said. This had a real crushing effect on her. She was a Senior and old around the eyes and used to getting her way in affairs of the heart. "I'll have to think about it," she said, wandering back to the toilet to make up her mind. The place was all decorated in candles and velvet paintings of slick Mex matadors. Needless to say, my blood was up. Then she came back, toothpick stuck between her teeth, and said okay, which left me light-headed and sweaty. I followed her back to the bedroom which was also decorated: stuffed pandas and movie posters (which spoke of Tormented Passion and Love That Blinds). "Don't go nowheres, Donald," she yelled. I was on top of her by this time, pants and Jockey shorts at my ankles. She had her eyes closed and wasn't breathing much. You could tell she was enjoying it. When they were doing it, I sat in the living room and played Johnny Mathis records. Afterward, driving home in the pick-up, I was grateful. "Thanks," I said. Donnie T. gave my shoulder a big squeeze. "Ain't nothing," he said. That's the kind of guy he was.

"How you know it's love?" I said now. I was feeling jealous, us having been pals so long.

Donnie T. pointed to his temple, knees and chest. There was dizziness, weakness and furious thumping, respectively. I felt shameful.

That evening, James Bond took me and Duc Lap over to Mimi's Flamboyant where I got stupid on 33 beer. James told everyone that Duc Lap was a Rising Recording Star doing a tour of charity and goodwill. The ladies went loco trying to be friendly to him and toward midnight he got on stage to sing Country and Western. Duc Lap did his damnedest to sound hurt and broken in despair, but you could see he was in his element, beer and closeness and willing women.

I passed out before he got to the part where the hero takes it in the ear.

For a week I saw little of Donnie T., but me and Duc Lap were making the rounds. James Bond was trotting us around like celebrities, even buying Duc Lap a purple and turquoise

Cowboy outfit with hat and chaps. The notoriety just swelled and Duc Lap was spending every second crooning, standing in the limelight, and writing love lyrics. *Stars and Stripes* even did an interview, called him the slope Hank Williams. After that, he was insufferable.

One night our paths crossed, Donnie T. and me. The change in him was remarkable. Hair cut and clean-shaven, he looked as wholesome as a tomato. You could see he wasn't getting any Intelligence out of Lucy.

"What say, D.T.?" I began. He was in the john, popping pimples in a fit of self-admiration. "Let's you and me go back to work, huh?"

He didn't say anything, just rubbed on a little Jade East and was gone. It was real grim.

Then, after two weeks, he surprised me.

It was late and I was asleep. Duc Lap was out being personable and noteworthy, posing for pictures and feeling grand. I was just the opposite: forlorn. I was dreaming of Donnie T. and me and fishing for carp in the Buffalo River. This was ages ago. We used to dig forts and tunnels in the sand bars, take a can of Sterno to bake beans, and sit around smoking Lucky Strikes and coughing. It was a youth dream, you know, brave and sentimental and lost. Then I felt this shaking.

There was Donnie T. and in the shadows a lurking figure I knew without seeing: Lucy.

"What'd you do?" I said.

Bribes had done the trick, he said. That and confusion and normal war mysteries had sprung her from the Detention Center.

"We're gonna get married," he said.

I pointed out the obvious: court martial, the stockade, misery, etc. It was like talking down a hole.

"I'm quitting," he said. "My fighting days are over."

It was early morning and a gorgeous moon was out, making me blue with homesickness.

"What about your mom?" Donnie T.'s mom was real

ugly, with all her brains in her chest, but real sweet and a charter subscriber to Art Thom's Rainbow Prayer.

"Regrettable," is what he said. "Now, come on, you're our best man."

"I ain't moving." Immediately Lucy began sobbing.

"What you mean?"

I reminded him of our plans. We were going to go down to New Orleans, blow off steam and count our blessings, then head out to the oilfields of West Texas. I had an uncle there who was a mudman. Me and Donnie were going to become rich, live in luxury, maybe buy a farm or a small city. It was the standard, uninspired hope.

"You're a fool," he said. "Now, shake a leg, Leon. We got a preacher already."

It was true, and twenty minutes later the three of us were standing in front of a Korean minister. He prayed, shook his fist over the happy couple, burped and it was done.

"Many happinesses," he said.

I was near tears. I could see my whole future going into the dumper.

Then the preacher's wife came out with a Black Market Polaroid and made us pose. "Birdie, birdie," she was saying.

Lucy looked radiant, and Donnie T. was, well, proud. He'd stolen a waiter's jacket from the Continental, so he looked real formal.

Then the camera went off like a phosphorus gun, leaving me blind for an instant.

"Bye, bye," Donnie T. said, pumping my hand. It was the famous adiós scene, you know, the two of us being tough and realistic and so on. But I wasn't up to it.

"Look what you've done now," I was crying. "Where are you gonna go, D.T.? They're gonna have your balls for this. Where will you live? You're stupid, Donnie T., plain stupid. Look what kind of a fix you're in now!"

But he wasn't listening, so I slugged him. We tussled for a

minute but he was fighting for a higher passion. Eventually, he sat on my chest. My cheeks were slick with tears.

"Here," he said, "you keep the picture."

And they were gone on a Honda into the darkness, me holding a snapshot of—left to right—the Korean preacher, the lovers and me. It was the worst moment in my life.

The Army was pissed, of course, losing a bona fide source of information and its number one tunnel rat, but took most of its displeasure out on Duc Lap. It was sad, him going from Entertainment Personality to grunt soldier in a day. Last I saw of him, he was sitting on the back of a deuce-and-a-half with a bunch of turncoat Friendlies, looking woebegone and heading for some fearful spot like Hue, some place full of dread and terror where he was sure to get a chest wound as a reward.

James Bond, he drilled me, but I pleaded innocence and apathy. "I don't know anything," I said. "Ain't no friend of mine." It was a touching lie which James saw through and sent me back to coaxing bad guys out of holes. But all my enthusiasm was gone.

I'd sit over those holes just like Donnie T., offering my advice and wisdom to those inside. This'd go on for hours. I'd speak to themes of mutual interest, like survival and valor, etc., maybe sing a bit from Uncle Roy and his Red Creek Wranglers. After a while, I'd just give up, pop in some CS gas, would snooze by some likely spot, then leg it back to my CO with another story of trying and failing.

Finally, Uncle Sugar saw the light and sent me back to the World.

Upon my return, I was uncontrollable, full of private crud and mean thoughts.

I went down to New Orleans, but without Donnie T. it just wasn't the party I'd planned on. Went to Texas, too, but the luxury was all gone before I got there. So, about the time the war stopped, I came back here, to Prairie Grove to work in the Purina store.

I see Donnie T.'s mom at the Kroger every now and again. Each time she looks uglier, naturally blaming me and the Pentagon for the loss of her boy. One time she came at me with a box of Tide and a can of solvent, her face gleaming with anger, her coat flying like a cape. "Where's my Donnie!" she shrieked, chasing me down the condiments aisle, her ruckus the focus of attention. "You!" she hollered. "Leon Busby, you coward. You let my Donald down."

I used to mind, but not anymore, especially now that I've got a love of my own. You guessed it: Betty Lou Greathouse.

Here's how it happened:

I got a postcard from Paris, France. From Mr. and Mrs. D. T. Bobo. It was full of gleeful news. Lucy and Donnie T. had two kids, Leon and Busby, all with Cong middle names. They were living in Ho Chi Minh City, escorting newsmen and making themselves useful to the new order. He was hoping life was good to me as it had been generous to him and his. Then he said: "Love has turned me around. You should turn too."

Last night, I did. I went down to the Creole Palace and worked up a whiskey frenzy, harmonizing with the band, shooting bumper pool. Everybody was smiling and taking me into their hearts. Then I grew horny and lonely and wet-eyed, and went outside to collect myself. Some minutes later I was sitting on the cement steps of Betty Lou's trailer. Nothing could have worked out finer: it turned out she was lonely too.

"Here's the truth of it," I began, telling her the whole story. To avoid embarrassing myself, I just pretended I was speaking to a tree stump or a charred hooch and that Duc Lap was translating.

Then the door opened. It was a classic moment. She was wearing a nightie and you could tell the years had been good to her.

"Come inside," she said, which almost made me explode.

The velvet paintings were still there, along with some driftwood and glass doo-dads and curios.

For a long time, we didn't do anything, just lay there on her bedspread, it being an awkward situation. Then we kissed, tender-like, and I felt a liquid warmth in my chest and went for her with a whoop. She reciprocated, whooping too. Oh, it was superior, the two of us moaning, me being sloppy and Betty Lou taking me to her chest with a sigh; and by morning, there I was, tired, planning and making promises.

Some of us take a long time to learn something. Others a short time.

Donnie T. knew that. I know it now.

BODY
BAGS

These selections are excerpted from the diary of a Navy flier, Lieutenant Frank C. Elkins. The message that concludes this chapter is self-explanatory.

Frank Callihan Elkins

Entries

JULY 28, 1966

Today we had our first aircraft downed, first aircraft for my squadron for the cruise. That damned Vinh again. Darell, Glenn, and I went in, and Glenn didn't come back. I hope that obnoxious son-of-a-gun is walking around down there somewhere, but I don't really believe it.

Darell was picking up a SAM radar and homing in on it for a missile shot when Glenn called, "Missiles away," and I heard him call again, "Keep it turning and hit the deck." We all scattered and watched the missiles explode above us. Then Darell popped back up for another shot. He fired two missiles and watched them impact; two good hits. Johnny and Harold, who were in another flight nearby, thought they heard "Maverick Two, good *chute*" on their radio, and therefore decided that someone saw a parachute. But nobody in the air would admit making the call, and we decided that perhaps Glenn had watched Darell's hits and had called, "Maverick Two good shoot" or "good shooting." It wasn't ninety seconds after Darell fired his missiles that we missed Glenn. All we really know is that his last heading was inland toward downtown Vinh.

I'm not as pessimistic about his chances as some, for if he took a hit and lost his radio, he might have glided in that direction (inland to the highlands). The hazards of ejection were less for Glenn, for he had been a paratrooper in the Army.

A few nights ago in our bull session, Glenn gave me a few hints about landing in water, and what you could do in addition to what we've already been taught. He feels much the same way I do about capture. Although we're taught that the best thing to do is to throw away your pistol if capture is imminent, since the NVN insist that captors go unharmed (it makes for their most effective weapon against our morale, the trials and threats to live captives), we both agreed that we would probably try to shoot it out and make like a one-man army rather than quietly march off to Hanoi.

I don't think Glenn is in pain. He's either out there evading like he's been trained to do, or he's dead, and killed quickly and without enduring much suffering. That's what I'd try: the long shot of escape, rather than the long shot of outliving and outlasting the brainwashing and rehabilitation.

What an odd place that Vinh is. Yesterday on that hop with Jack, not a shot or missile was fired. And today, no Glenn. Oh hell, you can't help hoping he's walking around down there somewhere . . . or maybe he got smart and headed for Sydney or Borneo. Not likely, but I hope so.

So last night I broke out the old guitar. A Kentucky boy on the line crew had been after me for a guitar session, and we wired our guitars through the movie projector amplifier in the ready room and had a good old Bluegrass hoedown, to the disgust of many of the city slickers aboard. I didn't give a damn for what they thought anyway. The Kentucky guy's name is Scruggs, and it's appropriate. He sang "Detroit City" and "Fireball Mail" like Nashville itself.

Glenn McWhorter, Ensign, USNR, killed or missing.

OCTOBER 10, 1966

This midnight-to-noon routine is killing. Really killing. We only seem to heckle the enemy and keep him awake and maybe make him keep his lights off at night, but we fly airplanes into the ground, into mountains, into the sea and lose sleep because nobody can get used to going to bed at noon. I'm getting sick of the whole affair. Still I try to remember that I asked to be here.

Just in the last week or so, the antiaircraft defenses seem to have doubled or tripled, and you get shot at now from places where even a month or so ago you could overfly with relative security. We've lost 10 per cent of our pilots and 20 per cent of our aircraft on this cruise so far, and we're not on our way home yet.

With luck, I'll make it home for Christmas.

OCTOBER 11, 1966

Wahoo, hurrah, and yippee! We're off the mid-to-noon for a whole week. Now it's noon-to-midnight, and that's so sweet it's like a chance to fly other than completely exhausted.

Sign on the ready room chalkboard: "Only 30 more Bombing Days till Christmas, get yours done early!" Sign number 2: "Flight Surgeon Sez: Get your annual physical, those not complying will be grounded (upon arrival in San Diego)!" Sign number 3: "Yossarian Sez: The Ironhand that was scheduled to be cancelled will brief 30 minutes early."

Night before last I took B-10 out on a night bombing hop and found and bombed a convoy of trucks. Stumbled around for twenty minutes not knowing where the devil we were, getting shot at from everywhere, looking for checkpoint 38. Finally gave up and decided to go out and get oriented and find something else. Heading out, I saw two lights, dropping two flares to mark the spot, and found the convoy.

On a later hop yesterday I took Jerry out and scared the devil out of us both. I led him through a couple of double-Immelmans, stalling out over the top of each one. Then I did some zero-airspeed, hammerhead climbs that always scare me. But then I did the grand finale which I never admitted to him that I had never had the guts to try before; I let down to low altitude over the water, getting lower and lower, 100 feet, then 50, then 20, then 10. Then finally I let my hook down and eased it down till the hook touched the water twice, and that was at about 350 knots. Great fun! I took Barry out today and did the same thing; but Barry did it too. I not only never did it before; I never heard of anyone's doing it. And when I saw Barry's hook touch the water, I decided that maybe I'd never try it again. When your hook hits, your drop tank is only about eighteen inches above the water.

It seems that we never go into A1 in the morning anymore but what there's another report of a Navy pilot downed. Just every day. Just count them off.

But now, glorious day, we're off the mid-to-noon for a week.

Night before last after I wrote Marilyn, while I was lying in bed for that six hours, I lay there and hated that night hop and hated that night hop and hated the strain of flying where you have to look in every direction at once and look out for yourself and somebody else and hated the Navy and mostly hated that doggoned night hop and the fact that I couldn't go to sleep so long that the very idea of a whole career in the Navy was so remote to me that I decided that I wanted out of all this, decided that the thing for me to do was go through three years of shore duty and then go back to North Carolina and do something; law, teach, anything, start a business, run the farm, and get out of all this. As far as that period of tossing and turning, rolling, forcing myself to lie still while I took first one hundred deep breaths in one position and one hundred deep breaths in another position in an effort to make my body go to sleep, as far as that four hours went, it was certain that the only thing for me to do was to get out. I thought of all the times when I was growing up, even in high school, that I was afraid of something and took the easy way out, of all the times I was scared and took the coward's way out, of all the times I didn't think I could look the other guys in the face and feel that I was quite the same stuff they were, fights I backed down from, loafing at football practice, loafing on the farm sometimes, or not putting everything I had into any one of a thousand things. I could think of all that, knowing that if I turned in my wings, that I'd have to live all my life in that same feeling of shame, having the medals but secretly knowing that I had given up because I didn't think I had the stuff to keep going when it got rough. And yet, it wasn't quite enough.

I had all that on the one hand, and on the other hand was that damned night hop coming up in the ink black that seems to belong exclusively to the night over here, the uncertainty that the airplane was going to make it into the air off the cat, the terror of not knowing or of having to find the exact right spot to coast in, of having to watch out not only for myself but to coordinate and control, to maintain order, to keep track of that all-important wingman, and to get back and find the ship and make sure that he got back and got aboard, and then to fly that ink-black approach and not break my neck on the ramp or fly into the water or fly into the sea or into a mountain or into the ground and see to it that my wingman didn't.

All these things can be done easily enough taken one thing at a time, but lying in bed knowing that you'll be required to do it all, it all lies on your mind at once, and you can't sleep and every minute goes by and you know that that's one minute more of precious sleep you lost and need to be safe and get the job done safely and yet you can't sleep and you just lie there and lie there and you can't stop thinking about it all and you toss and it never quits.

It would almost be a relief to get up right then and brief

and go and do it all, but you can't even do that; you just lie there knowing that when it's really time to go that then you'll be sleepy and tired out and unsafe, and there's nothing, absolutely nothing, you can do about it. It's horrible. And it happens every night, every night until you're off that awful schedule.

And now we're off that schedule for a week. The feeling of relief is inexpressible. Now I can know that although it'll be night flying and Vinh and Nam Dinh and Cam Pha and Haiphong and all the rest, it'll be a schedule on which I face things one at a time, doing each thing as it becomes necessary, living one day at a time, and getting enough sleep and rest to do it sanely and as safely and as much under control as possible.

Still in the back of my mind is the knowledge that sooner or later, a week, eight days, ten, and we'll be back on it again. That's what I came to find out: whether it was really just in my mind, or if I could really hack a combat flying billet, and what it was really like. So now I know. To tell the truth it's about what I expected—harder'n hell.

Scott and I had a discussion once. We're pretty honest with each other, and the subject of his having to prove himself to himself all the time and my having to do the same thing came up. I remember his laughing once and saying something like, "Well, it's true, I don't believe in myself enough to just say, 'Now, Scott, you can do as much or more than anybody else and you don't have to prove a thing,' I've got to show myself." And then he said, "But dammit I do show myself, and do prove things to me and as long as I can keep doing things other folks can't do and things I don't really believe I can do, where's the harm except in the fact that someday I'll fail to prove something—and I've done that before too—where's the hurt if I manage to successfully prove myself?" And I guess that's me over here.

I hate night hops, but almost only when they're the first hop of the day. And every time I walk up on that deck knowing what's coming up, it's like facing death. Hell, more than that, it is facing death; but I think I face it sometimes more heavy-hearted than other folks. I think I'm sometimes more cowardly about it than others, more hesitant. But dammit, I do it. So where's the hurt as long as I manage to get it done?

Yankee Station
12 October 1966

My Darling Marilyn,

I don't really have time to write a decent letter, but I just received your letters, and I wanted to write a thank you note. Or better, an I love you and am thankful for you note. I do and I am.

I'm sitting here in the room eating gee dunk because I didn't feel like getting dressed and then back into flight gear. That's because Robert McNamara, General Wheeler, and a bunch of other admirals and Army generals and captains and colonels are all aboard for the night.

The captain came over the intercom today and said, "Now we're just going to show them a normal day's operation," and now the aviator's chow line is closed.

I missed the big action this morning. Down to the south, Darell was hitting a truck park and was using his bomb computer. The computer fouled up and threw a bomb out into the boonies, and they got all sorts of gigantic secondary explosions. So everyone kept bombing that area and kept getting fires and explosions. It was probably a stockpile area for the DMZ forces. The next three launches were diverted into that area and got all kinds of results. Really a big day. I missed it all. My hop was traded with Joe so that he could escort the VIP's tonight, and I got a tanker hop which aborted. I didn't care; I'd rather give up the hop than do that escort duty.

Another bit of excitement occurred today when a number of motorized craft resembling PT boats were approaching the ship's steaming area from the north. We all figured that maybe we'd get some antisurface action, but they turned out to be Chinese motorized fishing trawlers. The *Constellation* found them first and was all set to sink them when pictures revealed that the single gun mount on the bow was really a crane.

Another A-D pilot down back in the woods. One a day.

I read and read again and again the things you said about the autumn, and it sounded so good I couldn't stop thinking about it. You can't know how much I wish I were there. Won't be long. Even so it seems so long. Tick-tick. It seems like a million years since I saw you last.

I'm looking forward to our cross-country trip to California. Maybe we can borrow sleeping bags and camp out a couple of nights. I love you so much I don't think we'd need but one sleeping bag or even use the other one if we had two.

Well, brief time for my flight. Taking Chip out again tonight. All my love, darling, and thank you again for your lovely thoughts in those two letters today.

I love you.
Frank

WESTERN UNION TELEGRAM

To: Mrs. Frank Callihan Elkins, Route One, Dunlap, Tennessee

I deeply regret to confirm on behalf of the United States Navy that your husband, Lt. Frank Callihan Elkins, 658100/1310, USN is missing in action. This occurred on 13 October 1966 while on a combat mission over North Vietnam. It is believed that your husband was maneuvering his aircraft to avoid hostile fire when radio contact was lost. An explosion was observed but it could not be determined whether this was hostile fire exploding or your husband's aircraft. No parachute or visual signals were observed and no emergency radio signals were received. You may be assured that every effort is being made with personnel and facilities available to locate your husband. Your great anxiety in this situation is understood and when further information is available concerning the results of the search now in progress you will be promptly notified. I join you in fervent hope for his eventual recovery alive. I wish to assure you of every possible assistance together with the heartfelt sympathy of myself and your husband's shipmates at this time of heartache and uncertainty.

The area in which your husband became missing presents the possibility that he could be held by hostile force against his will. Accord-

ingly, for his safety in this event, it is suggested
that in replying to inquiries from sources outside your immediate family you reveal only his
name, rank, file number, and date of birth.

                              Vice Admiral B. J. Semmes, Jr.
                              Chief of Naval Personnel

Tom Suddick's fiction stings. The war left no one untouched, and those who tasted its pain and destruction sometimes took their pleasure in strange ways, as with Jackel and his captive rat.

Tom Suddick

Caduceus

I. WHAT A JOHN WAYNE IS

Convulsing in laughter again, I fell backward and rolled atop my bunker as Greene spilled his third cup of coffee. On the sandbag next to my head, Sutherland, the radioman, pounded with his fist, shrieking and groaning in a helpless laughing fit.

On the next bunker the rest of the squad roared and jeered at the raving Greene in the trench between us.

Greene shouted a hawser of curses and kicked the side of the trench, splattering dirt into the coffee cup (he'd cut his finger making it five minutes ago), causing us to laugh even more uncontrollably. Rummaging in his pack for more instant coffee, powdered cream, and sugar, he started over again.

We had watched this exercise in futility every evening for the past ten days. Greene's coffee-making failures were the only entertainment at Con Thien—a defensive perimeter ringed with bunkers, connected with zigzagging slit trenches—and the only source of comic relief from the irregularly intervalled shellings that forced us to spend most of our time inside our bunkers.

The number of variations for ruining coffee that Greene could perform was positively artistic—though vaudevillian. So far this evening Greene had burned his fingers with the blue polypropylene tablets used to heat C rations, causing him to knock the water-filled cup from his makeshift stove; and he had twice kicked it over while searching for more sugar.

From the top of the opposite bunker, Jackel crowed, wiping tears of laughter from his reddened face. "Christ, Greene, don't ever learn how to make coffee. I'd probably go as crazy as Sutherland if you did."

"Oh shit, no," piped up Kaufmann. "If you do learn, we'll have to go back to torturing rats for laughs."

Greene glared up at them, then began gazing around, as if searching for something that he absolutely knew was there.

Sutherland elbowed me. "I think it's time for your offer of help," he muttered.

I jumped down into the trench. "Want a hand, Greene?"

"Yeah—thanks, Doc. I can't find my John Wayne, It was here just a minute ago." He rifled through the pile of C rat boxes at his feet, raising a flurry of cardboard and tin cans, jerking his head back and forth spasmodically in frantic search.

"You stuck it on your dog-tag chain," I said, hearing the others burst anew into laughter.

Abramson, the squad leader, stood up on the bunker top. "Hey, cummon, Doc. You're givin' him too much help and you're spoilin' the show."

I shrugged my shoulders and put my hands in my pockets. Greene smiled sheepishly, finding his tiny can opener, and extracted another tall, olive drab can from the rubble at his feet. Cutting the lid open, leaving enough uncut to form a handle, and dumping the contents—a package of powdered chocolate, some crackers, and a small tin of peanut butter—he converted the can into a coffee cup.

"You'll need another stove, too," I observed, to the groans and Bronx cheers of the rest of the squad, noticing that the one he'd been using was practically filled with water, scorched cream and sugar, and half-burned but useless heat tabs.

Greene cut small holes around the bottom of a short B-2 unit can to make a stove. "Ah shit. I'm out of heat tabs."

"Here," I said, bringing out of my pocket a plastic bag of C-4 that Sutherland had torn out of a claymore mine. "This stuff works faster."

He rolled the C-4 into a ball and put it in the stove, filled the cup with water from his canteen, dropped in the instant coffee and sugar, lit the C-4, and jumped back as it flared blindingly, bringing the water to a boil almost instantly.

I smiled up at the rest of the squad. They perched, squatting on the bunker top like helmeted gargoyles, their eyes focused on the boiling brown water, widened in suspense. Anxiously, almost breathlessly, they waited for the stove to explode, or for Greene to reach for it and burn his hand again, or for him to stand and stumble again, or for the infinite number of this comedy's bizarre twists of error that would send the seething cup splattering to form another dun-colored stain at the bottom of the dry clay trench.

II. WHAT JOHN WAYNE-ING IT IS

But I noticed suddenly that Abramson's eyes widened in a different direction.

Outside the perimeter.

Then all our eyes looked overhead as we all heard the all-too-familiar—a long, hollow swathing noise like a giant band saw.

Well inside the center of the perimeter, an ARVN artillery command post built of empty shell boxes exploded into flame and splinters and screams.

We all dropped to the trench bottom and scramble-crawled to bunkers.

Inside, I saw Sutherland curling at his place in the corner of the bunker wall that faced the outside of the perimeter—he believed that fewer shells fell in that area. I preferred to stay just to the left of the bunker door, believing that to be the safest place in case of a cave-in. Sutherland and I used to debate our preferences at length, but we decided that the arguments were rather academic since, as he put it, "We can only be proven wrong one way."

The rounds came in salvos of five. "Heaviest yet," I noted to Sutherland, trying to make conversation. From many days in this bunker with him, I knew he was an excellent conversationalist under fire, and I liked talking during a barrage. Sutherland was always considerate in that he never said anything without my speaking first.

He squirmed around to face me, putting his back to the corner of the bunker, wincing and jerking with every blast outside. I could see that this barrage was inspiring him with a fascinating topic. "Doc," he began, "have you ever thought about how many ways 'John Wayne' can be used?"

The bunker jerked and shuddered like an old elevator; dust dropped through the overhead and swirled chokingly around us.

Sutherland continued. "I mean, linguistically speaking, it's almost as versatile a word as 'fuck.'"

"Sure," I grimaced. "Like, 'fuck this incoming.'"

"Right," snickered Sutherland, "or like, 'I wish those fuckers would stop their fucking firing.'"

Everything shook, and the explosions were loud enough to blot out every other sound as the Viets raked our area with their guns.

"Yeah, the motherfuckers," I screamed as the salvos passed by and walked to the middle of the perimeter again. "This is really fucked."

"Oh, what the fuck. We could go on forever," shouted Sutherland. "But I was talking about how fucked up John Wayne is. I mean, he's a can opener, he's a method of firing a machine gun, he's a rifle sling, he describes heroic lunacy, he . . ."

A round fell very near and a couple of bags burst open, spilling their sand like toy dump trucks on the bunker floor.

"Fuck!" I shrieked.

"Fuckin-ay!" yelled Sutherland, pulling a bullet from his magazine. "Looks like we'll have to John Wayne it." He put the bullet between his teeth, bit down hard, and laughed maniacally.

III. WHAT A CADUCEUS IS

"Oh yeah," Sutherland said, jerking out of his mania and taking the bullet from his mouth. "I noticed you've lost the serum albumin from your Unit One."

I lit a cigarette, looked at my medical bag in the corner, and discovered he was right, then I glanced up as I thought I heard the blasts decrease in number, giving me time to think.

Despite my knowing Sutherland, I could never get over his having half a brain. He knew just as much about medic work as any corpsman I'd ever seen. The rest of the squad thought he was insane and they didn't like him very much. But they mistook a developing intelligence for lunacy.

Even in the eyes of his seniors he was considered a trifle odd. But they couldn't deny his competence. Only a few days ago, I had heard Lieutenant Campbell, the platoon commander, describing Sutherland as one of the few men in his command worthy of that most uncommon of military distinctions: a diddly shit.

He was a radical change from the hospital school where the instructors treaded into our brains a sense of superiority to the marines. "They don't call them grunts for nothing," they used to say with smirks, as if we'd have all the superstitious respect

from the grunts that a medicine man enjoys in a primitive
tribe.

So when Sutherland came on knowing all that he did about
my job as well as being better than professional at his own, I
was always thrown for a loss. "You know too much,
Sutherland," I exclaimed and ducked from another set of
blasts. "'A little learning is a dangerous thing,' and . . ."

"Yeah," he said, grinning, "live dangerously: Go to college and drop out after your third year to join the crotch."

"I'm not bullshitting. You going to leave this place insane
if you don't get killed."

"Who doesn't? Come off it, Doc. I hear this 'What's a guy
like you?' line too much. Shit, it's worse than a movie. What
about you? You're more educated and all that crap than anyone else here, but you'll go nuts or get zapped. You think that
caduceus on your collar will protect you like some kind of
medical Saint Christopher medal?"

The ARVN artillery started firing back finally and our own
mortars began firing as well, adding dull staccato thuds to the
sharp explosions.

"By the way," he coughed from another billow of dust,
"I've been meaning to ask you why doctors chose that as their
symbol. It's supposed to be the scepter of Mercury. What the
hell does that have to do with medicine?"

I couldn't help laughing. I roared as hard as I had at Greene's
incompetence with C rats. Sutherland always brought up the
weirdest topics—consistently during barrages. The day before,
he had speculatively discoursed for forty-five minutes on the
menstrual periods of female elephants.

But nobody before had ever bothered to ask about the caduceus—not even myself. I was caught in a three-way bind:
trying to control my laughing, which was beginning to give
me stomach cramps; trying to cover myself by squirming and
curling closer to the bunker wall; and trying to talk to Sutherland to put my mind off the barrage.

"It's supposed to represent," I began, as the earth jumped violently and I heard an air-splitting explosion that couldn't be anything but the ARVN ammo bunker, "the 'Wings of Mercy, delivering the Staff of Life, from the Depths of Hell.'"

I heard shards of metal screaming through the air like thousands of blindly wielded scythes. "It can also represent the staff of Moses, turned to a serpent before the flight of liberty from the pharaoh."

Sutherland snickered triumphantly in his maniacal manner, sneering his words from the corner of his mouth. "Right. Just like I thought. It means about as much as 'fuck' and 'John Wayne.'"

IV. JOHN WAYNE COOKIES

The salvos became smaller: four rounds, then three, two, and finally one lone shell, knifing a long noisy arc through the air, crashing louder (it seemed) than the rest, as if trying to justify being last.

The land-line phone clacked in its box with its horrible rattle. Sutherland answered it: "Good evening, Vietnam War. Right, this is Checkmate—Abramson's got the radio in the next bunker—use your radio, he's got mine with him—because this bunker was closer, that's why."

I looked outside. In the darkness I could see only smoke, curling and swirling windlessly, filling the air with the stench of cordite and charred wood.

Moving outside, carrying my Unit One, I began to see light appearing over the top of the trench line on both sides. Outside the perimeter, over the DMZ—some two thousand meters off—Huey gun ships rocketed the Viet artillery positions while dropping flares, suspended lights that lit up the area like night baseball.

"Anybody hit?" I called, hoping not. The squad came from their bunker—first Abramson, then Greene, Kaufmann, and Jackel.

Kaufmann shook his head. "Nah—we're okay. But the gooks sure caught the shit. Lookathat," he said, jerking his head toward where the ARVN battery used to be. It was a pile of blasted boxes, burning wood, twisted guns. The fire lit up the inside of the perimeter.

I started to climb from the trench. "Better see if . . ."

"No way, Doc," Abramson said. "I just got the word over the radio that everybody stays in the trenches, no exceptions. Seventy-five percent watch tonight."

The squad chorused a groan. Three people out of four on watches all night meant sleep loss for all of us. Especially in this shorthanded squad.

I came down and squatted in the trench as Abramson went on. "And we've pulled the LP for tonight. Jackel and Greene, you're up. Sutherland and Kaufmann had it last week. The rest of you get to your holes. Doc, you can sleep if you like."

Abramson turned to go to his hole and chuckled. "Greene, look."

We all looked to where Abramson pointed and saw Greene's coffee, standing atop its C rat stove at the bottom of the trench—unsullied, untouched by the barrage.

"'S' probably cold," muttered Jackel.

We all anxiously watched Greene creep toward the coffee cup, stalking it like a panther. I had never seen stealth more excellently performed—Greene was almost graceful. He crouched over the coffee and took a deep breath, as if he were about to disarm a cobalt bomb.

"I'll check its heat with my finger," Greene gloated. "No, wait. It might still be too hot and it'll burn my finger and I'll knock it over." He looked back at us, smiling and seeking approval. Then he looked through his pile of rubble, producing a John Wayne cookie—a chocolate covered hockey puck that came with three fillings: coconut, vanilla, or maple. He held it up to us and pantomimed dunking it like a doughnut.

"Brilliant," exclaimed Sutherland.

Greene dipped the John Wayne cookie into the coffee with

the surehandedness of a brain surgeon. Then, scrutinizing it, he carefully extracted the half-coffee-soaked disk and brought it to his mouth as we waited watchfully.

"Not hot, but at least warm," said Greene casually, just as the coffee cup tipped, spilling onto the trench floor.

V. YOUTH IN ASIA

Deciding the bunker was too damned hot, I chose to try sleeping near Abramson's sandbagged fighting hole, knowing fully that I'd end up talking to him to help him stay awake. To ease the squad's pain from lack of sleep, Abramson himself would stay up all night. He was just that way.

We watched Jackel and Greene crawling out of the trench and into the dark, toward the listening post past the edge of the wire, where they would fight with themselves to stay awake all night and hope that the Viets wouldn't come.

Abramson and I talked the usual shit:

"How short are you now, Doc?"

"About four more months."

And:

"When do you get out?"

"Soon as my tour's over."

"Shit. I still got two years to go."

And:

"What did you do on the outside, Abe?"

"Hung out."

An advantage of being "the Doc" was that everyone looked upon me as being different—but accepted me even though I wasn't a marine. And being different made me easy to confide in.

I listened to Abramson tell me of his trial for petty theft at age nineteen. How the judge had offered him either a year in prison or four years in the corps—with a gunnery sergeant standing beside him in dress blues.

Like a bartender, I'd heard everyone's life story at one time or another. And what occurred to me as I listened to Abramson was that he talked of his trial as if it were one of the happiest times of his life. He even laughed about it.

After a while, I found myself drifting in a half sleep that carried with it a dream of writing on paper that sometimes spoke to me, with my own voice.

"You aren't young anymore," the words of my voice said. "None of them are either—not Sutherland, not Abramson, not Jackel, Greene, or Kaufmann. You're all old men. The movies lie; there are no young men in war. You're nineteen or twenty, and you become old with your first case of Viet shits. "Your youth drops purgatively out your asshole during your first week in Vietnam. And you realize that from then on you're vulnerable—and you're old because of it. Being vulnerable makes you, at any second, as old as you might ever be."

"Doc," Abramson said, shaking my shoulder and waking me from the sleeping voice, "LP's got movement out there." He jerked his head toward the wire.

Sutherland popped his head out of the bunker that housed the land-line phone. "They're coming in, Abe," he said. "They won't use a signal flare, so we better pass the word."

I heard stage whispers transferred from fighting hole to fighting hole down the line, "LP comin' in."

Then Abramson froze as we both heard the hollow, tom-tom-like beat of mortars outside the perimeter. There were no more whispers. "Incoming!" Abramson yelled.

Elongated swishes sliced over our heads, followed by dull explosions that rocked the center of the perimeter and grew louder, creeping toward our backs.

We crawled on hands and knees to the bunkers. Inside, Sutherland talked on the radio, peering out the bunker's embrasure, watching for Greene and Jackel. "That's affirm," he drawled in the unagitated monotone peculiar to radio operators. "Lima Papa is trying to get in, but, nope, there's no

show yet. Will advise when . . . Oh Jesus!" His eyes widened
and I could see a flickering light on his face.

I rushed to the embrasure to look out.

Trip flares attached to the wire popped on like blinding
fireflies; they lit up the front of the perimeter and billowed
smoke from their burned magnesium that hovered about three
feet from the ground. Below the smoke, I could see silhouettes
of legs running confusedly about, frantically starting and stopping about seventy meters off.

In front of the legs, I saw Jackel and Greene—two weird
shadows like savages dancing before fire—running toward us.
But a burst of automatic fire came from out of the fog—one of
the shadows froze and writhed with the impact of every
round, as if the bullets entering his body were all that kept him
on his feet. I watched him fall, and watched the other shadow
drop to a crawl, trying to drag him in.

"This is Checkmate," Sutherland yelled into his radio.
"We've got heavy troop movement in front of this position—
automatic weapons, satchel charges, the works."

The rounds continued to explode outside the bunker, but
we wouldn't be able to remain inside any longer. Sutherland
shouldered his radio, grabbed his rifle, and headed outside
without a word.

I followed him and heard the rifle fire snapping and buzzing above our heads. Looking out, I saw the advancing
Viets—still sixty meters or so off, not having their assault lines
formed up yet—screaming and firing and throwing grenades.
Our line opened fire and the Viets began dropping.

Twenty meters from the trench, I saw Jackel and Greene.
In the light of an overhead flare, I could see that it was Greene
who was hit. Jackel dragged him, not even knowing if he was
still alive.

There wasn't time to think. All I remember is wrapping
my Unit One around my shoulders, drawing my pistol, and
crawling from the trench. I watched the assault line carefully,

gambling that they'd be too tied up with the withering fire from the trenches to notice me crawling on my stomach.

I finally reached them. "Get outta here, Jackel," I screamed over the firing and Greene's groans. "Cover us on the way in." Jackel rolled to one side and began crawling backwards, his rifle pointed toward the advancing Viets. "Cummon, Doc!"

Greene's body was torn and battered from at least fifteen rounds—his left arm twisted behind him, attached to his shoulder by a thin shred of muscle; both his legs were shattered and jagged pieces of bone gouged through his flesh; a gaping hole the size of a football in his stomach belched forth blood until the ground beneath him was saturated. His groans became screams with every tug of my hands.

Each scream, increasing in pitch, hit me like a hammer—a judge's gavel that ruled beyond doubt that he couldn't possibly live.

I looked up to see two Viets not ten meters away—the only ones to get this close to the trenches.

From behind I heard the sharp clacking of Jackel's rifle. I fired myself and heard the rounds thudding into their bodies, snapping their bones. Greene screamed my name and writhed in terrified pain.

And in a split second everything ran through my brain. Greene couldn't live until morning—he'd be damned lucky to live until we got back to the trench; we'd never get him to an aid station in time—no chopper would try to land at a place that was getting overrun; his sobbing screams told me how much pain he was in—but morphine would just put him to sleep, during which time he'd die; and dragging him like this was just tearing his body apart even worse than the rounds already had.

Still fifteen meters from the trench, I reloaded my pistol with another magazine and continued to crawl and drag, turning to fire at the Viet assault line and trying to deafen myself to Greene's delirious and choking screams.

Finally, I was deaf, and numb, and blind. In fact, it even felt like it was someone else who turned, put the pistol to Greene's temple, and pulled the trigger.

VI. C RAT

Like a low-budget horror movie where the monsters only come out at night, the attack stopped when the sun rose.

But the horror lingered, hanging over Con Thien like a plague. Smoke and flames burped from bunkers that had been blown up by Viet satchel charges on the heaviest-hit side of the lines. Transformed into treaded flame, two amtracks flared and smoked, filling the air with a stench like bus exhaust.

Chunks of Viet flesh hung gorily from the barbed wire, an outdoor butcher shop, and hundreds of Viet dead lay scattered in grotesque, armless, legless, and headless death between the wire and the trench line.

Next to the command post bunker we deposited our own dead. I carried Greene's body there myself and rolled it in a waterproof poncho. With its blasted legs sticking out like a badly dressed store mannequin, it lay among the thirty-five others waiting for the choppers that would carry them south— to be placed in green cocoonlike bags, from which they would emerge only at Graves Registration.

Our side of the lines had been the lightest hit—Greene was our only casualty. And I thought about that as I walked back to the bunkers. Nobody would ever know, except me. Could I tell anyone? Could I tell Sutherland?

I knew I'd have to sometime. "Yes," I thought, "Sutherland will understand. Who else would?" I looked for him in the bunker, but it was empty. Then I looked out toward the wire.

The squad walked along the line of Viet dead, followed by a mule—a motorized, four-wheeled flatbed cart. Abramson led them, shooting each of the bodies as his squad drew near them, in case any were still alive.

As I walked closer, I saw Sutherland, Kaufmann, and Jackel loading the corpses onto the mule, flinging them by the arms and legs—the ones that had arms and legs—building a stack of bodies that tangled like a toy box full of discarded dolls.

They loaded the last dead Viet on the mule, and we all watched as the driver headed for the huge pit that the bull-dozers were already digging. Mules from each side of the lines converged on the pit. They backed toward it until they dumped their loads and then drove off for more.

"Sutherland," I called.

He turned toward me with the dazed and exhausted eyes shown so often in photo essays on war and ran past me toward the bunker. The rest of the squad gathered around me as we watched Sutherland grab his entrenching tool and begin fran-tically digging a hole. His arms threshed up and down like a man mad with greed, digging for treasure, until he suddenly threw the short shovel aside, dropped to his hands and knees, and vomited into the hole.

"Doc, what's the matter with Sutherland?" Abramson asked toward sunset. "I mean, is he flippin' out? I gotta know."

Sutherland had spent the last four hours sitting atop his bunker, arms wrapped around his knees, rocking back and forth, staring at the wire.

We had spent the entire day counting bodies, collecting their gear and weapons, and dumping the carcasses into the huge pit by the command-post bunker. It had gotten to Sutherland worse than it had to anyone else.

"I mean," continued Abramson. "I always thought he was a little dingy. But he's valuable—he's a damn good man."

"Let him sleep it off," I said. "He's got a case of fatigue, but he'll be okay when they pull us out."

I knew where Sutherland was—like me he had toured the lines in the early morning and had seen everything. I was there myself. I couldn't stand without dizziness, couldn't eat without gagging, couldn't think without seeing flames and blood and burning flesh—and Greene's face, just before I put the round into his brain; a face that feared death and begged for it at the same time.

Kaufmann ran up and jerked me by the arm. "Cummon, Doc—we got one." His face contorted, eyes widened with brutality. "Look," he said, pointing to the front of his bunker, where I saw Jackel on his knees, bending toward the ground.

Drawing nearer, I saw that Jackel bent over an anthill, where red ants ran about like a frightened mob. From the top of the anthill protruded the head of a rat, squinting from the few rays of sunlight left.

"Kaufmann," Jackel growled, "gimme your John Wayne."

"Little fucker," he addressed the helpless rat. "Get into my bunker, eh?" Kaufmann threw him the can opener and sat atop his bunker to watch.

Jackel took a box of C rations and opened it, strewing the contents at his feet. With the John Wayne, he opened a small tin of grape jam and poured it over the rat's face. Then he sprinkled a package of sugar around its neck. "Ants'll just love this," he chuckled from the side of his mouth.

In spite of myself, I watched this with fascination—wishing the ants would leap immediately onto the rat's head, eat sections of its eyes, and tear its flesh. I wanted to see that rat picked clean, as if it could make up for everything.

Abramson and I moved to the top of the bunker to watch. As I leaned back, I bumped into something, and I turned to see Sutherland. He looked at me, then shifted his glance to the anthill.

The ants scurried at the base of their hill; only a few came anywhere near the rat. I jumped from the bunker top. "Jackel, give me that B-2 unit."

I took out a John Wayne cookie, crumbled it in my hands

like a cracker for soup, and sprinkled a trail from the rat to the base of the anthill.

Slowly, the ants were attracted by the cookie and they moved up the hill, gathering the crumbs as they went, until they swarmed over the rat's head.

Completely.

Grunts' lives were sometimes spent far too frivolously in Vietnam. Josiah Bunting, who served with the Ninth Infantry Division in the Delta, provides a poignant fictional account of one man's death. As Bunting once said, "I wanted to show what a decision made by an ambitious general meant to those who had to execute the decision."

Josiah Bunting

The Lionheads

Kien Hoa Province
Republic of Vietnam
2300, 14 March 1968

"They're sealed in there."

"Yeah, sealed. Who the fuck told you that?"

"I heard it. I heard Lieutenant Haney say Colonel Plowman told the CO the whole battalion's sealed in there."

"Come on, Compella, you know what it takes to seal a VC battalion in a place like that?"

"Whip it on me."

"How 'bout a lead fence twenty feet high with a cement foundation ten feet deep. With no breaks. Maybe one division U.S. standing on top of the fence, each man with an M-60."

"What about the rivers? How'd they get across them at night? We got thirty, forty boats in the rivers."

"If they want to, if they're even in there, they'll get out."

But the prognosis, as Major Claiborn reads it, remains good. Robertson agrees with him. It is 2300. The three exhausted companies of the 1st Battalion are on line, "A" Company's right "anchored" (as the after-action report will describe it) on the Rach Ba Nho, its left positions tied in with Bravo Company, whose left in turn is Charlie Company's right. This last unit's night positions stretch directly south to the north bank of the Song Sao. The aggregate is about 350 troops, subtracting the losses of the morning's ambushes and subsequent fire fights. The battalion holds the eastern side of the "seal," river to river, a distance of 1000 meters.

Two kilometers to the west, the 2nd of the 71st is likewise on line, stretched bank to bank, facing the 1st Battalion. Its casualties are negligible—six wounded—but if there is an attempt at a break-out, they will have to stop it. The two rivers are cluttered with boats: ASPB's, Monitors, ATC's, the revving of their engines as they back down or lumber out of each other's way suggesting a huge sportscar rally. From Claiborn's present vantage point, from the grease-penciled map-sheet propped against the bulkhead of the CCB, it does indeed appear that the VC are "sealed." Yes, some will get out, men who can hold their breath a long time, he reflects with a shrug, a few small parties of desperate confused soldiers who will crawl through the deadfall, get through the 2nd Battalion's line, and exfiltrate to the west; but no more than these. How can they? "If I was COSVN I'd relieve his ass," he says quietly, thinking of the VC commander. "If you're lucky, they won't have to," somebody says.

Gunships have been overheard, off and on, for almost an hour. The two 105 batteries at BRADLEY have been shooting into the encirclement since 2130, halting their fires only when the gunships come over. There is even a chance a 155 battery can make it to Cao Sang by daylight. That would really do it.

And all the while, the gunboats, cruising in a miniature parody of "line ahead," have been throwing everything—cannon, .50's, .30 cal, into the objective area. It is impossible that the 317th can survive.

Horne, Logan, and Compella share a position on "A" Company's extreme right, barely ten meters from the Rach Ba Nho. They are all that remain of their squad. And they have just begun thinking they've got it made. Relieved and exhausted, they are pleased to follow Lieutenant Haney's curt orders: "Anything you see moving in front of you, any sound in the river past your position, shoot it. Otherwise stay where you are. No more than one man sleeps at a time. For Christsake don't shoot unless you've got something to shoot at."

There it is. Logan dully remembers a briefing map. "They'll never try it out this side." The night is hot and dark and stinking. Horne, his head against Compella's thigh, sleeps deeply. Compella has been lying on his belly for an hour now, behind an M-60, its barrel propped over a log. Logan stares through the clutter of vines and deadfall at the open space that is the river. Directly to Compella's front, perhaps 400 meters into the bush, the supposed positions of the VC remain targets for every support weapon the MRF disposes.

The scene, hazy and recessed, more visible to the imagination than sight, gives no clues about the enemy. The flares disappear, and it is black again. Over the 1st Battalion's positions, perhaps 400 feet up, a gunship bats through the air, back and forth. Compella tries to guess its position, looks up through the skeletal gaps in the canopy, sees nothing. Suddenly, however, a stream of what looks like solid tracer escapes the gunship, molten pink, its hot liquid shaft probing the inside of the encirclement. The gun makes a brooding sound like the hum of a dentist's drill from the waiting-room. And the shaft seems to probe like a drill, each pitchless burst a question curtly phrased: Are you there? Do you feel? And when the question has been asked, and no answer given, it poses its question in a slightly different idiom, in a new tone, getting at the hidden targets from new angles. Suddenly the shaft touches a nerve. The patient screams for an instant, regains his composure. Compella and Logan can only guess where he is. Apparently satisfied, the shaft disappears groundward. Still the 105's do not fire; save for the boat noises and the invisible slapping of the gunship rotor it is silent again.

Again. Refreshed, the dentist having selected a new drillhead, the engine returns to work, the pink shaft angling down, probing once more, this time from a point immediately over Compella. He has a sudden recollection of Dr. Gray back in Torrington, a calm man who talks baseball when he walks over to the sideboard to get a new drillhead: "Malzone is a complete third baseman, hits for power, guns his throws like a cannon, steadies the pitchers down. OK, Paul, open up again, huh?" "Is this the last drill?" "No, second to the last; it may hurt, I'm close to a nerve." And the fiery small hum preens itself again in the back of his mouth. "He hit one out of Fenway Sunday that went over *every*thing, green monster, screen, everything." Paul's fingers tighten around the ends of the chair-arms, the drill stops. Dr. Gray walks over for another drillhead, the last one: "That was no Fenway home run."

The gunship, still overhead, still unsatisfied, probes again, asking its questions at length now, less patiently. The shaft flickers down, becomes solid, more intense. Suddenly the gunship is Compella, Sr., standing at his boy's back, coldly angry, speaking invective to an older boy who has just slapped his son. The father has taken up the argument, and having resolved it, disappears.

His son squiggles, changing position, looks over at Logan. "Look at that shit. You hear what Haney said, a mini-gun like that, on a chopper at 500 feet, could put a round in every square foot of the Ann Arbor stadium in thirty seconds."

"Keep your voice down. That's no fuckin' mini-gun. There's no bunkers in the stadium."

"Whatever it is."

Again the gunship, this time farther away. It spits another

long pinkness, the longest one yet, still refusing to acknowledge its failures. Finally it stops altogether, the shaft at last announcing its resignation in driblets. The gunship moves out of hearing.

A flare pops softly over the encirclement, and again the landscape defines itself in a flash, the light fading bright to hazy ochre. Through the cluttered skeletons of burnt trees Compella stares, ignoring the night-vision warnings. But still there is no movement. What do they do, he wonders, just lie there? Why don't their wounded cry out? They must be dug in, but if their bunkers along the river were that good they couldn't have spent much time preparing bunkers where they are now. No way. They can't tunnel in there; two feet down it's water. All they can do is scrape and burrow, pressing their faces to the mud, hoping it's the man on either side of them.

The flare has signaled a new inning for the artillery, and Compella hears the reports of the guns at BRADLEY, waits, waits, the rounds at last searing through overhead, rushing down. The earth shakes with the blasts and seconds later, like rain on metal, the spent shrapnel slaps the broken canopy overhead. The explosions seem without definition, monstrously compressed roars. The whole sequence begins to repeat itself, again, irregular but without letting up—a distant guttural sound, silence, a sucking rush overhead, the blast and shock in front, metal on palm-frond, shards falling around them.

Logan and Compella lie facing each other, heads up against the log, pressed close to the ground. The artillery barrages begin to roll forward, away from their position toward the western part of the encirclement.

"Compella," Logan whispers. "Were you at Division before you came down here?"

"For two days."

"What's it like?"

"Whaddya mean, what's it like?"

"Ever see the General?"

"Yeah, I saw him. I saw him one morning in a briefing."

"Did he say anything?"

"He just asks questions and listens. He doesn't say anything."

"I mean, what does he do?"

"He runs the Division, whaddya mean, what does he do?"

"Like, just shouts at people and they run around and do it, like that? Do they get incoming at Division?"

"Once in a while. You were at the Young Lion Academy."

"The Young Lion Academy. What kinda shit is that? The Young Lion Academy. They brainwash your ass. The Young Lion Academy. They try to make the whole thing a big game, like a joust, all that shit. Like the Rams with those horns on their helmet, you know, in football, all that halftime jazz. Biggest bass drum in the universe. Everybody prancing around, then they go out and get their ligaments torn to shit and their collarbones broken."

"You're a cynic, Logan."

"Keep your voice down."

Compella senses movement in front of their positions, like a tiny stirring of water.

"Y'hear that?"

"Yeah, maybe it'll rain."

"I thought it didn't rain at night."

"Sometimes it does," Logan answers, "God gets pissed off."

"You're a cynic, Logan."

"Shit."

The gunship returns again and begins reworking the VC battalion.

Major Claiborn and Lieutenant Colonel Plowman are orchestrating from within the CCB, manning the radio consoles in the well-deck. They shift from one net to another with practiced ease, secure and comforted in their expertise. They coordinate the fires of boats, gunships, artillery; record SIT-

REPS from the company command posts, trying to evoke a clear picture of the night battle. Robertson studies them from his field-table, drinking his coffee out of a canteen cup. He sifts through the grating fogs of static, taking in the transmissions, rarely speaking, hearing the shower falling on the overhead.

He can abide most ambiguities, but this one is different. There is a VC battalion not five clicks away, a ragged unit pounded and churned into mud. There can be little exfiltration tonight, so the odds are good that his brigade can sweep through in the morning, collect the weapons, and count the bodies. The battle has cost the brigade a certain price, as always a terrible price, but not as terrible as he had promised General Lemming. The friendly casualties will be "moderate" ones on the after-action reports, moderate enough for Lemming to claim a significant victory. The point was, he considers, that the absent helicopter company could have reduced them almost to nothing, could have kept Colonel Plowman's "A" Company out of the boat ambush. However.

Moths and bugs clog the tiny bulb overhead. The light is bleak, dreary. The Colonel clasps his hands behind his head, leans back, listening, remembering . . .

> O Western wind, when wilt thou blow
>> That the small rain down can rain?
> Christ, that my love were in my arms,
>> And I in my bed again!

and says: "What's it look like, Plowman?"
"Beautiful. Best night operation I ever saw."
"Good."

To Compella's right, 100 meters in front of the position, a .50 cal on board a Monitor fires into the north side, the river side of the seal, hoarse popping blasts of five or six rounds each, a short break between fusillades while the gun traverses.

The tide is in, so that the gunboat has direct fire into the VC, doesn't have to worry about wasting ammo on the riverbank. All the same, it does little but reassure the Americans on line at either end; the VC are not in the habit of walking around in their night positions when taking fire. The Monitor keeps it up for five or six minutes, firing into the blackness and the rain.

Some of the night sounds don't fit the pattern. Compella shifts back onto his stomach, lifts up on his elbows, slowly, his eyes rising just above the top of the log. He drags the stock of the M-60 tight into his shoulder, sighting on nothing, squeezing, squeezing the hand-guard and the narrow part of the stock like a baseball bat.

"Hey, Logan? How 'bout that? Y'hear that?"

"No," Logan whispers. "I told you, they're not gonna come through here. Maybe the river, along the bank, but not in front of us."

But if they did, Compella wonders to himself, if they did, could we hear them? He remembers a drill sergeant at Polk. "For example, during the Korean War. The Chinese would blow bugles or play records on loudspeakers, right in the middle of night. This was the way these people had of trying to demoralize an opponent, trying to scare the hell out of him by making him think there were large numbers of Reds. The Japs would do the same kind of thing, like in the John Wayne movies: "Marine, you die." This is what you call a crude form of psychological warfare, and it didn't shake our people up in 1944 or 1952, any more than if the VC did it it would shake you up now. What you know you're not afraid of. But the VC don't do that. Those people are smart as hell. They've been playing their little game a long time. You down there in nametape defilade, you asleep, just like you'll be some night in a NDP and Charlie'll zap your ass." The soldier in Compella's basic training company was sitting in the second row of the grandstand at Fort Polk, getting his night indoctrination. He was falling asleep in the warm dusk, and, staring at the ground, was trying to strike an impression of rapt, musing concentration. "You don't look at the ground, you look at me! Needle-dick Nick the bug-fucker, aren't you, Private? You're gonna go to sleep in Vietnam, aren't you? Ain't gonna be any bugles in Vietnam, you better listen up at night, you got me? You listen for every fucking rustle in the night . . ."

But as the night wears on in Kien Hoa, in the lulls of shelling and aerial machine-gunning, the rustles of the night merge in a sibilant unvarying regularity. Compella, anyone, can only react to the promptings of his imagination, unless the VC were to get desperate, and being desperate reveal themselves. In which case, hell, he's got nothing to worry about. Logan said it: they'd never come through here.

"I wish we had a starlight scope."

"They're all in the drink. Got shot down. Three hundred dollars apiece, twenty-four of them. They went down in a chopper. They won't come through here."

In a starlight scope you saw the enemy moving as you saw men moving on the bank if you were under water, through an amber haze. Then you lost sight, surfaced, made the bank, found yourself unhurt, and, being unhurt when others were dying, felt a terrible exhilaration. I made it through that, I made it through that, Compella thinks, and when the morning comes I will have made it through the whole thing. A soft gravelly sound to his right. Horne turns over in his sleep. "They won't come through here."

"The fuck they wouldn't!" Compella is up on his knees, screaming like a savage. He cocks the gun desperately and fires a long stuttering burst into the clearing up ahead. Logan rolls up, slams the M-79 shut, fires too, drops beside Compella to help feed the M-60. Out of the haze a dark rush of figures comes toward them, one stumbling, another pitching forward on its face. A third, only a charging outline, detaches itself from the cluster, skids sharply to Compella's right front, regains its balance, skitters toward the riverbank in a crouch. Jarred awake, Horne grabs in the wet for his M-16, and, reaching it, crumples without a sound. Compella can only keep firing at the dissolving forms still in front, moving toward them. He dimly senses Logan has gone after Horne's weapon, is firing toward the river.

All the forces resist, as in a dream. The moment lengthens to hours, the expectation of completion and safety somehow undergirding everything as it happens. The guns responds, but somehow distantly, as if fired by itself; the after-images of the scrambling forms remain. But are they people, are they still there?

A long burst off to the right, splattering into the river. Logan is dealing with the VC in the undergrowth along the bank, the VC now sinking into the bush, maybe dead, maybe wounded, perhaps already in the water. He is back alongside Compella, brushing against him. "Jesus," he says, but not loud, not scared, just the word. He feeds Compella's gun, firing now at nothing. At there. It stops. A cloud of silence settles closely about them.

"You get that guy in the river, Logan?"

But Logan did not get the VC flying toward the river, and suddenly, a scarlet viscous bubble created from nothing, there wells up in Paul Compella's skull the agony of a death wound, exploding as from within, pushing and blasting out with a terrible force. A long sliver of bone, rent up and out through flesh, plops across Compella's right eye, its end stuck to the wound like a hangnail. "Logan," he says, and crumples onto the log.

"The fuck was that?" Haney is alongside Logan, more angry, it sounds, than concerned. Like the others he has not expected VC probes on the east side of the seal. Jarred out of his dozing he has crawled forward to Compella's position.

"I said what the hell was that?"

Logan, shaking, nudges his shoulder and points at Horne and Compella. "They tried to come through here. Horne's dead. Compella's breathing. Look at his face . . ."

"Alright, we'll get him out of here. Hang on. You alright?"

"I'm alright."

"Give me the radio."

"Cheetah 6, this is 3."

"This is 6. Whatcha got?"

"3. We got one KIA, one bad WIA, over."

"Roger that. What's your situation?"

"3. They tried to come through my right, along the river. Nothing now."

"How many, Logan?" Haney asks.

"Four, Sir, four or five."

"Four or five, 6."

"Roger. You got VC KIA on the position? Over."

"Negative, none I can see. Wait." He looks at Logan, who shakes his head. "Man on the position says unknown."

"This is 6, ah, get the WIA out. My position twenty meters from route GREEN. We got a boat here. What is condition of WIA? Over."

"3. Critical, repeat critical. Will get him out, over."

"6. Try to confirm enemy KIA, over."

"Negative at this time. WIA is Compella, PFC, joined unit yesterday. Out." And to Logan. "Joined the unit yesterday, right?"

"Yes, Sir, joined the unit a couple days ago . . ."

Command Boat
Kinh Giao Thong, Kien Hoa Province
0030, 15 March 1968

On the CCB, now tied up on the west bank of the Giao Thong about 1000 meters behind the 1st Battalion positions, Robertson senses the rain has stopped. He reaches out, clutches Lieutenant Colonel Plowman by the elbow.

"What's your casualty situation right now?"

"Unchanged from 1800, far as I know, Sir. Last I have is sixteen KIA, sixty wounded. Bad. Not as bad as I thought; most of the wounded aren't serious. What's the story on 2/71?"

"Six wounded, very light. You went in first, you were the bait, I guess. The VC went after you. Probably cleared their positions on the south river as soon as they heard the ambushes on the Rach Ba Nho this morning. Your people got it again, more than they could handle, more than they deserved."

"Not more than we could handle, Sir," Plowman says gently, a little truculence in his voice. "We'll do it again if we have to."

"You did fine, Jim, you know that," Robertson says quietly, reading the bone-weariness in his face. "Get some sleep, flop on the mattress over there. We have any trouble tonight it's not going to be your people."

"I will. Thank you, Sir." He walks over and sinks onto the mattress.

Claiborn and Robertson look at each other, both shaking their heads.

"Tiger 6, Cheetah 6, over."

Major Claiborn answers for Plowman. "Roger, Cheetah."

"Cheetah 6. VC probe on my right at zero-zero one-five. I got one KIA, one WIA. No further enemy activity. Am evacuating US WIA by riverine."

"Roger, Cheetah. Out." Claiborn turns around abruptly, staring at Robertson: "Should I wake up Colonel Plowman?"

"No. Don't wake him up. Let him sleep."

It was a good encirclement. The 1st Brigade had stolen a leaf from Colonel Morton's book. At 0220 the 155's registered, honed in on the enemy position, began pounding away. With textbook synchronization the other support fires were registered, locked in, fired, lifted. The gunships returned four more times during the night. The monitors on either river kept up their shelling almost without pause. At either end of the terrain pocket the two battalions slept, watched, waited for VC attempts to break out, wondering if the bastards were really still in the pocket. But in the sad pre-dawn grayness, the supporting fires lifted for the last time and the last flare fired; they understood that, at least, if the VC were still inside and alive, there would be no attempt to break out. At 0700 Colonel Robertson ordered his units to sweep toward each other and determine what the night of shelling had done to the 317th. He and Claiborn went up in the C and C to oversee the operation.

Preliminary body-counts and a complete absence of resistance indicating a more than substantial victory, he ordered the battalions to complete their sweep, backload, and return to the Mobile Riverine Base. Then he flew home to the *Samson*.

The results of MRF operation 18-68 were tersely summarized late on the afternoon of 15 March in a combat after-action report the industrious Knapp prepared for Robertson's approval. The report stated:

> . . . helicopter assets being unavailable, the brigade abandoned its original scheme of operation for search-and-clear missions in Cao Sang District, Kien Hoa Province. The targeted enemy unit remained the 317th Main Force Battalion.
>
> As originally schemed, 2d Battalion, 71st Infantry, was to have conducted beach assaults on the south bank of the Mekong (Song My Tho), moved overland to a pick-up zone, there to await airmobile movement to a landing-zone immediately west of the objective area. From this landing-zone the battalion was to have deployed into blocking positions oriented east, thereby creating a seal anchored on the south

bank of the Rach Ba Nho and the north bank of the Song Sao. First Battalion, 71st Infantry, was to have conducted beach assaults on sites on the north shore of the Rach Ba Nho, 200 meters west of its juncture with the Giao Thong; from here it would have swept west, toward the 2d Battalion's block.

As noted, helicopter assets were denied, and the plan had to be changed. First Battalion, 71st Infantry, landed at the sites originally selected for it at 0720 hours, 14 March. This landing was opposed. One ATC was crippled, losing power and unable to steer; the platoon aboard suffered heavy casualties, such as to render it combat ineffective for some hours. The remainder of the battalion made good its landings farther up the Rach Ba Nho. During this landing phase of the operation the battalion took 11 KIA and 31 WIA, the majority of those killed from the ambushed platoon.

. . . Second Battalion, 71st Infantry, meantime, had moved in riverine convoy down the Giao Thong, turning west onto the Song Sao. It was not ambushed. Its beach assaults were unopposed. By 1200 hours, 14 March, the companies of this battalion were in their assigned blocking positions and the seal was made. The battalion's casualties to this time were six wounded.

First Battalion, 71st Infantry, was deployed into its blocking position by 1230 hours. Supporting fires into the encirclement then intensified, continuing without substantial pause until approximately 0500 hours, 15 March. Enemy exfiltration was detected at one point only, on the extreme right of 1/71's block, the battalion sustaining one KIA and one WIA.

. . . At 0700 both battalions commenced to sweep through the objective area, completing their search at 1100. On orders of the brigade commander, the units then backloaded and returned to the MRB.

Preliminary estimates establish enemy losses as follows:

VC KIA, by BC	158
Hoi Chanh	2
VC captured	11
VC weapons captured	120 (110 indiv; 10 crew-svd)
Other	90 lbs. medical supplies 15 lbs. documents

. . . Operation 18-68 must be accounted only a qualified success. The provision of helicopters, which would have enabled the brigade to proceed according to its original plan, would have minimized friendly casualties and enemy exfiltration.

For the Commander:

★ ★ ★

The report was taken to Colonel Robertson for his approval only after a long argument between an exhausted Major Claiborn and a fresh, outraged Captain Knapp. Good soldier that he was, the S-3 recognized the polemics were justified by what had happened. But combat after-action reports are not supposed to be polemics. They must recite the facts, and the facts only. Division knew that Robertson had tried, and failed, to get helicopter assets for his brigade; no sense of tearing off the scabs of barely healed wounds by reminding Division of an old and acerbic controversy. Besides, it would probably mean Robertson's relief from command. General Lemming's decision to withhold a helicopter company hurt the brigade and the brave sailors who had carried it to the objective; on the other hand, the River Lions had achieved an exceptionally large body-count. Robertson's stock would rise automatically, if he kept his mouth shut. Lemming might listen to him next time around. Why jeopardize the prospect?

"Because, goddamit, I want it to be a matter of written record. Alright? Lemming's not going to put his arms around Colonel Robertson just because we killed a bunch of VC in one battle. Nothing's going to change."

Claiborn hasn't the heart to kill the report. "Alright, Knapp"—he stops drumming his fingers on the desk—"we'll take it to the Colonel."

U.S.S. Samson, APB-58
Thoi Son Anchorage
1700 Hours, 15 March 1968

Claiborn and Knapp find Colonel Robertson sitting alone in the immaculate study, watching the smoke of his cigar drift toward the open porthole. His hands are folded together, thumbs under his chin, elbows resting on the dining-table. From the pontoon below the distant murmur of the troops' conversation can be heard, but the punctuation of laughter and wisecracks is gone. They are standing in the gray haze drinking beer. In spite of his exhaustion—he has not slept for forty hours—Robertson appears calm and rested. He is uncharacteristically spruce in fresh jungle fatigues and clean-shaven. Without looking up he is aware of their entrance, and pointing at the Commodore's closed door, as if sensing the urgency of their visit, gestures for them to talk quietly.

Claiborn is solicitous: "Excuse me, Colonel. We're sorry to bother you now. Knapp has written up the preliminary after-action report. I assume you've been in touch with General Lemming?"

Still staring at the porthole Robertson nods. "I've talked to the General. He was up at 2d Brigade all yesterday, but I called him this afternoon."

"Is he pleased?"

"Pleased. Is the General pleased. Does it please the General. Will't please you to rise, Sir? We'll meet the company below. Interesting way of putting it, Charles, is the General *pleased*?"

"You want us to come back later, Colonel?" Neither Claiborn or Knapp has ever seen the *gamin* in him; only heard about it.

"No, my friends, it pleases me that you should stay. You *do* wish to please your Colonel, do you not?" Still he does not look at them. They shift uneasily on their feet. Claiborn decides this is not an attractive side to the Colonel's character but writes it off as fatigue.

Robertson finally tears himself away from the play of motes, snaps out of himself. "Yes, Charles, the Great Man is pleased. I trust neither of you is preparing to upset him?" He suddenly turns toward them, staring archly.

"I can't say that, Sir. Captain Knapp has written up the combat after-action report. It has to go out on the C and C at 1800, or whenever the rain lets up. You want to look at it before it goes up? You should look at it, Colonel."

"I should look at it, huh, not to mention sign it?" Knapp hands it to him like a schoolboy handing a bad report card to his father. The Colonel puts on his half-rim tortoise shells, spins around on his chair, takes the report and studies it.

They strain to pick up his reactions to the controversial paragraphs, Knapp self-righteously hoping it will provoke arguments. But the Colonel finishes without a flicker of disapproval on his face and resumes staring out the porthole.

"You know, Knapp," he says finally, "when I heard you

and the Major come in here I expected you were going to ask me a question. Not the one you asked, not ask me to read a report, but to ask me something no one's asked me since we went into Kien Hoa. An important question, too, one might even say the *only* question. You know what I'm thinking about?"

Claiborn and Knapp stare at each other. "No, Sir," Knapp replies, sorely disappointed in himself.

"You don't, huh? Your Colonel is not pleased." He turns back to them. "O.K. We've played games long enough, afloat and ashore. How many'd we lose out there this time, Charles, sixteen killed, seventy-odd wounded, not counting the Navy?"

"Yes, Sir."

"I'm thinking about one of our friends in a high place, higher than General Lemming. I'm thinking of our distinguished visitor, the one allergic to helicopters, the one we went out again to prove the concept of riverine mobility for. You recollect now who I mean?"

"Jesus. He never came. The son of a bitch never came."

"No. He never came. Yesterday at 1400 he got in a C-130 and flew up to Da Nang to decorate some marines. This afternoon he flies back to Washington." Robertson's voice is cold, without expression. "Only don't call him a son of a bitch. He doesn't know, probably will never know, what went on here yesterday in his behalf."

With a dramatic flourish Knapp flicks the ballpoint out of his fatigue-jacket pocket and hands it to George Robertson, who signs his name to the report. "Send it up to Division. Put an 'Eyes Only' on it and address it to the General, not to G-3. Don't make any changes. Save a copy for me."

"Yes, Sir," Claiborn says.

"I can make it worse, Colonel," Knapp notes.

"No, send it as it is. Don't change a word." He looks out the porthole again and puffs on his cigar.

"Thank you, Colonel."

"Get out of here, both of you. Go have a beer. Get pleased."

5:30 P.M. The afternoon monsoon now buffets Kien Hoa Province and the Song My Tho. It is a great gray swirl, the waters coming down as if from huge sluices, warm sleet pelting the remnants of the 317th escaping to the south, and the U.S.S. *Samson*, buttoned up against the storm. It is like the desperate punishment of some frustrated God, Robertson reflects, hearing the rain against the skin of the ship. But the punishment, the daily afternoon scourge, is neither lengthened nor intensified from day to day. For almost a week the monsoon rains have come in the late afternoons; the dry season is finished. The rains will be a part of the 1st Brigade's operations for the next five months.

Most of which, Robertson supposes, he will spend at some desk in MACV Headquarters near Saigon. What did the troops call it, tolerating the presence of the officious colonels and majors from MACV who were always flying down to look at the Force? Hollywood West? It was as if one of the five sides of the Pentagon had been lifted out of its foundation, flown halfway around the world, and been deposited—aircon-ditioning, coffee shops, uptight staff officers and all—in the war zone. That's where Lemming will send him, he reckons, calling one of his cronies, telling him he's got a colonel who can't cut it as a commander, asking him to find Robertson a place. Maybe in G-4? He could supervise the distribution of jockstraps to the troops, or perhaps oil of citronella, responsi-ble for the whole expeditionary force. For the General is cer-tain to relieve him; he does not brook insolence, and the Knapp after-action report, which Robertson had endorsed and dispatched directly to the General, is nothing if not insolent. True, but superbly insolent.

Robertson lies in his bunk and stares up at the overhead, too tired to sleep easily. He calculates the time and sequence.

The report will go direct to the General (as soon as the mail ship can take off, when the rain stops); it'll be in his hands by 1830. Lemming will finish his drink, excuse himself in his courtly way, drive from the General's mess to the helipad at Division, and fly out to the *Samson*. Then there'll be the inevitable showdown. He'll be out here by 1845. It won't be a shouting match: just those deadly eyes trained on him, several quiet words, and it will be done. Perhaps even the promise of a medal for a sweetener. Robertson turns onto his stomach, dozes.

There is suddenly a hand on his shoulder, importunate and nervous. He frowns against the light streaming in from the study and sees his friend Claiborn's face staring down at him. No need to ask what is meant, for Claiborn, sensing what is to come, says: "We're behind you, Colonel." Robertson points at the study. "Is he in there?" The Major nods. "Tell him I'll be right out." Claiborn leaves, closing the door behind him. Robertson gets up, splashes cold water on his face, puts on his fatigue jacket, and steps out into the study.

There is no noise. The rain has stopped. The sunset can be seen through the open porthole. No one is in the study but Lemming, sitting on the table facing the door of Robertson's stateroom, staring at him with a look of dedicated hatred as he walks out. He says nothing, waiting for Robertson to start talking, perhaps half-expecting a quavering apology. But that is not in Colonel Robertson's mind. He has another plan.

"It's nice of you to come down, Sir. I have an idea you'd like to see the wounded down below." He glances pointedly at his watch. "The dispensary closes to visitors in fifteen minutes. It'd mean so much to the troops if you'd say a few words to them."

Lemming doesn't want particularly to see the wounded—plenty of time for that later—but he is outflanked and knows it. "Alright," he says amicably. He ambles over to the passageway door (he is not to be hurried) and calls for his aide. "Terwilliger, what'd you bring down in the way of decorations? You got some bronze stars for valor and some purple hearts? Colonel Robertson and I are going below to talk to some of Colonel Plowman's wounded." He turns to Robertson. "Plowman's wounded come here, don't they?"

"Yes, Sir. They come here."

Terwilliger pats the canvas kit bag slung over his shoulder so Lemming can hear the clinks of the medals inside, and the three of them snake their way together down through the ship, naval ratings and soldiers popping tight against the bulkheads as they recognize the two stars on the General's cap. "How are ya? How are ya? Good to see ya," he says to them. Just above the waterline, under the wardroom, is a beautifully equipped dispensary, cool, shining, and antiseptic. A corpsman in the waiting-room looks up from his *Cavalier* and comes to attention as the officers enter.

"Unnerstand you've got some of my boys down here," Lemming says. "Like to see 'em for a minute or two."

Some of my boys, Robertson thinks. The bastard. He follows the General into the ward.

On either side of the narrow ward are beds, ten to a side. Lemming walks all the way to the far bulkhead, letting the troops see him—those that are awake and able to see—turns around, and heads slowly back up the aisle, stopping in front of each bunk. The first trooper has had a kneecap blown off by a booby-trap, and his leg is extended on an aluminum support at an angle of 45 degrees to the mattress. The soldier, sensing the General's business, has laid his newspaper on his chest and is propping himself up on his elbows when Lemming stops before him.

"How're you feeling, son?"

"Good, Sir, real good."

"How'd you get hit?"

"I got it jumping off the ramp of a tango boat. They had command-detonateds on the bank."

"Give you any pain now?"

"Nah, not now, Sir. No pain."

Lemming nods, drops his eyes, smiles. "Where're you from, son?"

"Owatonna, Minnesota, Sir."

"Ah, yeah, that's beautiful country out there. One of my boys goes to college in Minnesota."

"Yes, Sir? Where's that, the University?"

"No, Carleton College."

The soldier nods at the General. "Kid's got some smarts, huh?"

"Ah, he's a worker."

"Beats working here, I guess."

"I guess it does." The string is up; there is a long pause in the conversation, neither Lemming nor the PFC from Owatonna knowing how to continue. Finally the General turns to Captain Terwilliger and asks him for a purple heart and a bronze star with "V." The aide hands them over, each decoration already fitted out with a stationer's clip to save the General fumbling with a catch and pin. Lemming moves around to the side of the bed, leans over the soldier, and attaches the decorations to his pajama pocket, saying, "Well, we're real proud of you, real proud."

"Thank you, Sir."

Real proud, Robertson thinks. The General says "really proud," or "really delighted" when he talks to his staff officers. With the troops he gets in that homey Shenandoah touch. *Real proud.* The man's a master.

The party moves off, down between the bunks, working its way back toward the waiting-room. The same conversational sequence is repeated over and over, the words changed slightly so that the soldiers in adjacent bunks don't catch the routine of it. How're you feeling, son? How'd you get hit? Where you from? Biloxi? Moline? Salt Lake? Laramie? Great country. Man could settle down there and live real good. We're real proud. Captain Terwilliger, please? Thanks. We're real proud. Goddamit these kids are lions, aren't they, Robertson?

At last they come to two bunks partitioned off from the others. Neither of their occupants is conscious. General Lemming reaches down for the clipboard hanging from the crank at the foot of the first bunk and reads the medical history of Paul Compella since 2345 last night. "This one's critical, General," the doctor advises, adding in a voice just above a whisper, "I don't know if he's going to make it. Bad head wound."

"Why wasn't he sent to 42nd Surg? Maybe he'd be in Japan by now."

"He was operated on last night around 0300. We don't want to move him yet."

"Is there brain damage?"

"Extensive brain damage."

Goddamn shame, Lemming thinks, but says nothing further. Again he looks over at Terwilliger, takes the decorations, and clips them onto Compella's blanket, staring at the soldier's face. It reminds him of the face of a male nun, the adhesive taut across his forehead. He turns and looks at Colonel Robertson, pursing his lips as he shakes his head. Real slow-like, Robertson thinks.

"I think I saw this kid once, Robertson. Didn't he used to do briefings at Division with Major Sorenson?"

"Very briefly, yes, Sir. Only for a day or two, I think. He'd only been in-country for a week."

"Yeah, that's right. Damn shame. Nice-looking boy."

"Yes, Sir, real fine kid."

"Well," the General turns back to the surgeon, "notify Colonel Robertson and me as to any changes in his condition."

"Of course, General."

The party leaves the ward.

Down at the far end the soldier from Owatonna without a kneecap has been listening and watching the officers' progress through the ward. From time to time he has reached out to his buddy in the next bunk, making whispered comments about

it. Now, as the door closes behind Lemming, he catches his
friend's eye again.

"Fucking prick," he says.

It is done without eloquence, without apparent anger,
without remorse. Colonel Sadler is the name of the new brigade commander. Robertson's executive officer and Major
Claiborn will stay on for the time being. It takes time to break
in a new CO in the riverine environment, sometimes too
much time, doesn't it, Robertson? The Colonel will get his
Legion of Merit and the General likes to think he has enough
drag up in Saigon to get him something decent at MACV.
Hell, he's only got, what? Six months left in-country? Perhaps
he could meet his wife in Honolulu for a week before reporting up to Saigon. Make a fresh start.

"But I'm obliged to warn you, Robertson, that insubordination of this sort may not be tolerated by other commanders. The airmobile company you didn't get went to Morton's
brigade, and Morton's got a major fight on his hands right
now. The assets weren't wasted. And I can't say that I think
your casualties were significantly greater in Kien Hoa than
they would have been if you had had helicopters."

The *post hoc* variation, Robertson thinks, sensing that Lemming already believes it.

"I'm not going to ruin you on your OER, either. No,
you're not getting a clean bill-of-health. In fact it's unlikely
that you'll ever command anything again. But you'll survive if
you learn this lesson. A star is not out of the question.

"I've got to go. I haven't relieved many commanders,
George, and I've never done it with malice. We've got a mission in this war, and anything which creates friction, slows
down its accomplishment, has got to be eliminated. A commander who drags his heels is infinitely more dangerous to us
than the VC."

"What's the mission, General?"

But Lemming ignores him, shakes Robertson's hand before Robertson can withdraw it, and is gone.

No hard feelings, you understand.

THE SOLDIER

YES. Why do we all, seeing of a soldier, bless him? bless
Our redcoats, our tars? Both of these being, the greater part,
But frail clay, nay but foul clay. Here it is: the heart,
Since, proud, it calls the calling manly, gives a guess
That, hopes that, makes believe, the men must be no less;
It fancies, feigns, deems, dears the artist after his art;
And I fain will find as sterling all as all is smart,
And scarlet wear the spirit of war there express.

Mark Christ our King. He knows war, served this soldiering through;
He of all can reeve a rope best. There he bides in bliss
Now, and seeing somewhere some man do all that man can do,
For love he leans forth, needs his next must fall on, kiss,
And cry "Oh Christ-done deed! So God-made-flesh does too:
Were I come o'er again" cries Christ "it should be this."

GERARD MANLEY HOPKINS

Headquarters, Twelfth Infantry Division in Vietnam
0850 Hours, 10 April 1968

On the walls of General Lemming's office, behind the great desk, are patterns of pale rectangles, the impressions left by pictures and framed citations and personal maps and plaques removed this morning after hanging there for fourteen

months. Sergeant Kowalski has taken them down, wrapped
them in tissue paper, and packed them. He has already polished the desk once more, removing the clutter for the last
time. Into the footlockers go the bibelots: the elephants and
the bronze Balinese dancers, the cigarette boxes and swagger
sticks, the folders and calendars and pads—all the souvenirs.
The polished artillery-shell ashtrays will stay behind, the
thoughtful gifts of one general to another.

Lemming likes indoor places, remembers their ambience,
their smells, the way the light angles through the windows
onto their floors and furniture. He will particularly miss this
office, from which he has commanded what some officers
have told him was the best fighting division in Vietnam. A lot
got done here. What a pleasure it was, working with Colonel
Murphy, with Crauford and Terwilliger and the young battalion commanders who came by to talk modestly of their tactics and their body-counts. All of it was pleasure, all the
activity that went on in this room—even, he reflects, the
things that annoyed him at the time. For in all the activity he
was at stage-center, could control things—the deployment of
battalions, the giving of solatium, the sequence and direction
of a reporter's questions, the way his staff carried out his orders, the building of base camps, the formulation of new strategies.

Of course some blood's been spilled here (not as it was up
in the Nineteenth Division, where the headquarters people
were actually killed and wounded in rocket attacks), but that
blood was not wasted. No. You cut out dead tissue so that
healthy tissue might grow. You destroyed some careers in the
process, careers just beginning to fulfill their early promise:
but better here, he thinks, here in the Twelfth Division while
they're still light colonels and majors than somewhere else
later on. Other careers have been made, by the bold stroke of a
pen or the attachment of a medal to a deserving breast. His
own has flourished. He has orders to the *Strategic Warfare Stud-*

ies Center at Fort Cuhlman, where he will be commandant and director, and he will go there as a lieutenant general.

But first there will be a long leave in Sequenoy. The Shenandoah is ripening now in the early spring. The rolling meadows are green and spongy; the young colts are beginning to skitter along the fences, over the hills. There will be time to sit by the great rough-stone fireplace and dip into the military history published in the last eighteen months, time to walk along the route of Jackson's Army of the Shenandoah, perhaps even to write an article or two about the Vietnam War. And time to love the good ample woman who has been his wife for thirty-four years. And still more time to attend the graduations of sons and nephews. "This is General Lemming," the headmasters and professors will say, introducing him around to the parents and alumni. Not cornflakes manufacturer Lemming, or company director Lemming, or country lawyer Lemming, but "my good friend, *General* Lemming—you probably saw him on the ABC Evening News, did you not? Katherine, you must be so proud, so happy to have him home safe. We all slept better knowing you were leading our kids over there, General. Perhaps you'll say a few words to the graduates?"

Kowalski and the Chief-of-Staff and the aide come and go, carrying things out, putting a few more papers in the "In" basket, working quietly so as not to disturb him. They correctly imagine he wants to be alone with his thoughts before he goes out to be decorated. General Paunce has already been briefed at length: he is ready to take command of the Lionheads. For Lemming it is now only a matter of clearing the last papers from his desk, of signing the last pieces of paper.

His affectations to the contrary, paperwork has never really bothered him. It gives him a sense of detailed control. He has been signing letters of condolence now for a long time, never blinking at the invariable last line of the form letter: "We who are left will carry on the struggle to bring freedom to Vietnam." That is sufficient placebo. In deep mourning you don't think about the politics too carefully. And he has been writing and endorsing letters of recommendation and officers' efficiency reports for years. In his benevolent mood of this morning he makes no written demurrer to the extravagant language used to describe the activities of his officers by those writing their efficiency reports. What the hell? But, Christ, you could name a fleet of battleships after the qualities his commanders and staff perceive in their subordinates: "intrepid, brilliant, valiant, indefatigable, invincible, gallant . . ."

On the efficiency reports are tiny little men standing tall. One little man stands at the top. Under him two more little men. Under them four. Under them thirteen more. Sixty. Thirteen. Four. Two. One. If the officer you are rating is a great friend, or if you know him to have been a great soldier, or if it eases your conscience to give him a handsome boost, then make a check next to the one little man at the top. He stands alone. And, odd thing, all the efficiency reports he goes through this morning have checks next to the one little man at the top, standing tall.

He looks up, watching the motes tumble in the shafts of light from the window. It'll be crowded at the Chief-of-Staff's desk in a few years. All his officers seem to be bound for the top.

He shrugs, signs the last of them, turns to other papers. Combat after-action reports, draft "Lessons-Learned pamphlets" (a PET milk can makes an excellent booby-trap, if properly configured), brigade and battalion SITREPS, District Intelligence Briefing abstracts, body-count mimeos, weapons stats. He initials them all with his big GSL. *I have seen and wish to make no obtrusion.* On to other papers. He reads through the personal notes from his friends, agreeing easily with their testimonials to his achievements as Commanding General. Without looking up he reaches over to the "In" box, feels for more papers, finds only one.

We all slept better knowing you were leading our kids over there.
He slides the last paper in front of him. Shit. A Congressional.
It is a letter dated 5 April, from the Office of the Chief of
Legislative Liaison. The usual inquiry about a soldier, rou-
tinely sent across his desk by his own request, like all Con-
gressionals. They can get a bit sticky, but he likes to keep up
with this sort of thing, flatters himself that he knows more
about what goes on in his Division than any other commander. What are the troops complaining about? Lots of times
their complaints are legitimate ones that the company commanders might have, should have taken care of themselves.

The language of these letters is always careful and re-
strained. Congressmen do not as a rule write generals in the
field on such matters; rather, they channel their inquiries
through a colonel in Washington. The colonel and his as-
sistants gently pose the questions to the leaders in the field:
"Why Specialist Four Herbert has written no letter home in his
three months in Vietnam; why PFC Johnston is sent to the
field despite his severe foot diseases; why Specialist Five Don-
ovan wasn't transferred to MACV Headquarters; why PFC
Paul Compella, deceased, was not promptly med-evacked out
of the combat zone to a hospital with facilities better able to
treat his wounds. It is felt by the deceased member's parents
that such procedure would have saved the member's life."

Compella, Compella. Lemming bites at the eraser on his
pencil, trying to remember the soldier, trying to connect the
name with a face. Wait a minute. Yes, now he's got it: the
handsome soldier on the boat, wounded in the Kien Hoa
Sweep . . .

"Excuse me, General, COMUSMACV's chopper is five
minutes out."

"Is the ceremony all laid on?"

"Yes, Sir. Are you ready? We've got your stuff loaded on
your C and C, ready to go."

"Thanks, Chuck. I guess we'd better get down to the ceremony."

"Looks like you're leaving a clean desk for General Paunce."

"The least I can do for the poor bastard."

"He's got a tough act to follow, Sir."

"Thanks, Chuck, it means a lot to hear you say that. But he'll have you here to keep him straight. He'll do alright."

"Thank you, Sir."

"There's one item. A Congressional. Parents want to know why a trooper didn't get proper medical treatment, one of those."

"You want Mason to draft a reply?"

"Yeah. Good. He's done a lot of those. You sign for Paunce. Don't start him off with a Congressional."

"Yes, Sir."

General Lemming stands up, tidies his jungle-fatigue jacket, carefully wraps the pistol belt around his waist. He walks slowly toward the office door.

"I'll miss this place. You ready, Chuck? You did a great job here. You won't be forgotten . . ."

"Thank you, Sir." He starts to say something more, but realizes his voice will crack if he does.

"Jesus Christ, don't be maudlin. Let's get outside."

Gallo Memorial Cemetery, Torrington, Connecticut
0930 Hours (EST), 10 April 1968

To people from other parts of the country Connecticut seems to arrange itself into two societies: suburban New York City—Darien, New Canaan, Westport, Ford Country Squires, the "Consciousness II" liberalism of a commuting society living over its head; beyond this, beyond a circle with perhaps a sixty-mile radius pivoting on Manhattan, the rolling spare Berkshires—Litchfield County, poets' retreats, the boys' boarding schools. There is more to the state than this. There is, for example, the grimy Naugatuck Valley, running south to north across the western part of the state like an ugly scar, a skein of old milltowns—Derby, Seymour, Naugatuck, Ansonia, Waterbury, Torrington, Winsted—industrialized communities of third-generation Italian and Polish Americans. The Connecticut war dead are mainly of this culture. For it is not Hotchkiss School or Greenwich or Pierson College that supplies the one-one bravos to the infantry battalions in Vietnam.

And in Torrington a Requiem Mass has just been sung in St. Peter's Church, and a funeral procession of perhaps seventy-five cars is moving slowly off the inlet road to another, narrower, driveway. Mrs. Raymond Compella, in the leading limousine, sees the awning ahead, three men standing under it, two of them priests and another in military uniform. The figures are motionless, their hands identically fig-leafed over their topcoats. They watch the line of cars move toward them, their heads bobbed forward so that they seem to be looking up at the procession. On Mrs. Compella's right is her husband Raymond; and in front of them their two daughters sit facing them. No one says anything. In the front seat Frank Ruselli, godfather of the deceased, nods over at the awning, and the driver pulls up fifteen yards away. Mrs. Compella is dully conscious of the car's heat curling up around her ankles.

Slowly the family gets out on either side of the car and walks toward the awning and the gravesite and stands across from the priest. It is a gray day, gray and windlessly cold enough for the breaths of the mourners to show against their topcoats. Blotches of old filthy snow are caked and layered around the bases of the tombstones where the early spring sunlight has never been. Mrs. Compella is vaguely aware of the asymmetry of the graveyard skyline: crypts, tombs, a mausoleum, headstones set randomly and crowded all around. The larger the stone the less the love, she thinks. The priest looks over at her with a determined but infinite tenderness, an expression she somehow connects only with the eyes of the anaesthesiologist looking down at her the morning Paul was born. So rapid has been the passage of years. The city had the same mayor then as it does now.

What was it she had read years ago, an account of Polish Jews going in groups to be shot into a trench, one of the girls saying to a soldier, over and over, "twenty years old . . . twenty years old." And now Paul, nineteen. The priest reads from his Missal. She remembers her son in the New Haven Arena three years ago, fiercely quick, eyes shooting sideways, head up, the right hand knowing, controlling the dribble as he brings the ball up court in a delirium of screaming and heat: Torr-ing-ton! His calf muscles flexed over his socks as he pushes off, elbow cocked, hand over the back of his head, "Shoot! Shoot!" and the ball springing off supple fingers and then arcing down from the rafters, its flight broken only by the webbing of the net.

How could he know what he was doing? Was there even a civics class at Torrington High? Time slides by in a changed expression: Paul at ten, holding his mother's hand at this very graveyard, the same hand her husband clasps now. Her mother's funeral.

She has not heard what the priest was saying. Now he blesses the casket, two hundred mourners watching in a stillness broken only by his toneless voice and the drone of a plane miles away. A flag folded into a cushion is placed in her hands. Some begin to turn away, to walk to their cars, and suddenly what she has dreaded begins to happen.

A voice cracking like a caw: "Please wait, wait . . . I knew him. He was vice-president of his class when I became principal. I want to say . . . he was a good and a kind boy . . . When I walked into the classroom the first day I was at the high school he came up to me and shook my hand. He introduced me. He always did things like that and I loved him for it." Mr. Lewis in his grief is conscious of his audience, unhappy in their taciturnity, in knowing what their bumper stickers advertise, that one of them last week had told him Martin Luther King's murderer should only have to pay a fine for "shooting coon out of season," that the older mourners have soldiered across Europe in the infantry and regard Paul's death as somehow just and as an honor to the city.

"For what, for what? . . . This hideous war . . . Is there a purpose? . . . What did he die for? For nothing? What did he do?"

Frances Compella has taken everything on faith all her life. Vietnam, certainly; her husband had explained it to her driving back from Bradley Field the day their son left them. See, if we don't stop them there they'll get Jap-an, which is our ally now, and Australia. How'd you like to see them on the Golden Gate Bridge shooting children? That's the way these people are, and you have to draw a line somewhere and we drew it *there*. No one else did, so we had to. Don't worry about him. He's smart. There's a picture in *Life* of this surgical ward they attach to the bottom of a helicopter and fly it right in to where they are. I think it was only 2 percent they don't save. No, Frances, Paul's no problem. Don't worry about it. A year from now we'll have him back here and be proud of him.

She knew he would be killed. Paul, at 5' 8", *challenging*, the announcer kept repeating. "Compella challenges Paine, who is 6' 3", dribbles up to him and shoots over his head." "Compella challenges Gregg with a high inside fastball and snaps it over the plate." Outside stadiums he didn't challenge anyone. But *there* he would, she knew. Thus he would die. No Communist would stride down the Golden Gate Bridge looking for children to shoot. No Red would get onto the island of Japan. She tried to make herself think he was safe, tried by acts of faith. But they never became rooted conviction, were choked from the start. She tried to believe what he was doing was somehow worthy, and sometimes fresh eddies of conviction had carried her along: a report of a bombed orphanage in Saigon, a picture in the papers of a tiny yellow child in New York for surgery and a trip to F.A.O. Schwartz, Paul's few letters—confident and disordered.

But it was no use. Her acts of faith were stunted growths, and on April 10th at the funeral only the thinnest stems connect her with them. Mr. Lewis cuts through them now as with a razor.

"For what?"

Now there remained not even that consolation to which she might have come to accommodate herself through the months and turning seasons ahead. No belief to cling to, no reason why to be believed, no certitudes. Only her husband now with his arm around her waist, taking her back to the limousine.

Headquarters, Twelfth Infantry Division in Vietnam
0930 Hours, 10 April 1968

Let us decorate our General, in front of his own Headquarters. He is in position already, standing in an almost geriatric parody of what he was taught at The Citadel thirty-nine years ago, his jungle-fatigue jacket hanging off his shoulders as if they were a broken wooden hanger. In spite of themselves, his staff takes an odd pleasure in seeing him like this, at attention, waiting for *his* superior. All the mornings of the long months past, precisely at 0725, they have come to attention as he walked through the Division office on his way to be briefed, passing their desks without looking at them, only absently saying "morning, morning," already absorbed in the challenges of the new day.

He is at attention on the sandy fresh topsoil in front of Division. Somewhere miles away a plane drones. It is, as always, hot and windy, and the lapels and shirttails of the General's fatigue jacket flap in the breeze. From where the staff and subordinate commanders are standing it is difficult to make out his face. The visor of his green baseball cap keeps his eyes and forehead hidden, but underneath, inside the shade, they imagine those eyes of his, corvine, deadly deep-blue, without remorse, not following the progress of the awards party as it moves slowly toward him.

The General who will decorate him with the Distinguished Service Medal is an august shuffling presence, a U.S. Grant in faded green poplin. He makes his left-face awkwardly in the sand, and his aide hands him the decoration which he has carried—yes, on a cushion. From somewhere behind the assembled staff, flinty and disembodied, a voice begins a familiar incantation:

> By order of the President, the Distinguished Service Medal is presented to Major General George Simpson Lemming, 040618, United States Army, for exceptionally meritorious service while serving in a position of great responsibility as Commanding General, Twelfth Infantry Division, from February 1967 to April 1968. During General Lemming's tenure as commanding general, the Division, largely as a result of his intrepid and imaginative leadership, achieved unequaled success in furtherance of its mission to eliminate Viet Cong insurgency in its assigned area of operations. It established and developed four major base camps, created a logistical base capable of sustaining its manifold combat and civic action operations, successfully conducted its search-and-clear mission against an aggressive and capable enemy, inaugurated a program of civic-action operations which have brought new friendship and understanding between American forces and the people and armed forces of the Republic of South Vietnam, and by unfailingly skillful airmobile, riverine, and conventional operations cut major enemy supply routes in its area of responsibility. During the period of

General Lemming's command the Division and attached forces conducted combat operations resulting in 9456 enemy killed, captured 820 Viet Cong and North Vietnamese soldiers, accounted for 190 Hoi Chanh, destroyed 12,230 structures known to have been built or occupied by the enemy, captured 12 tons of enemy documents, and conducted 4000 separate civic-action operations ranging from the rendering of simple medical treatment of indigenous personnel to the construction of 32 new elementary schools and 8 hospitals.

The Twelfth Infantry Division particularly distinguished itself during the enemy's recent TET offensive and in the weeks immediately afterwards. In a time of great crisis it stood firm against the repeated onslaughts of the enemy infantry, seized the initiative from him, and eventually routed him from the Division area of responsibility. General Lemming personally directed and coordinated many of the operations of his assigned maneuver elements during this period, repeatedly exposing himself to hostile fire, inspiring commanders and troops alike by his visionary leadership, unremitting courage, and great stamina.

General Lemming's service as commanding General, Twelfth Infantry Division, is in keeping with the highest traditions of American military service and reflects great credit upon himself, the United States Army, and the United States of America.

By direction of the Secretary of the Army, /s/ Stanley R. Resor.

A few crackles from the loudspeaker, and it is shut off.

Now the theater commander has clipped the medal to the General's pocketflap, and he stands back a foot or so and their hands grope, as they study each other's faces, grope and lock and pump. Nelson and Collingwood. MacArthur and Wainwright. It is an intensely personal moment for them both, a mutual, relieved affirmation that what each knows the other to have been doing for the past thirty-five years is worthy and true and of good report. Now the senior General's left hand goes out and clasps Lemming's elbow. They are smiling at each other, hard, as if proclaiming together that, by God, some things *are* sacred in this collapsing world of 1968, and friendship among brave warriors is one of them. The small band to their left breaks the quiet with a Sousa march and the Generals awkwardly turn, lurch into a jerky cadenced step, and stride together off the field.

August, 1971

Except for Paul Compella, all the characters who figure prominently in the narrative survived their tours in Vietnam.

George Simpson Lemming is at Fort Cuhlmann with the war studies group to which he was assigned in April 1968. He is hopeful that he will be reassigned as Supreme Commander, Allied Powers in Europe. His book, *Memoirs of an Infantry General* (nothing in it to prejudice his chances for the SHAPE job), was published in January 1970 . . .

Charles Murphy, Lemming's Chief of Staff, is a brigadier and an assistant division commander at Fort Lewis. His oldest son was caught blowing grass at the Virginia Military Institute, dismissed by the authorities, and is now a PFC in Germany.

George Robertson is living off his pension and his wife's money at Sea Island, Georgia. He has become a great reader of W. H. Auden and Thomas Love Peacock.

Charles Claiborn gained early promotion to lieutenant

colonel. Then, against the dire warnings of Infantry Branch, he turned down his assignment to the War College in favor of a tour of duty as deputy professor of military science at Columbine University, Cranston, Montana.

Philip Knapp, Robertson's former plans officer, is involved in the defense of Daniel Ellsberg. The firm of Churchill, Berman, Garrison and Hunt, Los Angeles, considers his services worth $35,000 a year.

Alden Jacobs failed to secure advancement in the naval service and is a buyer for Chipp, Clothiers. His sloop *Invicta* recently finished fourth in the Newport-Bermuda race.

The new gymnasium at Torrington High School is called Compella Memorial Gymnasium, and Paul Compella's bronze star was melted into the wall plaque soldered underneath the press box.

THE REAR

Humping through the bush, lugging a rucksack, rifle, 15–20 magazines of bullets, a Claymore mine, four hand grenades, a gallon or two of water, assorted military odds and ends, and getting shot at is no picnic. Along with getting back to the World and going on R & R, many grunts dreamed of a job—any job—in the laid-back, get-over, fat-cat rear.

Tim O'Brien

Dulce et Decorum

Tim:

How does one respond to such a letter as that? July was always a hot month, sweaty kids running through the streets with sparklers, but where are they now, tell me? With you, I fear; some of them still shrilly laughing, a sordid patriotism racing in their souls.

I suppose if we gain anything from this unsought experience it will be an appreciation for honesty—frankness on the part of our politicians, our friends, our loves, ourselves. No

more liars in public places. (And the bed and
the bar are, in their way, as public as the floor
of Congress.)

For honesty has become something wholly
other than childhood innocence or adult aspira-
tion. Rather, because there is no time, no cause
or reason, for anything but truth, honesty has
become fundamental to life itself. We must be
honest or be silent.

And especially for you, living in your terrible private world, mercilessly made public to
death, I try to be honest. I am in Vietnam, but I
am not in combat, and I'm sometimes conscious enough to be grateful for that. Having
sought the answer to why we are both here and
finding none, I now ask why you are out there,
doing the battling, and not me. Again, no answer. Would I willingly risk those few moments again at Fort Lewis, when two decisions
were made that fated two lives? Would I risk
the chance to persuade you to enlist for an extra
year to avoid the infantry for the possibility
that you might have persuaded me not to? And
would I now be there beside you, or instead of
you? The whole thought of wishing for the
chance over again is just as absurd as the actual
act.

How far into this must we go to find meaning? Here, I want desperately to help you. To
give you a ticket to a place I know in Norway.
And there is nothing, absolutely nothing, I can
do but encourage you to be honest, as you have
been.

But here I am in Long Binh, this sprawling,
tarred, barbed-wire sanctuary for well-bred
brass and well-connected lifers. What they are

doing to win or end the war, I don't know. As for my own contribution to military history, I spent the first month in Asia as a legal clerk, helping the army to chastise its pot smokers and nonconforming, often futilely proud black soldiers.

At night, I spend time on guard or waiting on standby alert. There's no reality to it. Long Binh is not the war; it's not really part of Vietnam, not with all the cement and Pepsi-Cola and RCA television sets. One night last week I watched a spectacular fire fight—gunships sending down red sheets of metal, then there was a long gap of blackness, then the sound reached me, just a buzz. I imagined you out there. I'm only an observer, Tim, audience to a tragic Fourth of July football game.

Erik

A new man, another southerner, took charge of Alpha Company in early August. He had been in command for only an hour when he marched the men into a mine field. Then the dust-off helicopters were there, taking away a dead man named Rodríguez and a cripple named Martínez. They were Spanish-Americans, bewildered companions. They'd spent time together snapping Kodak pictures of each other in gallant, machine-gun-toting poses.

But when all that happened, I was in Chu Lai, looking for a new job. Captain Smith, probably feeling guilty for having copped out on a long-standing promise for a job sorting mail in the rear, had given me a three-day pass and a wry grin. He wished me luck. I hitchhiked around the sands of Chu Lai, showing off letters of recommendation from Captain Johansen and Alpha's first sergeant, trying to talk someone into taking me on. But the army has plenty of mediocre typists. I couldn't

change a tire, and no one wants a tired foot soldier anyway.
There were no offers, and I rejoined Alpha Company.

If foot soldiers in Vietnam have a single obsession, it's the
gnawing, tantalizing hope of being assigned to a job in the
rear. Anything to yank a man out of the field—loading helicopters or burning trash or washing the colonel's laundry.

Unlike the dreamy, faraway thoughts about returning alive
to the World, the GI's thinking about a rear job is not dominated by any distant, unreachable, unrealistic passion. It's right
there, within grasp. You watch the lucky ones wade into a rice
paddy and toss their packs into a chopper. They grin and give
you the peace sign. There is a self-pity, an envious loneliness,
when they are gone.

GI's use a thousand strategies to get into the rear. Some
men simply shoot themselves in the feet or fingers, careful to
mash only an inch or so of bone.

Some men manufacture ailments, hoping to spend time in
the rear, hoping to line up something.

And one man maintained a running record of the dates
when rear-echelon troopers were due to rotate back to the
World. When one of those days came near, he'd send back a
request for the man's job.

But the best route to a rear job, the only reliable way, is to
burrow your nose gently up an officer's ass. Preferably the
company commander. If an officer takes a fancy to you—if he
thinks you're one of his own breed—then you're a candidate
for salvation. But you've got to spill over with clear-headed-
ness; you've got to bleed with courage, morbid humor, un-
questioning forbearance.

For the soul brothers, that route is not easy. To begin
with, the officer corps is dominated by white men; the corps
of foot soldiers, common grunts, is disproportionately black.
On top of that are all the old elements of racial tension—fears,
hates, suspicions. And on top of that is the very pure fact that
life is at stake. Not property or a decent job or social acceptance. It's a matter of staying alive.

With either the hunch or the reality that white officers favor white grunts in handing out the rear jobs, many blacks react as any sane man would. They sulk. They talk back, get angry, loaf, play sick, smoke dope. They group together and laugh and say shit to the system.

And this feeds the problem. Pointing at malingering and insubordination by the blacks, the officers are free to pass out jobs to white men. Then the whole cycle goes for another round, getting worse.

For Alpha Company, the phenomenon finally hit a point when the circle was spinning so fast, with such centrifugality, that it blew apart.

Alpha's first sergeant was hated by the blacks. Rear assignments, they said, were going to ol' whitey, and they intended to do something about it. "Damn first sergeant's responsible," they said. "He's the Man, we'll get him."

When we lost four men one day, the first sergeant saddled up and took a chopper out to join us until replacements came in. He was a tall, even-handed man. He seemed to hate Vietnam as much as anyone. His National Guard unit had been activated, and he'd been torn away from his town and friends, same as the rest of us, by politics and circumstance. We were mortared the night he arrived. He crawled on his hands and knees with everyone else. To be fair, the first sergeant may not have been a leader, but he was quiet and helpful enough.

In the morning we began searching villages, moving through two or three of them. We moved across a broad paddy. The company was formed in a long, widely spaced column. The first sergeant, probably to show us he had guts and could take charge, walked up front with the company commander and the RTO's, and we moved slowly.

I was watching the first sergeant. He lurched backward, and dirt and a cloud of red smoke sprayed up around his thighs. He stood and gaped at the short explosion. He didn't say anything. As if he were trying to back out of the shrapnel

and noise, he took three steps. Then his legs disintegrated under him, and he fell heavily on his back.

It exploded right under him. No one felt any particular loss
when the helicopter landed and we packed him aboard.

That evening we dug foxholes and cooked C rations over
heat tabs. The night was hot, so instead of sleeping right
away, I sat with a black friend and helped him pull his watch.
He told me that one of the black guys had taken care of the
first sergeant. It was an M-79 round, off a grenade launcher.
Although the shot was meant only to scare the top sergeant,
the blacks weren't crying, he said. He put his arm around me
and said that's how to treat whitey when it comes down to it.

In two weeks, a black first sergeant came to Alpha.

Except for one or two of them, the men in Alpha Company were quietly, flippantly desperate for a rear job. The desperation was there all the time. Walking along under the sun,
pulling watch at night, waiting for resupply, writing love letters—we thought and talked about all the rear jobs waiting
back there. We were not all cowards. But we were not committed, not resigned, to having to win a war.

"Christ, you *know* I'll take anything they give me," Barney
said. "I'll shovel shit for 'em during the daytime and drink me
some beer nighttime, no problem. They send me to Chu Lai,
and I'll stack bodies at the morgue. I'll toss bodies and bloody
shit around and just drink it in, they give me the job. There it
is."

And Bates and I would pull radio watch together some
nights. "When Chip and Tom got it—that damn mine—that
did it for me. Nam was some kind of nervous game till they
got blown up. I wasn't even there then. Jesus, I was just listening over the radio. But, damn it, that did it. I knew those
guys. I'll take my job back there, anything."

So, along with the rest of Alpha Company, I followed the
new commander during August, hoping for a rear-echelon assignment and trying inconspicuously to avoid death. It seemed
odd. We weren't the old soldiers of World War II. There

wasn't anyone or any reason to write a *Guadalcanal Diary*. No valor to squander for things like country or honor or military objectives. All the courage in August was the kind you dredge up when you awaken in the morning, knowing it will be a bad day. Horace's old do-or-die aphorism—"Dulce et decorum est pro patria mori"—was just an epitaph for the insane.

Alpha spent most of August on top of a stubby, flat hill to the north of Pinkville. It was an old corn field, a dusty and hot place without trees. We ran patrols during the days. At night we were mortared. It was a sort of ritual. The sun went down, we ate, smoked a little, played some word games, and at about ten P.M. the mortar rounds came in.

It was hard to keep a decent foxhole in that corn field, the soil was so chalky. The sides simply caved in on you. In the end, we dug narrow sleeping trenches and just lay there, half-asleep and sometimes talking to one another, wondering when the barrages would stop.

The whole thing was so well coordinated and timed that we learned to urinate in the first hour after sunset so as not to be standing when the explosions started. No one was hurt during the nightly sessions, but it was frustrating. Looking down into the paddies, we could see the red flashes of the mortar tubes, we could hear the ploop of the rounds shooting out.

They sprayed our hill with 82mm rounds for twenty seconds, then packed up and went home. We called for gunships and sent our own mortar fire on them, but it was always too late. It was almost better to turn in the trenches and go to sleep.

Despite the ten-o'clock attacks and all the heat and dust on the little hill, the month of August was not bad. No one was killed. Few were seriously hurt. Sunstroke and blisters, nothing worse. It was God's gift. We lay there at night, listening to metal tearing through the hedgerows and shrubbery; impact craters only yards from our sleeping holes.

Resupply choppers brought in hot meals daily. We guzzled cases of iced beer and sodas. Morale was high—we were in a bad place, but no one was being mangled, and we were blessed. Nothing could go wrong. On one early-morning patrol, we chased two Viet Cong into a bunker. The company commander and a lieutenant threw in grenades and emptied magazines of M-16 ammo into the hole. They threw in more grenades and fired more bullets. The bunker seethed with smoke. They stopped, and our Vietnamese scout called in and asked if they would surrender. The Viet Cong threw out a rifle. Some GI's went down and pulled them out. One—a young, riddled boy—was dead. The other was older, barely alive. He coughed blood and oozed blood through black spots and torn, rust-colored flesh where the shrapnel hit. He pleaded with the scout to save his life. Our medics tried to patch him, but it was clear he would die. We began cutting down a tree to allow space for a medevac chopper. Then the man died. We left him sprawled out there; chickens were pecking away at the dust around him when we went away.

Back at our corn field, the scout went through the old Viet Cong's papers. "That VC—he VC district chief," he said. "Big man. Mean bastard."

"No shit?" the company commander said. He grinned. "Hey, we got ourselves a VC district chief. Killed a VC honcho back there."

The company commander was elated. He called battalion headquarters and gave the news. We stayed up late that evening, talking over the kills, congratulating ourselves for being tough, stealthy, lethal soldiers. But, when it got late, we quieted down, and everyone admitted it was coincidence and fortune. And, of course, at ten P.M. we were mortared.

Near the end of August, helicopters carried Alpha Company to another hill, this one alongside the South China Sea. A refugee camp was being built there, and our job was to watch civilians clear the land and put up huts. Although the place was less than a mile from our corn field, we were not mortared—only an occasional sniper—and it turned into a vacation. We sent out one patrol. A mine-sniffing dog went along. The dog stepped on a mine, and it blew his trainer's foot away.

It was there beside the ocean that I got my rear job. They wanted a typist in battalion headquarters; they wanted me. I dug a six-foot-deep foxhole that night, and I slept in it. In the morning Barney came to wake me and said I was a lucky sonofabitch. We went to the sea and swam, ducked some sniper bullets on the way out, and I threw my gear into a helicopter, and it was done.

Rich by Vietnamese standards, GIs found their wads of currency could buy not only stereos but also women. If any one factor ruined the image of the GI in Vietnam, it was the fact that the American presence spawned vast battalions of prostitutes. Anderson's acount is unfortunately only too accurate.

Charles R. Anderson

The Thing Most Missed

To the continuing frustration of American men in Vietnam, not all social needs could be answered in the rear. The lack of women was a constant problem, gnawing away at the composure of nearly every man. Since the average age of battalion members was under thirty, almost every man would be sexually active if he were back in the World around girls and wives. In Vietnam, of course, that pattern of activity was disrupted completely. The desire was there but opportunities for expression were virtually nonexistent. Strip shows were hardly satisfying since they were all look and no touch. In this respect alone assignment to the rear was worse than duty in the field. The grunts had their desire for women either eliminated or reduced to a minimum by the danger and the exhausting work involved in surviving in the bush. But the men in the rear had plenty of time, and they were rarely too tired to think about the girl or wife they wanted to be with.

There were several ways of dealing with the sex drive in the rear, none of which was any more than temporarily adequate. For one, a guy could reread the battalion's circulating library of pornographic novels and "skin mags"—magazines containing little more than pictures of female skin. Or, if all issues were checked out, a guy could rearrange and stare at his personal collection of pictures which he had thumbtacked to the wall beside his rack at bed-top level. The pictures were of completely or half-nude girl friends or wives.

If a man couldn't find a girl in the States willing to pose nude in front of a camera, he would have no choice but to resort to the simplest and most widely practiced method of dealing with the desire for women. He could stare at an underfed, prematurely aged, Vietnamese woman and fantasize her into Raquel Welch.

If a guy wanted a real girl, not a fantasy, he had to break the rules. Every base in the rear had a rule against anyone being outside the compound after dark. To enforce the rule every base had a high fence around it and an armed guard force on duty twenty-four hours a day at all entrances. But the guards were human, too, and they felt the same needs as everyone else in the compound. They could usually be counted on to look the other way at night while a hole developed in the fence between gates and a few men snuck out for some boom-boom time down the road in Dogpatch. The military's response was to put Dogpatch off limits. Any GI caught in or only walking past such an area at any time, not only at night, was subject to arrest and court-martial.

Those who headed for Dogpatch at night had to think about another, though unofficial, kind of penalty. A collection of some of the wildest rumors ever dreamed up were in constant circulation among troops in the rear. While it is most probable the rumors did not originate in the military, it is just as probable their circulation was never discouraged, for they

promised such horrible experiences for any American ventur-
ing into Dogpatch that their effect was to help enforce the off-
limits directive. According to one, the residents of Dogpatch
were very anxious to slit American throats. Another warned
that the Vietnamese offered GIs whiskey mixed with ground
glass. Another had it that local prostitutes had broken glass in
their vaginas. According to still another, prostitutes not fitted
with broken glass would give GIs incurable varieties of VD,
and the victims would be quarantined for life on a small island
in the South China Sea, never to see the States again. But official policy and unofficial propaganda had little effect, and
periodic MP sweeps through Dogpatch areas netted the un-
believers and deserters.

A more satisfying way of dealing with the sex drive, and
one that did not involve the risk of arrest and court-martial,
was related to making that run over to the Freedom Hill PX.
On the way back to 3d MPs, the driver would often decide
that since Vietnam was such a dirty, dusty country, and since
the colonel hated to see his vehicles get dirty, he had to stop at
a water point for a quick wash and service. A water point was
a place near a well or a small stream where the Vietnamese
washed jeeps and trucks for the Americans. The groups of
Vietnamese working at the wash point always included two or
three women somewhere between the ages of fifteen and
forty-five, and four or five boys about seven to twelve years
old. There was no official connection between the wash points
and the Americans; the former were strictly free-lance operations.

The wash points were not really wash points. True, the
boys splashed water on the jeeps and trucks but they didn't
pay much attention to how much dirt they left on the vehicles.
The wash points were only the newest variations on the old
prostitution theme. While the young boys splashed water on
the jeep, the driver went back into a shanty made of Coca-
Cola cases with one of the women. That's what he meant by
"service" when he said he had to stop for "a quick wash and

service." If you could have seen what the wash point girls looked like, you would understand how desperate Vietnam could make a guy.

None of those methods of dealing with the lack of women was particularly involved. None of them was very risky, and none was new. They had been practiced by troops far from home in nearly every time and place. But there was one man in 3d MPs who used considerable imagination in solving his problem. The most elaborate scheme for dealing with the need for women that I ever heard of was dreamed up by one of our excess career sergeants. His plan was also one of the most damaging to the American effort in Vietnam, and to postwar Vietnamese-American relations.

We all knew him as Sergeant Ski because none of us could pronounce or remember any more than the last three letters of his very long Polish name. And as far as we knew, no one except his parents and the administrative clerks, who kept all the service record books up to date, ever even knew his complete name.

Sergeant Ski had begun his first tour as a skinny and scared PFC more than three years before; he had finished as a skinny, but not so scared, corporal. He had begun his second tour as a lean and mean senior corporal. That tour was cut off after five months when Sergeant Ski stopped several hundred steel fragments from a North Vietnamese mortar round—with his buttocks. Back in the World Sergeant Ski had liked the Purple Heart medal, the American food, and the promotion to sergeant he was awarded, but he hated the desk he had to drive and the papers he had to shuffle in his postconvalescent leave assignment. The personnel officers at Marine Corps Headquarters probably drooled when they saw Sergeant Ski's request to go back to Vietnam—not very many men wanted another year of the Nam after their first. Even fewer wanted another tour after their second, especially after the *Tet* offensive of 1968. Sergeant Ski began his third tour in the Nam no longer lean and no longer mean. He came prepared to collect the benefits he felt the U.S. government and Vietnam owed him from his first two tours. He had served his time in hell— he had already walked through miles of rice paddy and over dozens of hills, and he had caught an assful of hot metal. Now he was going to cash in.

Shortly after Sergeant Ski joined 3d MPs the bennies started rolling in. There was all the steak and ice cream and beer he wanted plus the club, movies, USO shows, and the Freedom Hill PX. And after he was back only one month Sergeant Ski was notified that very soon he could announce himself as *Staff* Sergeant Ski. With combat pay—an extra seventy-five dollars a month—and a promotion in his pocket, Sergeant Ski was beginning to feel like somebody. "Who was it said 'war is good business?' . . . yessir, I sure would like to meet that guy someday," he could be heard to say in the club some nights.

Unknowingly, General Westmoreland, General Walt, and Lieutenant Colonel Palooka helped Sergeant Ski make up for the lack of female companionship in his life. Those commanders had for years been letting Vietnamese enter American bases during the day to earn a subsistence income by performing a variety of services for American troops—translate English to Vietnamese and vice versa, serve food and drinks, cut grass and hair, wash and iron uniforms, polish boots, make beds, and sweep out hooches. About ninety percent of the Vietnamese who came onto the bases were women and most of those were hooch-maids engaged in the last four of those jobs. Every day about fifty Vietnamese came into the 3d MP compound.

Sergeant Ski was in the battalion less than one day before he discovered that two Vietnamese women were the maids for his hooch. One was about forty-five, the other about twenty. Neither was attractive by either Vietnamese or American standards, but after two weeks Sergeant Ski's impression of the younger woman changed from "ugly and filthy" to "acceptable" ("She'll do in a pinch—Ha!") to "pretty damn sexy when you really take a look at her."

Sergeant Ski's job was to counsel prisoners in the brig every day and to serve as duty warden for one eight-hour shift every other day. The counseling never took more than three hours, and Sergeant Ski preferred to serve as warden at night, so he usually had every afternoon to himself. That was plenty of time for him to think of a way to get at the girl in his hooch. His first move was to visit, at night, the hooch of the navy medical corpsmen attached to the battalion. For a bribe of a bottle of whiskey, a luxury not allowed junior enlisted men in the combat zone, one of the corpsmen gave Sergeant Ski a broken stethoscope, an operating room mask, and the Vietnamese word for doctor, *bac-si*.

The next morning after finishing with his prisoner, Sergeant Ski tried out his technique. He went to his hooch at about eleven. The hooch was empty except for the two women. Sergeant Ski took an extra pair of boots from under his bed and gestured the older woman outside to polish them. Now only the younger girl was inside. Sergeant Ski went back inside, put the mask over his mouth and nose, and hung the stethoscope around his neck. Then he walked over to the younger girl and announced his new profession: "*Bac-si, bac-si!*" The girl turned to him with what would be judged an expression of complete bewilderment in any culture. She understood his words but not his costume, not his timing, and not the place. She might have understood his purpose if she could have seen the lascivious leer behind his mask. Sergeant Ski repeated himself. "*Bac-si, bac-si!*"

When the girl failed to move, Sergeant Ski moved her. He led her over beside the bed, sat down, and stood the girl in front of himself. Then he began a longer speech, mostly in English. "Now just relax, sweetheart . . . I'm a *bac-si*, see? And I gotta make sure you got none of them weird diseases people get over here, see? Now just hold still."

Sergeant Ski began somewhat professionally. He took the

girl's hands and pretended to examine the backs, the palms, the fingers. Then he went to her head and looked into eyes, ears, and nose, and down the throat. While he "examined," Sergeant Ski kept talking. "What's your name, sweetie?" The terrified girl could neither understand nor formulate an answer the American "doctor" would understand.

"You don't have no name, huh? Okay, I'll give you one." Sergeant Ski then pronounced several times a slang word for the female genitalia. "That's your new name." He repeated the word until the girl said it a few times, then he proceeded with his assault.

Now Sergeant Ski was ready for other areas, the areas whose existence had caused him to devise this whole charade. He raised the girl's blouse above breasts that had probably never been covered by a bra. "Here, hold up your shirt so I can check your heartbeat . . . oo, not bad, not bad at all." He touched the end of the stethoscope at a few places on and around the soft brown mounds before him. Then he dropped all pretense of medical concern and covered the bare skin before him with both hands for a long time.

By now Sergeant Ski was breathing heavily and sweating freely. He no longer saw any need to hold up a facade of professionalism; he ripped off the face mask and stethoscope. And the girl now knew that the foreigner who could not control himself was not a doctor. But, comparing his size with hers, and fully aware that there were very few men inside the 3d MP compound willing to help her, she let the attack continue.

"Everything's all right up front, now let's check down here." Sergeant Ski let the girl's blouse drop and jerked her black silk peasant's pants down around her knees. Here he found the only undergarment the girl wore, a pair of plain white cotton panties. The plainness of the panties took his mind off what he was doing for a fraction of a second. There was nothing embroidered on the white cotton—no little pink hearts or cutesy messages ("Never on Sunday") as he had found at other times and places. The panties soon joined the pants around her knees.

The fat, panting sergeant couldn't believe what was happening—this girl, this real live female, was standing before him naked as a jaybird and not saying or doing anything to stop him! He had put on the doctor act half expecting it would do no more than get the girl's attention. He had come prepared to struggle for every feel. But here he was experiencing something as good as the wildest fantasy he had dreamed up in a long time!

As fast as he could cover the short distance to the target area, Sergeant Ski's hand was between her thighs squeezing, probing. At this new extension of the assault the girl's leg muscles tightened and she turned to one side, falling away from, more than protesting, the continuation of her humiliation. Sergeant Ski quickly killed what he thought was the beginning of a delayed protest with a twist of his probing hand and a viselike grip on the thigh which was moving away. The girl's hips jerked back to the proper position and the sergeant continued.

Through all of this the girl was thinking, but of things much different than those racing through the frenzied mind of her tormentor. In her naive farmer's daughter's mind, a mind that had never been exposed to formal education, she was wondering why it had taken so long for something like this to happen. She had heard from her friends that this kind of thing happened all the time. But her first time had not happened until today, over two months after she began coming to this camp. "I am luckier than most girls," she concluded.

She was also wondering if there was some way to stop this kind of activity. Ever since she had been working here she had thought American men were much nicer than Vietnamese men, but now she wasn't sure, she wasn't sure. She had heard that girls who tried to stop men like this lost their jobs and could not work in any other American camp, but if she lost her job her six younger brothers and sisters wouldn't have enough to eat. She had to keep her job, she had to. But there must be a way to stop this unkind behavior, there must be a way. If only she had been able to go to school, then maybe she could think of a way, but that was not to be. As the oldest daughter she had had to begin working almost as soon as she could walk. Such was the fate of the poor in a country that knew little else but war and bad harvests. But there must be a way to stop this unkind behavior, there must . . . there must.

After many more long seconds, a combination of associations and impulses came together in the gray fog of Sergeant Ski's brain and reminded him that it was time to refill his huge stomach. The sergeant took his hands away from his victim. "Everything seems to be okay, sweetie, but I'll have to check every once in a while just to make sure," he announced, his entire body running in sweat. Then he ambled out the door toward the mess hall, his wet face framing the broad smile that all men without women recognize as "conquest completed."

The girl slumped to the floor, crying softly into a sleeve of her blouse. With the other hand she gradually pulled her clothes back in place. She slowly stood up, took a deep breath to suppress her sobs, and began remaking the bed her attacker had wrinkled with his excessive weight.

In the next few days there were more "examinations" by the self-appointed "doctor." They were finally interrupted one morning when Sergeant Ski was met on the way to his hooch by Bill Thomas, the battalion S-5 officer. Sergeant Ski straightened out of his slouching walk and saluted. "Morning, Lieutenant."

"Morning, Sergeant Ski . . . I want to talk to you for a few minutes."

"Sure, Lieutenant . . . come on over to my hooch. I was just gonna wash up for chow."

"Right here is fine," Thomas snapped. "You better keep your hands off the hooch-maids; they got plenty to do without you manhandling them."

Sergeant Ski reacted to Thomas's reprimand as he reacted

to all criticism—he turned his eyes off Thomas to the dark
hills in the hot distance behind the brig. He found he didn't
hear very well if he wasn't looking at the source of a sound.
Thomas continued through a lecture he had delivered many
times before and expected to deliver many times more.

"And every time one of you guys grabs a hooch-maid or a
waitress they go home and tell their family and pretty soon
they hate us as much as they say they hate the VC, and when
the VC come along and ask if they want to help fight the
Americans they're more than willing, more than willing, so
this fucking war goes on and on . . ."

Sergeant Ski responded as he had been conditioned. He saluted, barked a "Yessir!" and stomped off to his hooch.

The sergeant was already in a rage when he reached the
entrance to his hooch. He marched in, muttering, "Where is
that little bitch!" When he found her, he grabbed the collar of
the maid's blouse and jerked her away from the row of boots
she was polishing. Her blouse tore and she uttered a small
scream. "You better learn to keep your mouth shut!" He un-
derlined his words with a hard slap across the girl's face and a
kick on her shins. The beating probably would have continued
had another sergeant not entered the hooch and reminded Sergeant Ski of the time. "Hey Ski, let's go to chow."

After a few days, when no punishment of any kind came
from the colonel or anyone else, Sergeant Ski knew he was
free to grab his hooch-maid anytime he wanted. And there
was no longer any need for the elaborate doctor act. The only
change Sergeant Ski made in his actions after Lieutenant
Thomas told him to leave the girl alone was to drop the crude
name he had given her and call her Baby-san. There wasn't
much the 85-pound girl could do against the unwanted ad-
vances of the 230-pound sergeant, and so they continued.

Most members of the battalion thought Sergeant Ski's assaults on his maid were funny, a light break in a boring routine. And many others in 3d MPs were doing the same thing.
The few who worked for or supported S-5 and the Civic Ac-

tion Program thought otherwise, and Bill Thomas put their thoughts into words.

"That fucking perverted sex maniac Sergeant Ski did it again this morning. I'd have to run five MEDCAPs to make up for every one time he grabs his hooch-maid, and to do that I'd have to stay in this fucking war twenty-five years!"

The attitude of those who were doing the same thing Sergeant Ski was doing was "we Americans left the highest standard of living in the world, we came ten thousand miles to one of the most fucked-up countries there ever was to save these people from communist brutality and to show them how to raise themselves to our level of civilization. We Americans are doing these Vietnamese a favor by just coming over here and the least they can do to show their appreciation is put out with a little nooky now and then and keep their mouths shut."

So, because of people like Sergeant Ski, the Vietnamese hated most of us a little more each day, S-5 fell further and further behind in its efforts to win friends, and the war went on.

None of us who sympathized with her knew how Baby-san continued to take all of Sergeant Ski's abuse, but she did. She never said anything and she never looked at him. Her self-control, her hiding of her real reaction to what was happening to her, was both amazing and pathetic. She just kept ironing or sweeping as Sergeant Ski's hands roamed over her, probing, pinching, massaging. She probably told herself Sergeant Ski's abuse was preferable to starvation. Our Western minds couldn't think of any other rationalization.

Those of us who tried to protect her from such abuse gave Baby-san our respect as a consolation for her humiliation and our failure. She would always be reserved a special corner in our overall memories of Vietnam.

When word about Sergeant Ski's doctor charade got around, most members of the battalion expressed sympathy with his need for women and admiration for the novel way he had used to satisfy that need. One of the senior sergeants, however, laughed when he heard about it and considered it a waste of time and effort. Sgt.-Maj. Garrett Snell knew there was a better way to get around the colonel's regulations and get some female companionship inside the compound, a way that did not involve the risk of getting caught. It was Sergeant-Major Snell's belief that a staff NCO, if he really was worthy of being a staff NCO, that is, should be able to satisfy his need for women without attracting the attention of young lieutenants and other incompetent do-gooders. Sergeant-Major Snell immediately set about acting on his belief, and because of his position in the battalion he could be sure of cooperation from many quarters. Sergeant-Major Snell was not only the senior enlisted man in 3d MPs—there is only one sergeant-major in a battalion—but also the marine with the most seniority in the entire battalion. He had enlisted in the marines in mid-1940, more than a year before the attack on Pearl Harbor, according to the way most of us referred to that era. Sergeant-Major Snell, however, dated his entry as "back about the time Christ made corporal." Now serving in his third war, the sergeant-major had over twenty-eight years in service, a full decade more than the colonel. Understandably, when Sergeant-Major Snell talked about what it was like in "the Old Corps," everyone listened.

The first thing Sergeant-Major Snell did to remedy the lack of women in 3d MPs was contact a couple of other sergeant-majors in the area, longtime buddies with whom he had served on several occasions before. From them he got the materials to build a small storage shed. Then he went to the colonel and commented on the growing volume of business in the club and how much they needed another Vietnamese girl to help wait on tables and how nice it would be to have another cute young female face around to take everyone's mind off the war. As Sergeant-Major Snell knew would happen, the colonel agreed and directed the XO to order another Vietnamese waitress from the FLC Indigenous Personnel Office. To make sure the system coughed up the right body, that is, a shapely, willing body, Sergeant-Major Snell went and talked to still another senior sergeant he knew in a strategic place, one in the office dealing with civilian labor relations, and told him to send along to 3d MPs the first likely candidate who walked in the door. The result appeared in the club one week later. Lulu could have made a priest forget his vows of celibacy. She was too shapely for a Vietnamese, mainly because she was half-Chinese. With her blouse-busting figure and rolling hips, all eyes were upon her as she walked to and from tables.

By the time Lulu came on the job, the new storage shed was ready for use, and it had been placed directly behind the club. That location, pointed out by the sergeant-major, was the most convenient, since the official purpose of the facility was to hold the extra cases of beer, whiskey, and soft drinks supposedly ordered to answer the alleged increase in demand in the club. In spite of that official purpose, the sergeant-major had a bed installed in the shed. At a secret briefing in the shed one afternoon Lulu was taught how to explain her trips from club to storage shed—"If anyone asks, just say you gotta get some more Seven-Up." The going rate for a quick roll in the rack with Lulu was passed around by word of mouth and business was off to a roaring start. On a typical night Lulu made between five and ten trips to the shed. She was allowed to keep half of her ten-dollar fee, and the rest went into a club "Improvement Fund," to which, no doubt, there was connected a pipe leading directly to Sergeant-Major Snell's pocket.

As everyone feared, word about Lulu and the storage shed spread throughout the battalion, and the lower-ranking enlisted men made known their desire that a similar arrangement be made at their club. Sergeant-Major Snell immediately rejected the idea and explained the exclusivity of the deal with one of the oldest truisms in the military: "Rank has its privileges."

Skin color seemed to hardly be an issue in the bush, but in the rear, the racial lines were often starkly drawn. This selection is a fair treatment of one of the most serious problems that the military faced in Vietnam.

Charles R. Anderson

Black and White

When viewed by outsiders, a military unit looks the epitome of conformity. All members work toward the same goal and under the same regulations, all activities are carefully coordinated, all members move together much of the time, and everyone even dresses and talks alike. To the outsider it appears that nothing divides the closed society of the military unit. Insiders, however, get a different view. They can see very clearly the differences between individual members: differences of age, regional or national origin, economic status, educational achievement, race, religion, and, of course, personality. During the Vietnam War the differences to be seen were especially sharp, not because of anything happening in Vietnam but because of developments back in American society.

The Vietnam War era was a time of rapid social change in

the United States. Racial and ethnic minorities—American In-
dians, Mexican-Americans, Puerto Ricans, and especially
blacks—were claiming the right to participate in every sphere
of American life on the basis of equality with the white majority. Behind the rapid social changes of the 1960s were decades
of gradually changing attitudes. In the years between the end
of World War II and the beginning of the Vietnam War the
view of minority members held by the white American majority changed. The picture of minority Americans, particularly
blacks, as simple people of limited ambition who would eventually enter the mainstream of American society and support
white values was questioned. Excessive sympathy and conde-
scension were dropped from white thinking. Persons of Afro-
American, Latin American, and American Indian ancestry
gradually came to be viewed as possessing the same talents as
those in the majority.

At the same time, of course, the views that minority
Americans held of themselves were also changing. Pride in the
accident of being born into an ethnic minority group replaced
shame. Assertive display of ethnic modes of behavior and
styles of dress replaced resigned acceptance of imposed norms.
A "get-it-now" urge to claim and exercise rights replaced a
docile patience with their subversion.

During the same period, and especially in the years between the end of the Korean War and the beginning of the
Vietnam War, the views of minority persons held by American military leaders changed less dramatically. Although the
military led the way in ending racial segregation when the
president ordered integration in 1948, the effects of the policy
were diluted by an unwritten quota system which governed
the assignment and promotion of minority members. Whatever complaints blacks and other minority members could
have made against the discrimination they endured were effectively muted, and the overwhelmingly white upper reaches of
the command structure continued in their belief that equality

of opportunity really existed and all was well in the ranks down below.

Throughout the period between the Korean and Vietnam wars the proportion of minority members in the military remained far below the minority proportion for the general population. Those minority members who did enter the military in this period generally accepted the values of the white majority and viewed military service as a method of gaining acceptance by the social majority. For the most part, they reinforced the stereotypes of minority personnel held by the military establishment. Those minority members whose self-view was changing in this period avoided military service because they believed it represented the surrender of one's individuality—one's "soul"—to the adversary social majority.

The change of values that occurred in civilian society in the decades before the Vietnam War and the most conservative views prevailing in the military set the stage for a confrontation between younger generation minority personnel and the military. What brought about racial confrontation in the military was the expanded draft call of the Vietnam War. Draft policy during the war exempted from military service those men who either were students or held certain jobs, such as teaching, that required a university degree. Since the proportion of minority members in universities during the 1960s was far below the minority proportion for the general population, the draft policy amounted to a form of discrimination. In terms proportionate to the white-to-minority distribution in civilian society, more minority members than whites were drafted. Large numbers of minority Americans who would never have entered the military if there had not been a war, those whose self-view had changed so drastically in the decades preceeding the war, were brought out of the inner cities and into direct and daily contact with an authority structure not equipped to understand or deal with them. Minority personnel, especially blacks, who answered the draft of the 1960s were much different from those who answered the call in the 1940s and 1950s. The former were highly sensitive to discriminatory treatment and not at all reluctant to complain whenever it occurred. The result was a double clash between, on one level, young black draftees and nearly all-white military command structure and, on the other, the same young blacks who had no interest in a military career and older blacks who were making a career of the armed forces.

While young minority draftees were expressing their ethnic differences, the military establishment gave its traditional response to individualism: "All military personnel are the same and will be treated the same. No exceptions." On the individual level, servicemen learned of the official policy when an NCO hollered at them, "There are no white marines or black marines in this unit! I see only green marines!" As is so often the case, however, there was a considerable gap between official policy and actual conditions. All of us in Vietnam wore the same green uniform but we were aware of other colors as well, chiefly black and white.

Although most members of all minorities exhibited some degree of ethnic identity, it was the behavior of young blacks that was most noticeable and that consequently contributed most to misunderstanding and confrontation. Five forms of behavior in particular brought about confrontations between young recruits or draftees from minorities and military authority figures. The first concerned styles of grooming. One of the first visible manifestations of the new pride among blacks was the "Afro" hairstyle. Preference for that hairstyle carried over from civilian to military life. But whereas in civilian life there is no printed and enforced regulation concerning the length and style of hair, in military life there definitely is. That regulation was one of the first challenged by young blacks on American bases the world over, and small unit leaders found themselves spending more and more time explaining and enforcing it.

Along with the new hairstyle came a new style of comb.

The Afro comb was shaped differently than its merely functional predecessor. Having few teeth and a long handle, it looked more like a stiff paintbrush than what most people recognize as a comb. The shape of the Afro comb made it difficult to fit in a uniform pocket, and that was why the new comb became a cause of confrontation. Uniform regulations of the Vietnam War period forbade putting anything in pockets that either made an outline of the object visible from the outside or protruded from the top of the pocket. The Afro comb was too long for uniform hip pockets; the black handle stuck out above the pocket flap.

Three additional practices did not violate any regulations but were so radically different from what racist authority figures considered proper conduct for minority members and what unprejudiced authority figures considered proper conduct for anyone in uniform that they made the entire command structure overly sensitive to actual violations. First was a style of walking called the ditty-bop. A direct expression of the new "I-am-somebody" pride among minority personnel, the ditty-bop was accomplished by exaggerating the normal roll and swing of hips, shoulders, and arms, and locking one knee.

A second unconventional but not illegal practice resulted when two blacks were ditty-bopping toward each other. Instead of greeting each other with a salute or a wave and continuing on their way, the two would usually stop and go through the elaborate ritual of "looking after my brother," as it was usually explained. The soul greeting began with the raised-fist Black Power salute, which then evolved into a rhythmical pattern of tapping each other's fists, palms, backs of hands, and chests, the entire sequence accompanied by equally pro forma phrases and questions: "What's happening, baby? . . . how's the (white) man treating you, brother? . . . keep them off your back, man . . ." The complete soul greeting between two men might take as much as two minutes, and if one man or group met another group, as much as ten minutes might be taken up in a process of recognition that whites usually accomplish with a one-second wave or nod of the head.

The third unconventional form of behavior was even more misunderstood than others. On off-duty time young blacks and other minority members would frequently gather by themselves in a hooch or, more commonly, outside around a bunker on their unit's defensive perimeter or in a bomb shelter, and talk about anything but the war or their unit's mission. The facts that no whites were invited to these meetings and that they usually took place at night added to the wondering and suspicion with which they were viewed by white authority figures. It looked as if young blacks were voluntarily segregating themselves, rejecting association with the white society their parents and grandparents had openly aspired to join. Whereas blacks had once fought against racial segregation, it looked as if they were now promoting it. To whites and older blacks who had for decades considered valid the goal of racial integration, the after-dark closed meetings were an upsetting development to witness.

Most white observers assumed, on the basis of little evidence and no verification, that such meetings and other new forms of ethnic behavior represented rejection of the goal of integration. The same observers then piled another unverified assumption on top of the first: since blacks were rejecting integration, they were therefore plotting its violent opposite—all-out war on white society and its military organization. Old fears about campaigns of vengeance against the white majority were aroused in the minds of many. Carrying such questions and suspicions, many small unit staff members and commanders were unable to see the new patterns of behavior exhibited by minority personnel as expressions of pride. Instead, they were viewed variously as evidence of disloyalty, unnecessarily provocative actions deserving a swift and harsh response, or outright violations of regulations.

Compounding the anger of whites who witnessed ethnic

pride was the selectivity employed by blacks as to the place of its expression. During combat operations in the field the behavior of black and white troops was indistinguishable. Everyone cooperated and many blacks and whites formed what the latter mistakenly considered close friendships. Once back in rear echelon areas, however, a change came over many blacks. They segregated themselves from whites during free time and occasionally became insubordinate. Many whites were bewildered to find blacks who had been friendly in the field suddenly turn hostile in the rear. The presence of the enemy in the field apparently caused blacks to postpone expression of their ethnic pride.

When the military made its legal response to those prideful expressions which were violations of regulations and orders—court-martial—the result was that a disproportionately large number of men arrested and confined to military prisons were blacks or members of other minorities. The proportion of prisoners from minorities in the 3d MP brig was consistently between forty and fifty percent, and the minority proportion in the Army Stockade at Long Binh occasionally went over fifty percent, although the proportion of blacks in the Marine Corps and the Army remained at or near fifteen percent.

Minority members who expressed their ethnic pride in various ways were not, in the early years of the Vietnam increased-draft period, consciously confronting the military authority structure. To their own minds they were only expressing pride, exchanging common experiences, or building up each other's shaky confidence. But later, when they saw how infuriating that behavior was to most white sergeants and officers, and how rigid the military's response to their prideful behavior was, increasing numbers of blacks and other minority members stopped thinking about contributing to the accomplishment of their unit mission or serving their country, and began playing a game with the adversary, mostly white military authority structure. The object of the game was to see how many authority figures one could anger and how close one could come to open violation of regulations without getting court-martialed. The reward was considerable prestige among one's peers. As more players entered, the game became more elaborate. What evolved was a kind of continuing tournament for underachievers. All definitions of achievement put forward by the military establishment were rejected. All rewards were shunned: liberty passes, duty assignments to which extra pay was attached, even promotions. To accept such rewards was taken as proof that one had renounced his ethnic identity and "sold out" to the adversary.

In time, reluctance to cross the line separating legal from illegal activities was dropped. Among the most bitter, minority in-group standards even developed to the point that one had to willfully violate regulations and be arrested in order to prove one's ethnic purity. According to this standard, one who had served a sentence in a stockade or brig was ethnically purer than one who had only been fined or verbally reprimanded.

During the Vietnam War then, the American military faced an unprecedented set of circumstances. At the same time that it was dealing with a numerically superior enemy force and a baffling cultural environment in Vietnam, as well as an indifferent or hostile civilian population in America, it was faced with a challenge from within—the possibility that military members from social minorities would withhold their loyalty from national policy goals and the military force pledged to carry out those goals. The irony, even the tragedy, of this development is difficult to overemphasize. The single social institution that had offered minority group members more opportunity than any other in American society since the very earliest days of the Republic was suddenly accused of being as discriminatory as the most unreconstructed corners of the nation, and was beset with an unprecedented level of insubordination by minority members.

While race relations in the military in general were a

faithful reflection of those in civilian society, there were certain differences in the racial situation between the various branches of service comprising the military establishment. Racial friction in the Marine Corps occasionally became sharp because of two features of that branch, one structural, the other regional. Because of its comparatively limited mission—to conduct and support amphibious operations—the Marine Corps offers training in fewer occupational specialties than the Army, Navy, Air Force, or Coast Guard. The needs of the Marine Corps are primarily in the ground combat and support specialties: motor transport, supply, armor, artillery, and infantry. Until the 1970s minority personnel in general had fewer educational and occupational advantages in civilian American society. Such persons had long recognized a side benefit of military service: the chance to learn useful job skills while at the same time being paid. But those who entered the Marine Corps in hopes of learning a marketable skill were highly disappointed to learn that no meaningful job training would be made available to them until after they had served a year or two, or (often) the entire initial enlistment period, in a field unit. There is, of course, no need in a civilian economy for infantrymen or artillerymen. Feeling deceived and used, many minority members were quick to see such policies as evidence of racism rather than the result of the "needs of the service" taking priority over personal desires.

American regionalism also contributed to racial tension during the Vietnam War. In the American South military service has long been considered not only a duty but an honor. While there has been no lack of persons from the North and West who consider military service an honorable activity, most conscientious objectors, draft-dodgers, and war protesters have tended to come from those regions. This regional difference in attitude became especially obvious during the Vietnam War, when every sizable antiwar demonstration took place in the North or far West. These regional attitudes affected personnel composition of the military: during the Vietnam War there was a higher proportion of southerners in uniform than the regional distribution of the American population would lead one to expect. Disproportionate representation in the military led in some quarters to a faithful reflection of the conservative racial views long characteristic of the American South.

The result of the southern character of the military was to heighten the suspicion and tension between young blacks in the lower ranks and white authority figures. Young blacks from large northern cities were brought into close contact with a kind of white man they had only heard about secondhand from parents or grandparents who had migrated from the rural South. White sergeants and officers from the South were brought into close contact with a new kind of black American—a young man completely unlike the docile figure they had seen in the formative period of their lives. Upon hearing a southern accent, many young blacks unjustifiably concluded that a cooperative stance toward the mostly white authority structure was futile; many felt justified in adopting a belligerent stance. Some senior sergeants and officers, unfortunately, fit quite well the stereotype of the racist red-neck of the rural South. The fact that many others did not fit that stereotype was overlooked by many suspicious and frustrated young blacks. Too often, southern accents and strict enforcement of regulations were taken as proof of racist intentions. What occurred with increasing frequency during the Vietnam War were sharp confrontations between the marine command and belligerent blacks over a wide variety of issues, including violations of uniform regulations, use of marijuana or drugs, and refusal to participate in combat operations.

In the 3d MP brig we had the worst offenders of all regulations, and judging from their actions in the brig, racial hatred was a contributing cause of their offenses. The guard force and anyone in a position of authority were subjected to a daily stream of abuse, much of it expressed in racist epithets. Every guard had heard at least one prisoner accuse him of being a "tool of the imperialist, racist, American establishment" or simply a "honky" or "white beast." Death threats by the least cooperative prisoners against guards were common and kept all alert for the possibility of a riot. The atmosphere in and around the brig was charged with a dangerous amount of tension, and the situation was not much different at brigs in other units and in other services. Clearly, something had to be done.

The response came from the Pentagon and applied not only to 3d MPs but to the entire American military. Instead of reinforcing the traditional response of arrest and court-martial, the military tried a new approach, by ordering each unit down to battalion level to form a Human Relations Committee. Between five and ten individuals representing all ethnic groups, and most ranks, were chosen to meet at least once a month. Given various labels (Race Relations Board, Equal Opportunity Conference), these committees all shared the same purpose—to improve race relations in each unit by encouraging members of all ethnic groups to openly discuss their views of each other.

The Human Relations Committees contributed much to the easing of racial tensions both in Vietnam and the United States. The unit committees offered the only informal setting in which military personnel of all ages, ranks, and ethnic groups could discuss behavior patterns they had seen each other exhibit without provoking derision or violence. By being given the chance to ask simple questions like "Why do you call each other brothers?" and "What did your parents teach you about black people?" both blacks and whites and other ethnic group members learned much about the perspectives of the others. As reports of Human Relations Committee meetings were sent up the chain of command and finally to the Pentagon, a number of Defense Department policies were changed. Soul and Latin music were added to jukebox selection lists to supplement the traditional country and western and rock and roll in all clubs on American bases the world over. Clothing, beauty products, records, and magazines appealing to minority tastes were added to the inventory of Post Exchanges. Clothing and grooming regulations for off-duty time were relaxed to permit use of ethnic fashions. But the Human Relations committees could not eliminate all racial friction. Despite the progress made, racially motivated incidents of violence remained depressingly common in the military.

While the idea of such committees was approved by nearly everyone concerned about race relations at the outset, some of the decisions with which they were initiated served to compromise their effectiveness. In most units, higher-ranking minority members were chosen to chair the committees. The reasons such personnel were chosen did not always reflect the spirit in which the Human Relations Committee program was initiated. Many commanders feared that minority personnel in their units were on the verge of open rebellion and they would, if faced with a situation in which they had to choose, give greater loyalty to their own ethnic identity than to their unit's mission or their nation's policy. They felt that by putting a black or Puerto Rican or Mexican-American in front of a group of younger generation minority members, the latter would somehow be less inclined to break regulations; the feared revolt, in effect, would be defused. By making such a decision, these commanders revealed their feeling that it was more important to forestall a revolt than to lay bare and examine the ignorance and suspicion which caused them (and many others) to fear a mass disaffection.

Other commanders threw the problem of race relations into the laps of higher-ranking blacks for a different reason. Some seriously believed that only blacks could really understand blacks and, by extension, older blacks had some special inherent ability to control younger blacks. One of the greatest successes of the Human Relations Committees was the revelation to members of many ethnic groups the racial myths that each preserves in an era generally considered "modern."

The effects of the practice of naming older minority members to chair committees and meetings of younger minority members were to only partially alleviate the reluctance of the latter to freely express themselves with a white chairman, to overlay the racial problem with the phenomenon of the generation gap, and to present the minority chairmen selected to solve this deep-seated, centuries-old social problem with a painful identity crisis.

Since higher-ranking blacks had decided years before the Vietnam War to make a career of military service (or they would not, of course, have reached a higher rank by the time of that war), young blacks usually viewed them as moral weaklings who had sold out to what was labeled the "white racist establishment." They were considered "bought men," shuffling Uncle Toms who answered "yassah" to everything the white CO ordered. Higher-ranking blacks were also, of course, older than first-term enlistees or draftees. They were thus subject to one of the truisms that so many young people of the 1960s accepted without question—"you can't trust anyone over thirty." Thus, for both their choice of career and their age, higher-ranking minority members were denied the confidence that could have enabled them to be more effective.

In addition, higher-ranking minority members chosen to chair the new committees were compromised by attitudes which they themselves brought to their new duty, as well as by tensions arising from their being placed between two groups to both of which they had long been paying loyalty Most chairmen genuinely wanted to make a contribution to the solution of racial problems in both the military and American society at large. But at the same time, most felt they were being placed in an impossible position—between a conservative authority structure trying to preserve itself and a radical force trying to alter significantly that authority structure. To support one side was to tear down the other. To favor the white authority structure was to deny the ethnic group that had given one life; to favor one's ethnic brothers was to reject the organization that had allowed one the best career opportunity open at the time of choosing. Torn between loyalty to country and career on the one hand and ethnic identity on the other, many committee chairmen were less than enthusiastic about their new assignment. Some decided to do no more than make a show of concern for their commanders to see and leave the real issues to someone else. Others felt they had been wrongly singled out to solve a national problem not of their making. Still others viewed young minority members as no more than loudmouthed troublemakers who had only exaggerated their own problems and were undeserving of all the official attention. Varying arrangements of such personal feelings and fears as well as other, extrapersonal forces, not the least of which was the fact that much of the effort to improve race relations was undertaken at the same time and place in which the military was trying to defeat an enemy and befriend a very foreign civilian population, combined to limit the effectiveness of the Human Relations program in its first years of operation.

From the perspective of the lifers (the officers and NCOs) Robert Chatain's hero had an "attitude problem," but his caustic view of his small slice of the war will be familiar to many who experienced the war from the bottom looking up.

Robert Chatain

On the Perimeter

ZONE

The tattered jungle beyond the barbed wire had been declared a free-fire zone in late June. Looking forward to spending at least five of my remaining ten weeks of war in permanent duty on the bunker line (the unofficial transfer was complete; even my "Visit Gay, Historic Vietnam" poster had been torn from the AG barracks wall and sent along with me to the ordnance company's security platoon, so determined was Colonel Hamilton to purge from his new command any taint of the pacifist subversion he had uncovered), I decided to free-fire.

I had access, over the weeks, to M-14's, M-16's, machine guns, grenade launchers, and an occasional pistol. The M-14 had been my weapon in basic training; I was a good shot.

With it I could cut down plant stalks at ten meters, hit beer cans and bottles at thirty; I drew beads on man-sized stumps and bushes as far away as I could see them and was sure some of my shots found their targets. I could also kill birds.

The M-16 I found disappointing. Its horizontal drift gave me trouble. Its ugly black stock was not long enough for my reach. The pistol grip fell awkwardly into my palm. Its sight was blunt. Obviously the weapon had not been designed for target practice. Remembering an old account of Marines dead on the slopes of Hill 881 with their M-16's broken down beside them, I wondered what it had been designed for.

The M-60 machine gun was a thrill. Fire at a patch of bare earth produced satisfying explosions of dirt, leaves, garbage, and anything else lying in the radius of my bullets. With a short burst one evening I tore a metal water can to shreds. The next night I opened up on the struts and wires of the old crippled powerline support tower I had begun to think of almost as a friend. Most of the rounds went through into empty air.

The powerlines were also a good place to aim the M-79 grenade launcher. If I connected, the grenades exploded high above the ground and fragmentation pellets clattered on the worn steel.

I discovered that pistols demanded more practice than I could manage without attracting attention. Free-fire was permitted, but some discretion was expected. Exorbitant waste of ammunition was discouraged. At the infrequent moments when a pistol found itself in my hand I shot at the rats foraging openly in the barbed wire for scraps of food. I never hit them.

I did this free-firing at dusk, after the trucks had gone back across no-man's-land through the interior perimeter gate into the ammunition depot; if the sergeant on my section of the perimeter called, I could explain that I was testing my bunker's arsenal. Firing after dark always drew such panic from the neighboring bunkers that I soon gave it up. Firing at dawn—I never fired at dawn. Dawn did not seem like the right time to fire.

Once I would have been ashamed to find myself willingly associating with these weapons. But I was alone. The guns were clean, well-made, efficient, impersonal. And I suppose that the problem of my former negative feelings toward weaponry had been solved. Guns were of some use, I admitted. In the proper circumstances I think I could have shot Colonel Hamilton without batting an eye.

FORMICARY

Lying one mild afternoon on a soft wool blanket spread beneath tall birch and thick cedar, my wife-to-be had outlined her ant theories. Ants, she said, are capitalists. They're disgustingly greedy. And they're middle-class. They work twenty-four hours a day hoarding food and adding superfluous tunnels to their ant-holes. Did I know that some ants tend gardens? That some ants herd cows? That some keep slaves? And, of course, ants make war. Armies march into each other's territories and attack instinctively. Individual battles might last for hours. (Finishing my circuit of the bunker without finding what I'd been looking for, I returned up the hill of sandbags and slid into the half-buried enclosure. It was already too dark. I would continue the search in the morning.) Are they brave? I asked. No, she said, they're not brave, an ant might think he's brave but actually he's just doing what all the other ants are doing. If an ant were really brave, he'd refuse to fight. (At dawn and again at dusk the cracks between the sandbags were alive with large black ants. I noticed no particular pattern to their movements. Each night I spent a few minutes covering the surface of the hill looking for the main entrance to their nest.) They'd throw him in jail, I argued. It doesn't matter, she said, he would know he was a moral ant. He'd be setting an example for the other ants. But, I said, suppose he doesn't care much about the other ants? He's still better off in jail, she said, he won't get killed. But if he doesn't want to get pushed around? Ants always get pushed around, she answered. Then, I said, he plays it by ear. We laughed. And ants don't hear very well, I added. (Later we made love on the floor of the forest, sunlight through the trees camouflaging our bare skin with irregular blotches of light and darkness; I stretched this recollection out to fill my mind for an entire watch, even forgetting the discomfort of sitting upon stacked ammunition crates.)

DISCOURSE

They liked to divide the members of the security platoon evenly along the length of the perimeter, no two "veterans" in any one bunker, and fill out the remaining positions with ordinary clerks on detail from the various units of Long Binh. Occasionally the roster put me with people from my old company, but usually I spent the night with strangers. In the intimacy of the bunker they could not keep their mouths shut. I had to listen, smoldering, to hours of rumor, complaint, prejudice, and platitude. By the time dawn carried them back to their safe barracks I would know whether they had been drafted or had volunteered for the draft or enlisted or been tricked into enlisting or railroaded by their local boards, their families, or the courts; I would have found out where they had received training, how they had come to Vietnam, what they thought they had discovered about themselves, God, and their country, and when they would get out; I would have heard some of their most interesting Army experiences; I would have been told their opinions on the manners and morals of the peoples of Europe, Asia, and the other places their uniforms had taken them, and I would have learned their attitudes toward the war, toward international communism, toward the peace movement, and finally toward the chance that they might be killed during the night, a possibility that I sometimes came to anticipate with pleasure long before they had finished talking.

MAZE

A rat's sleek head caught in the red beam of the flashlight triggered somber, fretful ruminations. How deep do they burrow? How many live in this hill with me? How do they know to avoid the pale yellow sticks of rat poison scattered in the corners of the bunker and outside under the clean starlight? Intelligent rats, well-fed on candy bars and C-ration tins, uninterested in poison. Their squeaks as they prowled around the base of my high perch on the stacked ammunition boxes. Their scuttling down below my dangling feet with cockroaches and scorpions. Don't reach down there, not for ammunition, not for anything. If you drop something, leave it until morning. Thousands in this mound of earth. Holes in the floorboards, holes in the walls, holes in the heavy timbers overhead. The sandbag slope alive with rats scurrying in the moonlight. Nocturnal. Remaining in tunnels during the day. Long tunnels, winding back upon themselves, coiling for miles. VC moving south in such tunnels, some captured with stories of traveling two hundred miles underground. Blackclad VC no older than fifteen sitting with their backs to dirt tunnel walls, singing. Underground hospitals. Operations underground, emergency lights flickering. Underground at Dien Bien Phu the wounded finding their wounds infested with maggots. The maggots beneficial, eating rotten tissue, leaving healthy. Time passing slowly. The wounded lying in darkness tended by blind worms.

I shifted my position. The rat vanished into its cavity.

TEST

Just before midnight the sound of a jeep on the perimeter road pulled me to the back of the bunker. Without hesitation I challenged the man who emerged; I was an old hand at the game. He identified himself as a corporal on official business. I let him climb the catwalk. He dropped into the bunker next to me and told me to relax. I relaxed. The corporal struck a match and studied his watch. I loaned him my flashlight. I saw that he carried a clipboard and a folded piece of paper. At what must have been precisely midnight, he ceremoniously handed me the paper. I asked him what the hell it was. "Black handicap message," he announced.

"What the hell is that?"

He seemed surprised. "A black handicap message," he repeated.

I looked at the piece of paper, unfolding it, and read only a small group of neatly typed numbers.

"It's a test," he said. "Don't you know what to do?"

Obviously I did not know what to do.

The corporal shook his head and sighed. "You guys are all supposed to know what to do with one of these. That's the way it goes, you don't know what you're doing, they don't know what they're doing, and I sure don't know what I'm doing."

"So what's it all about?" I asked.

"All right," he said, "you call your command bunker and tell the sergeant you've got a black handicap message. You read off the numbers. The sergeant copies them down and passes them on."

"Should I do it now?"

"Yeah, you should do it now."

I cranked the field phone, reached the sergeant in Bunker 12, gave him my information, and hung up. The corporal retrieved his piece of paper and turned to go.

"Hold it," I said. "What the hell is going on?"

He explained. A black handicap message tested the efficiency of communications along the chain of command. Originating in my humble bunker, those numbers would be passed from one headquarters to the next until they arrived at the Pentagon itself. Crucial to the test was not only correct transmission of the number series, but also the amount of time required to pass information through command channels. "Are you bullshitting me?" I asked.

"Would anyone come way out here in the middle of the night to bullshit you?" The corporal hoisted himself up out of the bunker and descended the catwalk to his jeep.

"Hey, how long does it usually take?" I asked.

"I don't know. A couple of hours. Who gives a shit?" He wheeled his jeep around on the narrow road and raced back along the perimeter into the night, anxious for the safety of the depot.

MIAMI

The passing of the broom from one bunker to the next was a time-honored ritual that had survived the earlier attacks on the ammunition depot, the physical deterioration of the bunkers during the months since their construction, even the coming of the monsoon and subsequent reduction in the amount of dust to be swept from the bunks and floorboards. No one remembered when the last inspection of the bunker line had been made, but still the broom passed every night. It was a good chance to catch up on the news.

"You hear about Fine?"

"No."

"Got orders for the Congo. Diplomatic mission. Far out."

"Hm."

"You haven't heard about the new offensive in September?"

"No."

"Supposed to be a big offensive in September, big as Tet."

"Hm."

"You hear about all the fucking money they dug up near Qui Nhon?"

"No."

"A hundred and fifty grand, all in fifty-dollar bills. The Treasury Department says there isn't supposed to be any fifty-dollar bills over here. We're paying for both fucking sides of this war."

"Hm."

"You hear about the Republicans?"

"No."

"Nominated Richard Nixon."

"Hm."

PERFUME

We lit up any time after midnight. No one traveled the perimeter road after midnight.

"Ah-ha!"

Voice and boots on the catwalk startled us.

"What is that delightful odor? Could it be—? Yes, I think it is!" A stranger climbed unhindered into our bunker. I was too stunned even to try to challenge him. But there was nothing to fear. He was a PFC from that night's reaction force, out alone for a hike and a smoke.

"We've got an IG. The fools are awake cleaning the barracks. I snuck out."

We got acquainted.

"Let me lay some of this on you people."

I inhaled.

The stranger went his way.

One of the two guards spending the night with me slept; in slow motion, the other climbed onto the upper bunk. "Jesus, what a buzz I've got. Wow, I can't stand up, I've got to sit down. Wow, I think I might get sick."

I draped my arm over the machine gun and bored into the luminous jungle with my eyes.

RELEASE

One of those nights of brilliant stars motionless above the earth whose grinding stones you can feel move beneath your feet. Even through thick-soled military shoes. The ground turning, tumbling around an axis fixed now nearly on the horizon, but not quite right, the wrongness more apparent at this latitude than farther north where the pole star hangs high in the air and a cold wind keeps your head clear. Eyes closed, you can hear the stones wrenching themselves slowly through each new alignment. The spindle has slipped from its proper place. The gears are binding.

I spent many watches completely outside the bunker, sitting on the roof or stretched full-length on the front of the sandbag hill gazing benignly into hostile territory. Sometimes I stood on the catwalk identifying stars and counting artillery bursts in the hills to the east. When it rained I crouched under the bunker eaves and caught the smells raised by moisture in the jungle and carried by the wind across clearings and through barbed wire. I did some undisciplined and inconclusive thinking. I daydreamed.

But the nights seemed to invite some physical participation, so from time to time I unbuttoned my fatigues and masturbated, stirring great clouds of sediment in my mind. From one of them I extracted this notion that the earth's axis had slid out of alignment and was wandering through the heavens. Under such celestial circumstances there could be no idea of progress, no notion of human accountability for human actions. Only the apocalypse could restore order. On subsequent nights I entertained further revelations of cosmic significance, all of which were cut short by the crisp sound of my sperm landing on the weathered canvas of the sandbags.

DUTY

"Hello?"
"Hello?"
"Hello?"
"Who called?"
"Bunker 18?"
"Right here."
"This is Bunker 15."
"Who called?"
"Ah, men, this is Bunker 17, ah, we've been notified of suspected movement to our immediate front, ah, I'm instructed to announce that, ah, we're going on seventy-five

percent alert, ah, this means two men will be awake at all times."

"This is Bunker 17, ah, everyone on the line acknowledge please."
"Bunker 15, roger."
"Bunker 16, we read you lima charlie."
"Bunker 20, roger."

"Bunker 18?"
"Bunker 18, right, seventy-five percent alert."

"Bunker 19?"

"Bunker 19? Bunker 17 calling Bunker 19, acknowledge please."

"All right, Bunker 19, answer your fucking phone."

"Bunker 18, will you shout over to Bunker 19 and wake those people up?"

"This is Bunker 18, sarge, 19 says they're on the line and can hear you okay, but you can't hear them."
"All right, 19, sorry. Stay on the line."
"Bunker 17?"
"This is Bunker 17."
"Bunker 17, this is Bunker 15, about this seventy-five percent alert: two men awake, one asleep only makes sixty-six and two-thirds percent alert. To bring it up to a full seventy-five percent I'm going to have to wake up eight and a third percent of the last guy."

"Just do the best you can, Bunker 15."

"Hello?"

"Hello?"

"Who called?"

"Is this Bunker 17?"

"This is 17."

"Bunker 17? Come in, Bunker 17."

"This is Bunker 17, I read you lima charlie."

"Bunker 17?"

"What, for Christ's sake?"

"Hey, Bunker 17, this is Bunker 20, there's something in our wire."

"What is it?"

"Too dark to tell."

"'Too dark to tell.' Shit, man."

"Who is that?"

"All right, 20, pop one, let's see what it is."

"Bunker 19, did you shoot off that second flare?"

"Keep observing, Bunker 18, I think it was a wild pig."

"You're a wild pig."

"Who is that? Let's keep this line clear, men!"

"Bunker 16?"

"Shut up. Go to hell."

"Bunker 17?"

"This is 17."

"Hey, Bunker 17, this is Bunker 20. All the crickets and frogs and shit have stopped making noise out in front of us. Bunker 17? Hey, Bunker 17? Bunker 17? What do we do? Come on, Bunker 17!"

AUBADE

You notice first the stilling of the night breeze. It happens abruptly; one minute your skin is cooled by the vague slow movement of air which began at dusk, the next it is not. From the jungle come tiny sounds previously masked by the whisper of leaves and branches. Then they, too, vanish. Nothing moves. Nothing. You look to the east, where you know the hills lie unevenly on the horizon you cannot see. You try to pick them out, straining to catch the first instant that they appear, staring where you think they will be; suddenly they are there, higher or lower than you had expected, the world has solidified and divided into two shades of black. Dawn is a livid, slowly spreading bruise on the face of the darkness. Birds rustle and murmur. The horizon fans to the north and south. In back of you is a strange murk, confused by several indefinable colors. Clouds form, hard shapes near the hilltops, soft shadows overhead. The sky turns blue, pink, light orange, yellow, pale gold. The buzz of a locust is followed by the flap of large wings. Details emerge in the land below the crests of the hills, some trees show their skeletons, brown and green are added to the spectrum of the visible. To the left and right other bunkers are gloomy neolithic mounds topped by thick slab roofs the color of very old rust. Flying insects rise in swarms to begin work. Grass and bushes sigh. The sky is light now, lightest just over the hump of the hill slightly to the north of east. Blue becomes white; white flashes incandescent as the tip of the sun blinds you. You turn your head away. The air is not clear; columns of smoke line the sky. Haze and fog lie in the low places. The river to the southeast is buried in white floss. Black dots of helicopters float in single file through the air above the hills, bringing night patrols home to their bases. A slight wind brings an oily smell to your nose. You itch. From somewhere comes the sound of an engine. The sun climbs. You face a day glistening, reptilian, fresh from its shell.

LOBSTER

"Imagine my surprise (the medic narrated loudly as four of us sprawled in a deuce-and-a-half tearing at top speed through the depot to breakfast), man, six months in this sewer of an outfit, you can't get a transfer out of here, you can't get TDY, you can't even get your ass attached to the fucking dispensary, so the complaints start up, I write some, everybody writes some, we get those Congressmen on the horn and we expect things to happen, you know? We got a union. I'm not shittin' you guys, a union. We make demands. We go up through channels like it says, you know, but we make demands. So one of our demands is about the crap we eat. That's our demand, right? Better food? Right. So last night, we head over to the mess hall, it's a Saturday and we expect hamburgers, figuring no C-ration hamburgers this time because the roads have been clear for three fucking weeks and it's about time the old ground beef turns up again. So we head over, and you know what they're serving? Lobster tails! Lobster tails? What are they doing serving lobster tails? What's going on? Drawn butter, the whole works. Lobster tails! Far fucking out. I figured that right after dinner they were going to tell us to line up for the ground assault on Hanoi, but I eat anyway. Figured they were going to make us paint the mess hall. Something like that. But I eat, and it's good, you know?"

ARMAGEDDON

Long, very hot morning, bird cries at regular intervals from the trees. Nodding over my book. When it comes, the attack rolls through the bunker line effortlessly. Some of us escape by hiding in the foliage on the other side of the road. The depot is destroyed. Long Binh's thousands of clerks are mobilized and fight holding actions for their positions. A general offensive throughout Vietnam threatens to bring down the Saigon government. Fresh U.S. combat troops are airlifted in. Unrestricted bombing of the North is resumed. South Vietnamese units sweep into the Delta and encounter fierce resistance. North Vietnamese troops emerge from Cambodian sanctuaries and strike Saigon in force. U.S. ships blockade Haiphong harbor. Communist divisions operating in the Central Highlands lay siege to isolated U.S. fire bases. A joint force of American, South Vietnamese, Korean, and Australian units engage main-strength Communist elements at the DMZ. Chinese troops join in the defense of North Vietnam. Laos is invaded simultaneously by American and Chinese armored columns attempting end-runs of the battle line. Russia calls an emergency session of the United Nations Security Council. In major clashes on both sides of the DMZ neither army gains clear advantage. Protracted artillery duels begin. Mass uprisings throw Saigon into chaos and South Vietnamese government leaders are evacuated to ships of the Sixth Fleet. A provisional government is established by neutralist and pro-Communist political leaders. High-level private negotiations begin at Geneva. Chinese and American troops withdraw from their entrenched positions along the DMZ. Formal peace talks are convened. Cease-fire is declared.

CZECHOSLOVAKIA

The well-informed were discussing current events over the field phone. I listened, but stayed out of it.

"If they've taken Dubček to Moscow he's probably dead by now."

"I just didn't believe they'd actually go through with it."

"The radio stations knew about it in advance and set up secret spots to broadcast from. They kept everybody cool."

"You've got to hand it to kids who throw stones at tanks."

"Well, there are good guys and bad guys in the Kremlin just as there are good guys and bad guys in Washington. The bad guys won."

A new voice cut in. "We should bomb the shit out of them."

"One war at a time, huh?"

PRODUCT

The C-rations had been packed a long time ago, everybody knew, but nobody knew just when, perhaps as far back as World War II. Most of the food tasted pretty good, considering. Inside the unmarked gray cardboard cartons there were tins of "main dish," various small tins (cheese and crackers in one, fruit dessert in another, etc.), and cellophane bags containing fork, napkin, salt, pepper, sugar, dehydrated cream, and ten cigarettes. Of the main dish selections, some were choice (tuna, ham), some not so choice (veal, hamburgers), some inedible (bacon and eggs). All of the tins were olive green; contents were printed in black according to a standard form, noun first, adjectives trailing with their commas. Brand name appeared only as a means of identifying the packer. I visualized dozens of cartoon factories turning out these uniform dark green tins and gray cardboard boxes, selfless owners and managers eschewing profitable competition to serve their country, patriotic stockholders approving, grim-faced workers unaware of any change.

In the bunkers we encountered one major problem with C-rations: the familiar ingenious government-issue P-38 can opener was not included in every C-ration box. In fact, finding a P-38 in your box was a little like finding a prize in a package of breakfast cereal. It was something to cherish, because those C-ration cans were *hard*. They conformed to *government specifications*. They were *tin cans*, not aluminum cans or vinyl-covered cardboard cans. With a good pair of pliers and a lot of time you could worry one open; artful wielding of a bayonet produced primitive but satisfactory results; blunt instruments cracked the cans but wasted most of their contents; shooting them, although entertaining, was not a good idea nourishmentwise; various other schemes occurred to me at various times, but a P-38 was the only guaranteed method of success. Without one, you might go hungry. I knew several men who carried them around their necks where they hung their dog-tags. One man wore a P-38 on the same chain with his crucifix.

GUIDANCE

Miller came out on what was probably to be his last twenty-four-hour guard duty, managed to find out which bunker I was in, and walked down early in the afternoon to say hello. He looked happy. "How many days?" I asked him.

"I won't tell you. You'll just get depressed."

Instead, Miller talked about the changes that had taken place since Colonel Hamilton had assumed command of the office.

"The man's insane. First thing, he decides he's got to have his own private partitions, and we do the plywood and mahogany stain thing again. He scrounges another air conditioner. He hires a new secretary."

"Suzanne's gone?"

"Downstairs. This new one is a real pig. Hamilton says he wants someone to serve his guests coffee."

"Good grief."

"Then he sets up new, streamlined organizational machinery, and I've got to type such gems as this."

I took the disposition form he handed me and read, "SUBJECT: Requests for Command Guidance. TO: All AG Officers. 1. It may be necessary on occasion for you to request command guidance from the Adjutant General concerning various problems which occur. 2. Effective immediately, no problem will be presented to the Adjutant General without the accompaniment of a proposed solution, regardless of the manner of presentation, i.e., written or oral. R. A. Hamilton, LTC, AGC, Adjutant General."

"Classic," I said.

"I brought it out to make you feel better. We're all going crazy. There's a new lieutenant now, he's floundering trying to figure out your filing system, he can't get through to the units because he doesn't know any of the clerks, it takes him three drafts before the Chief of Staff will let his letters pass, and, on top of all that, Hamilton hits him with this."

I took another disposition form. "SUBJECT: Adjutant General Liaison to Information Office. TO: 1LT Robert D. Wexler. 1. You are hereby appointed to act as my liaison with the Information Officer for the purpose of insuring that all aspects of my section to include those elements under my operational control and under my staff supervision are properly recognized for their accomplishments through the use of hometown news releases and articles for various service papers. In this connection it is not necessary nor do I expect you to write articles, edit articles, or in any way act as an information specialist. All I expect you to do is to insure that the Information Officer is made aware of newsworthy items occurring in this section. 2. In connection with routine items such as arrivals, departures, awards, and promotions you are expected to make DA Form 1526 available to those individuals desiring such information to appear in hometown newspapers and to offer such assistance as may be requested. 3. In performing these duties you are authorized direct contact with the Information Officer, this command, any branch in this section, and the Commanders of all subordinate units or their authorized representatives. 4. You will clear any request for other than routine individual hometown news releases with me before presentation to the Information Officer. 5. This appointment is not intended to consume your entire working day, in fact it should not take more than five percent of your time. If it appears that you will become involved for a greater period of time, advise me, in writing, of the reasons therefor. R. A. Hamilton, LTC, AGC, Adjutant General."

I handed the copy back to him.

"He's got everybody pissed off. No crossword puzzles on duty, so Major McCarthy spends all day at the PX. No reading on duty, so we all sit around like bumps on a log waiting for mealtimes to roll around. And these mad DF's keep coming."

"I know McCarthy's no use, but can't Major Inhalt do anything?"

"Major Inhalt is threatening to become Lieutenant-Colonel Inhalt and be transferred to MACV at Tan Son Nhut."

"What about Sergeant Kroeber?"

"He's short."

"Short? You mean he didn't extend again?"

"No, he says the war's over now and the horseshit's getting started."

We talked for a little while longer, and then Pete climbed out of my bunker and scrambled down the hill. I watched his listless walk along the perimeter road, annoyed that I missed him.

RAGNAROK

When it comes, the attack rolls through the bunker line effortlessly. Some of us escape by lying in our bunkers pretending to be dead. The depot is destroyed; Long Binh's thousands of clerks take to the woods. A general offensive throughout Vietnam panics the U.S. commanders and triggers full-scale bombing raids on Hanoi, Haiphong, the panhandle, and the Ho Chi Minh trail. We cross the DMZ and fight our way deep into North Vietnamese territory. Chinese troops enter the war and bring us to a standstill. Russian, Chinese, North Vietnamese, South Vietnamese, Laotian, and American aircraft battle in the skies. U.S. ships engage Russian and North Vietnamese craft at the approaches to Haiphong harbor. Our bombers strike at supply routes on both sides of the Chinese border. Fire storms destroy Saigon; the government falls. A provisional coalition government is formed. Plans are announced for the possible evacuation of all American troops from Indochina. The President of the United States is assassinated and right-wing pressure forces the new President to take strong military action in Southeast Asia. Our troops make amphibious landings along the North Vietnamese Red River Delta and strike directly for Hanoi. Chinese planes attack ships of the Sixth Fleet. Limited nuclear war begins. Landbased missiles are launched against enemy missile sites. China's government is destroyed. The United States suffers fifteen percent casualties. Russia suffers ten percent casualties. Ballistic missile submarines at sea are given orders to strike population centers. Everybody dies.

ORDNANCE

At four-forty-five, if I was in one of the bunkers on the eastern side of the depot, I pulled out my borrowed watch and began to count the minutes until the five o'clock fireworks display. I had watched this show often but was still not tired of it. During the day, trucks carried the outdated ammunition a quarter-mile from the depot and left it in a clearing I could just barely make out if my bunker was on high ground. Before the detonation a helicopter flew over the site. Then there were long moments of waiting; I could not trust my watch and never turned my eyes away from the spot. If I was still looking when the explosion came I saw the smooth hemisphere of fire, the shock wave bubble, the flattened trees and the wall of dust in silence until huge noise slammed into the bunker. Sometimes other, smaller explosions followed, but more often everything went up in one grand blast. HA-*BLAM*! Smoke poured into the sky afterward. What a great sight. And what a great noise! KA-*BOOM*! Terrific.

CHICAGO

First I heard that large demonstrations were planned, which was to be expected, and that the Mayor had announced he would keep order, which was also to be expected. Then I heard that twenty thousand troops would be on hand and that sixty black GI's had staged a sit-down strike at Fort Hood when ordered to go. From an amateur political analyst I understood that Gene had no chance, George had no chance, and if Hubert didn't take it on the first ballot, Teddy would get the nod. I was reminded that labor troubles in the city had affected transportation and communications. I discovered that the FBI had unearthed plans to dump LSD into the city's water supply. I read that the Unit Rule had been abolished, a "peace plank" had been proposed by a minority of the Platform Committee, and Georgia's Lester Maddox group had not been seated pending the outcome of a challenge by a rival delegation. A ser-

geant told me about a lot of violence in Lincoln Park. I found
out that the peace plank had been respectably defeated. I was
informed that city police had apparently gone crazy, injuring
hundreds of people. A crowd had been pushed through the
plate-glass window of the Hilton Hotel's Haymarket Lounge,
someone reported. I saw a remarkable *Stars and Stripes* headline
which read, "Police Storm Hotel, Beat McCarthy Aides."
There was speculation that newsmen were being deliberately
assaulted. I learned that Hubert Humphrey had received the
Democratic nomination. I was told of a silent candlelight parade by delegates from the Amphitheater to the Loop.

RIOT

The MP was unsympathetic. "We'll let them live in their
own filth as long as they want."

"You mean they're still loose?"

"Loose? Hell, no. They got one part of the compound, is
all. They're not going anywhere."

"Did some escape?"

He shrugged. "Hard to tell, with all the records gone. May
be a couple of weeks before they get a good head count."

"I wonder if a guy named Forbes was in the stockade."

"No idea."

"Larry Forbes. He was in for pot. I understood that they
were going to move all the narcotics guys to Okinawa."

"I don't know. I don't think so." He lit a cigarette and
glanced at the rain heading toward us.

"Was a guy named Haines Cook still there?"

"What, do you know everybody in LBJ?"

I chuckled nervously.

"The whole deal was chicken-shit," the MP said.

"But somebody got killed, didn't he?"

"Yeah. Big deal. One out of seven hundred."

"Out of how many?"

"About seven hundred, more or less. Give or take a few."

"In that one spot? I've seen it; it's only two blocks long!"

"It's a lot smaller than that now, and most of what's left is charcoal."

A few drops of rain fell.

"I've got to take off, I'm going to get wet," the MP said.

"Did you guys use tear gas?"

"Shit yeah."

"Many people get hurt?"

"Mostly them."

"How come you went in?"

"Well, what are you going to do? Let a bunch of militants take the place over?"

Rain was falling harder. On the road the other men in the detail struggled to secure a tarpaulin over the trailer-load of old ammunition they had collected from the bunker. At my feet, my new shells gleamed in their fresh boxes.

"What's the status of things now?" I asked.

"Most everyone is sleeping outside; the fucking Afros are fenced off by themselves. When they feel like giving their right names, they can come out."

"I guess technically it was the worst stockade riot in Army history."

The MP sneered. "Technically."

GARBAGE

As I approached the magic thirty-day mark, that date when I could no longer be reassigned, transferred, lent out on temporary duty, or otherwise fucked with, the orderly room sent me an outprocessing slip and told me to begin working on it. The next day an order arrived removing me from the guard roster and dumping me back into Headquarters Company as a nominal duty soldier, although I was expected to spend most of my time staying out of everybody's way. Reshevsky let me know that I was not supposed to report back to the AG Section. This was fine with me.

On the last night out I caught a ride from the bunker line directly back to the company area. Hart was driving; it seems that Colonel Hamilton had overheard one of his monologues on death and had reassigned him to the orderly room. I sat in the cab of the truck with him. His headlights didn't work and he wanted to make it back before the light failed; he asked me about a short cut along the perimeter road to the construction work at the new supply battalion warehouses. I had seen jeeps travel off in that direction, so we gave it a try. Hart must have missed the turn. We wound up in pitch darkness somewhere southeast of Long Binh looking for the 1st Aviation helipad. I spotted a glow on our left and we drove overland toward it. Hart bounced the truck through a series of shallow trenches and then we were in the midst of the Long Binh garbage dump. The stench was dizzying. Murky fires flickered and smoldered. Smoke blinded us. I climbed out on the running board and tried to tell Hart which way to turn. The engine stalled. Hart began to cry. I considered it, but collapsed instead into helpless laughter.

Sometimes tyrants do receive their just deserts, but even so the memories continue to lurk.

Tom Suddick

A Shithouse Rat

I finish washing my hands and reach for the handle above me.

It clatters under my fingers, and I hear it clack hollowly inside the tank as the toilet flushes with an empty whoosh. I sit again and stare into the bowl while the water swirls and swirls, disappearing with a strangled glug.

Happens about this time every week—sometimes twice—on Tuesdays and Thursdays. Maybe it has something to do with the Bronze Star. I don't know. I'm used to it, though. After five years I should be.

But it isn't over yet.

Next the remembering will start. That happens every time, too; like a recurring dream, and every bit as vivid.

So I stand up and get a fresh, clean white towel for my hands—I can't have them wet for very long—and I stare into the mirror. I flick the light switch on and off, making myself disappear in a snuff of darkness and then reappear in a blinding-white flash. On-off-on-off-on—my face looking like an old-time movie star's.

The flickering light helps me to remember. If I remember, I will be cleansed and I can sleep. I keep flicking the light switch, and I flush the toilet again. In the intermittent light I watch the water swirl and swirl downward.

A dun-brown pillar of smoke twisted and turned over the rusty barbed wire and ascended into a dusty sky. I watched it rise from the gaseous, flaming pit that bubbled and hissed and popped like a witch's cauldron, then went back to my reading.

It was not napalm from a village-turned-inferno by the ZIPPO tracks that caused the smoke to rise so grotesquely some fifteen meters from where I squatted with my complete Poe. Neither was it a burning tank transformed into a treaded ball of flame by a Viet land mine. Such sights were common in the field, but rare in Phu Bai, the rear area.

It was burning shit.

We had been in the rear for two weeks, resupplying and regrouping after our last operation. Burning shit was a more frequent sight here than burning villages.

The others were returning from their cigarette break. I heard their voices and the scuffling of their boots behind me, carried by the early autumn wind that raised mini-tornadoes of dust to mingle with the smoking shit.

"Whatcha readin' for, Sutherland?" I heard Kaufmann say, sneering. "You ain't in college anymore. If you wuz, you wouldn' be watchin' no burnin' shithole." The other seven guffawed like amused Neanderthals—all except the doc.

The gathered in a semicircle around me: seven other marines and the navy corpsman. We watched the smoke abate as the fire slowly died, leaving a thick, pasty blackness in the pit that glowed like a nearly spent coal fire.

The doc looked over my shoulder. He was always interested in what I read. "What is it today?"

"'The Purloined Letter.'"

Kaufmann crowed and chuckled. "Purloin—isn't that a kind of steak?"

I never knew why Kaufmann hated my guts. I just supposed that hatred was a way of life with him. He took every possible opportunity to harass me. And along with me he hated all college students, blacks, liberals, Communists, Mexicans, and, of course, Viets.

"Naww—that's 'sirloin.' 'Purloin' is a place in Iowa," snapped Jackel, one of Kaufmann's squad.

The others joined in the chorus. "That's Des Moines. 'Purloin' is where Lance Corporal Sutherland went to college . . . You dumb shit, that's Purdue . . . No, Purdue is someplace in South America . . . Wasn't Purloin a British general in the Revolution?" The laughter continued until the doc told us to cover the pit.

"Okay, let's get on the truck. We just have to do the other side of the base, and we can knock off for the rest of the afternoon."

On the truck we sat and bounced over the rutted road that ran a perimeter around the inside of the base. Huge, rusted, twenty-five gallon buckets rattled and slid around in the back with us. We sat on the edges of the back, keeping our feet up so the buckets wouldn't slam against our shins.

I sat in a corner at the very rear, looking out over the base—a marine shantytown of half-screened huts, made of plywood and galvanized aluminum roofing that made hundreds of mirrors for the sun. Each hut stood in straight rows that only the military seemed able to achieve. Dust clouds swirled in gritty arabesques between the huts and over them, coating the shiny roofs with a dull film.

The truck we rode raised more dust that settled over us all

like a screen, turning our olive-drab utilities to a sickly reddish brown.

It was like this twice a week. Every Tuesday and Thursday the marines in Vietnam dumped their shit. Two men from each squad, one from company headquarters, and me, the platoon radioman, were under the charge of Doc, the company corpsman.

The doc moved toward where I sat. "I've seen you on this detail for the last two weeks. You on somebody's shit list? No pun intended."

"Aww, Doc," Kaufmann piped up. "Don't pay no 'tention t' him. He's crazier 'n a shithouse rat. He volunteers for this detail every goddamned time."

"Jesus," the doc said, wincing at me. "What the hell for? You *like* dumping shit?"

"Course not. But it's better than the rest of the details—raking gravel between the huts, cleaning out the staff and officers' quarters, or digging sod to put around the mess halls for the colonel's beautification program. Besides, I can get the rest of the afternoon off so I can read.

"Figure it out, Doc. It's either work my ass off all day digging sod or dump shit for a few hours and get the rest off."

The doc grinned. "You're a pretty strange person, Sutherland. You read a lot of Poe?"

"Yeah. He writes about guilt a lot. Guilty characters are the most interesting kind. If you like, I'll loan this to you when I'm finished."

"Sure. No offense, Sutherland, but it's rare to find a halfway literate grunt."

I snickered and slipped the book into the left thigh pocket of my utilities and grunted.

The truck rumbled to a halt, and the doc turned toward the rest of the detail. "Okay, Kaufmann and Jackel, dig the pit over there by the corner of the wire."

The two grabbed shovels and grinned, leaping from the

truck, happy with escaping the handling of the shit buckets. The truck drove on.

There were only three shitters on this side of the base. Each shitter was built on a foundation of two-by-fours, about six feet off the ground. On the sides of the screened structures hinged doors of plywood closed over compartments that housed four-handled buckets, exactly like those we carried in the truck.

Each of us brought a bucket from the truck. They were fifty gallon drums cut in half. We pulled the full buckets from the compartments of each shitter, loaded them on the truck, and then placed empty buckets inside the shitters.

The others in the detail chorused their half-snickering gripes: "This is the shits . . . What a bunch of shit . . . This is a real shit detail . . . Man, Sutherland, you sure know your shit."

The stench was overpowering as we got back on the truck. Twelve buckets of shit and piss, replete with flies and making the air an ozone of gaseous nausea. A slight film of dust covered the top of each bucket as the truck drove slowly backward toward Kaufmann and Jackel. The pit was ready.

I had an odd tendency to be philosophical about this job. Like Hamlet at Yorick's grave, reflecting that everything returns to clay, I considered how everyone is united by shit: the colonel's shit mingled with the corporal's, the provost marshal's with the private's, the chaplain's with the cook's.

And I stared absently into the twelve buckets, reflecting that we rode on a truck that carried three hundred gallons of shit.

In those buckets my own shit mingled with the doc's and with that of the two or three others I could call my friends. Even my enemies were united with me in those buckets—inextricably bound with my shit. I thought about those I despised as I looked into the buckets and tried to imagine whose shit was whose. The oozy, khaki-colored shit would belong to Staff Sergeant Villanueva, who took ecstatic delight in throwing discarded C rations to Viet kids to watch them fight over food. The hardened globs with flecks of corn and nuts that looked like failed fudge could have come from Pfc Jackel, who had a fixation for destroying Buddhist temples. The long, tubular shit was probably Private Kaufmann's, he who favored white phosphorus grenades for burning the homes of villagers. The black tarry shit must have been discharged by Lieutenant Campbell, who enjoyed stuffing hand-illumination grenades in the shirts of NVA· prisoners. Here, in a variety as infinite as man himself, was all their shit. And I thought, "Yes. Everything in the Vietnam war boils down to shit."

We emptied all the buckets into the gaping maw of the pit, and the doc poured five gallons of kerosine on top of the oozy surface. He also poured some into the buckets and set them aflame with a match.

I turned to see Staff Sergeant Villaneuva drive up in his jeep. He stepped from behind the wheel and straightened himself to a pudgy five-foot-six. His utilities were starched and pressed superbly, and his boots gleamed with a spit shine like a wine bottle. On his belt, next to his polished .45 holster, hung two old-style pineapple grenades. The grenades were polished with Brasso until they appeared as golden gourds. Villanueva stood and stared at us, as if he couldn't imagine what we were doing.

The doc looked up to see him and grinned at me.

"'This is the excellent foppery of the world,'" I said, laughing, and the doc laughed with me as we watched Villanueva waddling into the G-5 hut—the civil relations office.

"What da fuck was dat?" bellowed a pfc in our detail.

"Villanueva," spat out Kaufmann. "Staff NCO of the PX. That sonofabitch's got more money an' gear than the whole fuckin' corps."

It was true.

Villanueva made his money off the Viet whores he brought in for the officers. He made money off the Viet concession stands that sold Cokes to thirsty marines at a dollar a bottle—a dollar-fifty with ice. He practically owned the PX. He sold supplies to the Viets—boots, blankets, even beer. Staff Sergeant Villanueva was a first-rate civil relations man.

It was a well-known fact that he kept the paperwork on all his holdings in the black box we could see in the back of his jeep. It was a sort of mobile file cabinet that he could take whenever he went to any of his concession stands or whorehouses.

And it was generally accepted among the lower ranks that Staff Sergeant Villanueva was a first-rate prick.

The doc went to the truck to get some paper to set the pit on fire.

Jackel snickered and elbowed Kaufmann. "Say, I wonder what ol' Villanueva would do if he found his box missin'?"

A fiendish gleam came to Kaufmann's eyes, and they both rushed toward the jeep. Jackel grabbed the box and Kaufmann helped him carry it to the pit.

Gathering around the yawning, shit-filled hole, the rest of the detail watched as Kaufmann and Jackel threw the box in. It sank slowly, then disappeared with a loud slurp. Until I saw them throw it in, I didn't know what they had in mind. I wouldn't have stopped them anyway, since I wasn't sure what Kaufmann and Jackel would do. Besides, I had no loyalty to Villanueva.

The doc came back from the truck, rolled up a copy of *Stars and Stripes* into a torch. He dipped the end of the wad into the kerosine, lit it, and threw it into the pit, putting *Stars and Stripes* to its best possible use.

Flames and smoke belched from the pit, and another duncolored pillar of smoke swirled upward.

I laughed inwardly at the thought of Villanueva's paperwork at the bottom of the six foot pit, where it belonged. The rest of the detail smiled knowingly at one another as they watched the bubbling, hissing fire turn the surface of the shit to a blackened patina.

"All right, marines," grated a voice from behind us. "Where is it?"

We turned to see Villanueva glaring at us, hands on hips, feet spread, his right hand menancingly near the grip of his .45.

"Where's what, Sergeant?" asked the doc.

"You know what, you squid motherfucker. Who's the ranking marine here? I don't wanna talk to no fuckin' sailor."

"Lance Corporal Sutherland, Sergeant," said Kaufmann.

"All right, Sutherland. Where's my strongbox?"

I looked around at the others, their eyes cast down. Kaufmann and Jackel looked at me through squinting eyes, challenging me to tell, and threatening me if I did.

"You pukes were the only ones close enough to my jeep. You took it." Villanueva drew his pistol and pointed it in my chest. The fire in the pit burned hot in my face as it grew bigger and I glanced toward it.

Villanueva caught my glance and a slow half smile came to his fighter face. "You two!" he said, pointing to a couple of privates in the detail. "Get a fire extinguisher. Now!"

The two privates ran for the G-5 hut and returned with a CO_2 extinguisher.

"Put out that goddamned fire!"

A private sprayed the pit and in seconds the flames were gone, leaving a thin, white, bubbly foam on the black-coated surface of the pit.

"Now, you're gonna do some diggin', Sutherland. You're gonna pull my strongbox from the bottom of that pit with your hands."

The doc jumped between us. "Sergeant, you can't make . . ."

Villanueva grabbed his shirtfront and threw him to the ground. "I can. Know what disobedience of an order during time of war can get you, boy? The brig officer's a friend of mine, and he can show you a real good time. So you better do it—I'm making that an order."

I gazed into his face, feeling partial contempt and partial disbelief, but saw the twisted, sadistic glee of a tyrant who knows he's in control. Since I'd been in the corps—where every one of your rights as a man are taken away and then returned over a period of years in the form of privileges—I had come to accept humiliation. But I had never imagined anything like this: to grovel through six feet of shit to recover a senior NCO's possessions—if anything, it was too literal. I had crawled through mud to recover the bodies of marines who had been dead and decomposing for days. I had lived with rats in bunkers while being shelled. I had loaded dead NVA on carts to be lined up for body counts. But I never thought it would come to this.

"Do it, Sutherland," Villanueva barked.

I was not about to do time in the brig. It was either dig through this shit or spend years harassed daily by the maniac guards for which the brig was so ominously famous.

I rolled down my sleeves and reached for a nearby pair of gloves.

"No. Barehanded," Villanueva snarled.

I tried to remember where I'd seen the box go down—I might be able to find it quickly and get it over without wallowing for a long time.

Kneeling at the edge of the pit, I looked up at the others. Some stood mutely gaping like toy store marionettes. Others stared at the ground. One ran for a nearby hole to puke.

I reached into the pit and felt the warm, oozing mess coat my hands and run between my fingers. I shuddered at the sensation, and I gagged from the stench of the blackened, kerosine-burned globs.

Flat on my stomach, I sunk my arms in past my elbows and felt a hard, flat surface with my fingertips. Fortunately, the box hadn't sunk to the bottom. I felt around for the edges and grabbed the corners. It took all my strength to pull it up. I held my breath against the smell, but I could hold it no longer and the fumes permeated my every sinus.

The box slipped from my hands as I puked and crawled backward from the pit.

I scarcely heard the explosions over Villanueva's screaming in my ear.

His screams were replaced by cries of "Incoming!" and the shrieks of rocket rounds. I saw the others scatter, running for the nearest bunker.

"Get back in there!" blatted Villanueva, kicking me in the side, I rolled and swung my fist, knocking his pistol into the pit and tackling him with my legs. A roar like two fast freight trains colliding in a tunnel deafened me as I climbed on top of Villanueva and wrapped my caked hands around his neck. He rolled, came on top of me, and I lost my grip. Straddling me, he smashed his fist into my face.

My mouth filled with blood and saliva, and I spat in his face as I saw his fist raise again. His shoulder seemed to explode in a mass of blood and he bleated in agony, his right arm dangling like a crimson rubber snake.

With all my strength I slammed my fist into his balls and rolled him into the pit. I looked around for cover, realizing that I couldn't drag Villanueva with me. He would have to take his chances in the pit.

The rockets still squealed and roared as I crawled toward the shitter. I didn't have time to get to a bunker, and there wasn't room for two in the pit. I hoped I would have enough cover underneath the shitter.

I saw that the Viets were walking their rockets further into the base, and I thought they would walk them out, so I started to run for the G-3 bunker. But I found I was wrong. The cluster of huts that housed G-5, along with Comm and G-2, was ground zero—the Viet's target area. I ran back for the shitter.

Rockets fell in a ghastly, grating rain, obliterating the huts, transforming them into geysers of yellow sparks and shaking the ground like a cataclysmic quake. Smoke and dust and pieces of wood and metal swirled and sang through the air in a hellish tempest. I screamed and screamed to let out my terror and to save my body from the battering concussion.

I watched the explosions, waiting for a break that might give me time to get to a safer position. A ball of flame billowed from the pit, and I saw Villanueva consumed in a vermilion cloud. I heard splats on the plywood sides of the shitter above me, and I saw burning globs dropping on the two-by-fours around me.

The rockets stopped. I could hear no more explosions or freight-train-like whisks. Out of the near silence I heard cries of "Medic!" and names being called and orders shouted.

I felt a hot throbbing on my left thigh and I winced, looking down to see my leg drenched in blood. Reaching into my thigh pocket, I pulled out my complete Poe; the pages were oozy with my own blood, and the shit on my hands mingled with the red smears on the cover.

In a gory heap, Villanueva's body burned half in and half out of the flaming pit. I limped toward him, stuffing my book back into my pocket, and dragged him out. With my shirt I beat out the flames on his torso as I saw the doc and four of the detail coming toward me, followed by Lieutenant Campbell.

"Sutherland! You're hit!" yelled the doc, grabbing me.

"Villanueva, he . . ."

"S'okay, Marine," said the lieutenant. "You did all you could. I saw you trying to pull him out. Doc, take him to sickbay—the rest of you men put out this fire and cover that pit."

I tried to speak. I wanted to tell them what had happened. "Lieutenant, I . . ."

"Don't sweat it, Sutherland. With that leg you'll probably be shipped out early. There'll be a citation in it for you, too."

I looked at the pit, slowly flickering. It flared brightly, then burned low, sending a gnarled, black cylinder of smoke, swirling, swirling, swirling . . .

I flick on the light and leave it shining brightly. My face is flushed and beads of sweat and globular tears make tracks over my cheeks. I taste salt and blood in my mouth.

The water in the toilet bowl is still, and I can only hear the soft rushing of the pipes.

I rush from the bathroom to my bookshelf. Inside my battered and stained complete Poe, the medal flashes its red, white, and blue ribbon in my eyes. The room begins to whirl, and I stumble back to the bathroom, clutching the Bronze Star.

I drop the medal into the toilet.

It clanks on the bottom of the porcelain bowl, and I reach again for the handle. The medal swirls in the water, around and around, until it vanishes with a watery gag.

Yes.

Now, after I dry off with another fresh, clean white towel—yes.

Maybe now I can sleep.

THE
REAL WAR

As in all wars, the innocents paid most dearly for our folly.

Tom Mayer

A Birth
in the Delta

The company was spread out behind a series of
dikes, taking a lunch break. The sun thrust down, glared with
steady eye-aching intensity off the muddy paddy water. Some
of the men had taken off their shirts, others wore undershirts,
which were dark with sweat. Now, resting, they had all taken
off their helmets. They were all also caked with mud to their
thighs. The mud was drying in the sun, beginning to crack.

The company had been in the field in the Delta for a week,
plowing across an interminable series of paddies, always
working through the muck and never along the hard packed
dikes, because the dikes were where you ran into ambushes
and mines and booby traps. Before this operation they had had
a one day stand-down, complete with warm orange sodas and
new uniforms, after having been in the field for ten days. Before that they had had a one day stand-down . . . etc.

The headquarters element was grouped in the center, around the company commander, Captain Harkness. Harkness looked to be perhaps eighteen, with the tanned athletic aspect of a life-guard or an assistant tennis pro, his face smoothly brown and his hair thick and blond, close cropped. His appearance was somewhat deceptive, for actually he was twenty-six, a veteran commander, now in the eighth month of his second tour. A paratrooper, an instructor at ranger school, a survivor of two dozen bitter firefights in the Central Highlands two years ago. He was studying the map—it often seemed to him he had spent the major part of his adult life studying maps—and half listening to the desultory luncheon conversation going on around him.

"I'll trade you ham and eggs for them Salems," said Corporal Blacksides.

"Fuck that," said Top Sergeant Himmlemann.

"You can have my coffee too."

"Shit. I got plenty of coffee."

"They give me the fucking shaft. I'm too fucking short." That was PFC Leyba, the radio man, who was scheduled to leave in three days. "They shouldn't have sent me to the field again. Fucking Roth didn't go on no operations, and I'm shorter than he was."

"Roth was a fucking fuck-up, Leyba," said Spec 4 Burns, the medic. "We need you."

"Fuck you."

"Ask the old man. You're indispensable, Leyba. They ain't never gonna let you go home."

"Watch your fucking lip. I'll fucking bust it for you."

"I'll give you my peaches."

"I don't know."

"Peaches, you asshole. You don't even like Salems."

"I got to think about it."

"Fucking eighty more days," said Rifleman Upshaw. He drew a line through the number 81 on his helmet. Many of the troops' helmets were virtually covered with numbers.

"You can't cross it off yet," said Private Prissholm, who was on his first operation. "We're not through the day."

"I can cross it off if I fucking want."

"Of course you can," Prissholm said. "But it doesn't mean anything."

"Shit."

"A can of peaches for a pack of fucking cigarettes, you dip. You don't even like the fucking brand."

"Maybe I don't like peaches neither."

"Don't shit me, Top."

"I never shit nobody."

The captain glanced at his watch, went over the map another time, making sure he had not missed some obvious ambush site. "All right, Top," he said. "Tell 'em to put it on."

"Where do we go now?" Prissholm asked.

"Across some more fucking paddies, you idiot," Upshaw said. "Where do you think we're going? On fucking R and R?"

"Put it on," Top was bellowing.

"Maybe we'll get us a fucking vil," Leyba said. "I like to burn them hootches."

"Rape, loot, pillage, burn," Burns said.

"Lay off that shit," Top said. "There ain't no fucking TV cameras around."

Men were standing up, slowly, drawing each move out, feeling the sweat begin to run again as they donned shirts, slid packs and webbing over shoulders, fastened buckles, slung ammunition containers and belts of machine gun bullets, placed the hated weights of the helmets. Harkness gave instructions to the platoon lieutenants over the radio. The point element, which was several dikes ahead, moved out. The company unfolded forward like an opening accordion. Harkness checked to either side that the flank security was out. They had not had a contact for two days, and he was not particularly expecting one, but he knew you got hit when you expected it least, and worked constantly to keep himself and his troops alert. Two or three kilometers ahead of them a treeline shimmered in the heat, a dancing band of cool across the glare. It could almost have been a mirage, but he knew from the map it was real enough.

It was headquarters' turn to move. One by one the men went over the dike, hesitated, and stepped down into the muck on the other side. The Delta was the most work of any place in the country, Harkness thought. In the mountains at least you were on firm ground. There were always twice as many heat exhaustion cases here. Several times he thought he had come to the end of his own rope. But you learned how to move in the muck, how to hop from one rice plant to the next and never, almost never, slide off into the gumbo, which might be knee or even thigh deep.

They slogged through the paddy and over the dike and into the next one and the sun kept pouring down. Some of the men wore sunglasses, but most did not bother. Glasses fogged up and you sweated so much they were impossible to keep clean. Every so often a man fell down, slipped off a rice plant and lost his balance and sprawled forward or sideways into the water and mud, then scrambled up swearing. They crossed one deep canal. They held rifles and ammunition overhead, but a machine-gunner, a Negro named Dillard, slipped going up the far side, slid back into the water on his chest, dragging weapon and ammunition through the ooze. Two men helped pull him out and they stopped while he cleaned the gun, wiped off the belts.

After an hour they stopped for a five minute break.

"I'm almost out of water," Prissholm complained. Most of the men were drinking deeply, carried four or five canteens on D-rings and webbing.

"Don't look at me, dickhead," Upshaw said.

"I wasn't asking for any. I just wonder when we'll get a resupply."

"Shit," Upshaw said.

"Maybe tomorrow," Burns said. "Maybe tonight. Maybe never."

"I could pill this paddy water."

"Sure," the medic said. "Put enough pills in piss and you could drink it."

"Don't shit this dickhead, doc," Himmlemann said. "He might try it."

"Top," Harkness said. "Make sure they're taking their salt."

"Right."

"I got plenty of salt pills," Burns said. "Iodine too. If anybody needs them."

"Good, doc," Harkness said.

"Blacksides, have you got some extra water?"

"How much you got left?"

"About half a canteen."

"You got plenty. Tell me when you're out."

"Thanks a million."

"Anytime, dickhead."

"This fucking operation eats shit," Leyba said. "It sucks."

"Nobody'll argue with you about that," Burns said.

"It's a goddamn ratfuck. I'm too short to get zapped on a ratfuck."

"You aren't going to get zapped."

"Fucking A I ain't. But you can't never tell."

"Don't sweat getting zapped, Leyba. I'll fix you up."

"Shit, doc. You don't know how to get a Band-Aid on straight."

"Well, motherfuck, just hope you don't have to try me."

"Now don't get pissed off."

"O.K.," Harkness said. "Let's move out. Get 'em moving, Top."

Harkness called ahead to the point and out to the flanks on the radio, told his people to stay alert, to watch the treeline. They were less than a kilometer away now. The map showed several hootches, which did not necessarily mean that there were people, or even hootches any more. However, Harkness was aware of how naked his people were coming across the paddies, how they might look through a pair of binoculars or a telescopic sight. He called Battalion, made sure they wanted him to push on. They did.

"It's typical," he said to Sergeant Himmlemann. "They haven't got a fucking blocking force so anybody in there can DD if they feel like it."

Himmlemann, his bull neck luminous with sunburn, the color of windblown coals, was too busy hopping from rice clump to rice clump to answer.

Leyba, slogging behind the captain, bent under the weight of the radio, loathed Harkness, focused his hate at a point between the captain's shoulder blades. He hated Harkness for bringing him out again, was sure he could have gotten him a dispensation. In fact, he had hated the captain for eight months, ever since Harkness had come to the company and made him a radio operator in the first place. The radio cut down into his shoulders and tendons, caused a burning sensation and numbness, almost as if the straps were eating their way through his flesh and sinew. He had humped the captain's radio and never gotten used to it: it was his ball and chain, an extra thirty pounds of knobs and transistors and batteries that nagged him like a lead growth. He had nightmares where he was drowning in a canal, floundering face down in brackish water, the weight on his back pressing him inexorably toward the muddy bottom. He thought of shooting Harkness if they got into a contact, a recurrent and favorite daydream. He had read about things like that happening, good soldiers shooting unjust officers in the field, in men's magazines. As far as he knew it had never happened in their brigade or their division. But there was always a first time. But they might catch him, and then he wouldn't deros, wouldn't ride the freedom bird, they would put him in LBJ, the Long Binh Jail. If he wasn't so close to leaving he wouldn't even mind that. Sometimes he thought anything would be better than the radio, than humping the boonies week after week with that dead weight on his back. He would shoot Harkness without a qualm if it weren't such bad percentages with only three days left.

Private Prissholm was simply miserable. He had gotten over being frightened—the first few days out he had been carried by sheer nervous energy, had imagined every odd shape and terrain feature concealed his doom, had not slept ten minutes—but now he was only tired, indescribably weary through his thighs and calves, and thirsty. How was he supposed to have known most of the water here was so saline as to be undrinkable, even when liberally laced with purification tablets? And even if he had known about that, how was he to have guessed that resupply would be so erratic? He assumed that somehow things like water and food got taken care of. This was, after all, the American Army, and the one thing everyone admitted Americans were superior at was logistics. That was supposed to be our genius. Six million cans of hair spray for the Saigon PX and air bases with ten thousand-foot runways of solid reinforced concrete every twenty miles up and down the country, but no water for one infantryman in the Delta.

He imagined a confrontation with the battalion lieutenant colonel, a mean-eyed Swede who affected a fatherly attitude, called everyone from his most senior major on down lad, in which he, Private Prissholm, told the colonel that it was a fucked-up Army that expected its troops to fight without water, and the colonel, amazingly, agreed with him, assured him it wouldn't happen again. Momentarily Prissholm was pleased with the vision, his victory, and then he thought that he was deluding himself. He was losing touch with reality. He was Michael Edwin Prissholm, college graduate, political science major, former vice-president of the sophomore class, and all of this, the colonel, the water, the muck, the heat, cretinous Sergeant Himmlemann, Leyba the obvious psychotic, Harkness who was running for eagle scout, everything since basic training, since induction, all of it was unreal, had nothing to do with the real world and real people. The only way to survive mentally was to turn off his mind.

Burns, the medic, was content. He was light, very lithe, and he was not weighted down with ammunition as were the other men, so he hopped easily, mechanically, from plant to plant. He had learned long ago how to turn off his mind, divert its focus, on marches like this, to concentrate his physical attention on the next step, never farther ahead than two steps, while he let the thinking part of his brain slip off on little trips. Burns was always well equipped with marijuana, and had even devised a way of taking it in public. He smoked Kools, the most noxiously mentholated of cigarettes, and he had discovered that by carefully repacking the tubes with a mixture of tobacco and grass the pot odor was lost in the menthol. He was so expert at this that it was completely impossible to tell one of his repacks from an original until you smoked it. He had smoked frequently in front of the captain, and had even considered offering him one just to see what would happen.

Now Burns was imagining being rich. He was a licensed chiropractor, a profession he had chosen for its large remunerative potential. He had just completed school when the Army drafted him. At first he had been indignant—at being drafted at all, then at not being treated like a doctor. They had no right to make him a mere medic while doctors were automatically officers and never left the air-conditioned hospitals. But then he had gotten over here, and all he cared about now was living through his tour so that he could go home to San Jose and start his practice. His Army record might even help bring in patients. Burns was a good California boy, born and raised there, and he happily imagined a weekend house in Santa Cruz where he could surf all year around. He would need a wet suit, for the water there was very cold, the Japan current brushed the coast at that point, but the surf was excellent. The house in Santa Cruz and a sports car—today he was torn between a Jag XK-E and a Corvette, with one of the new

Porsches running slightly behind—to get him there from San José. Maybe a helicopter. He had never thought of a personal chopper before. He would learn to fly, buy one of those Loaches like the colonel had. They couldn't be all that expensive. He pictured the house on the cliff overlooking the beach and the long waves breaking and his Loach skimming in over the hills and landing in front of the house.

Harkness was getting worried. They were closing on the treeline and he was reflexively worried. He had been shot at from too many treelines. He pushed the point out a little farther. In a few minutes he would begin to recon by fire, let his lead platoon shoot. If you shot first, even if you were wild, they would sometimes open up themselves when you were still out of effective range, give their position away. Usually, of course, they weren't there at all. And this time there might be civilians. Down here in the Delta there was always a chance of that. There were not supposed to be. Intelligence said they had all been moved out, but few things worked out the way they were supposed to.

It was precisely then that the point man in the lead squad, which was only 150 meters from the treeline, climbed across a grassy dike and tripped off a booby trap, a grenade with a wire attached to the pin. The fuse had been removed, and the grenade detonated instantaneously, blowing off the point man's right foot and sending fragments into his inner thighs and groin. The man behind got a few pieces in the chest.

There was a moment of general confusion, men stopping and crouching, trying to place the explosion, fix its type and source. Then a few of the new ones scurried headlong for cover, for the protective backsides of the dikes, and the platoon sergeants shouted at them to stay calm, to watch for trip wires. Harkness called to the point squad leader, asked what had happened.

"Fucking booby trap. Two WIA."

"Who?"

"Fraily. And that new guy. Walinski. He got a foot blown to shit and got it in the nuts."

"He was on point?"

"That's affirm."

It was usual practice to put the new men on point. It slightly minimized the risk for the veterans. The new men either died or were wounded or learned quickly enough to live until there was someone newer than themselves.

Harkness called for a Medevac, then called Battalion, told the colonel what had happened. They discussed the best way to proceed. They had to assume there were unfriendlies in the treeline. They could try to flank it, then drive in, or call in arty and air.

"There might be some civilians," Harkness pointed out.

"I know."

"S-2 says they got them out."

"I know that's what S-2 says. The province chief told him." The colonel paused. "It's up to you, lad. You're the man on the spot."

"Let's get arty and the gunships then. Maybe we can get an air strike."

It was better them than us, Harkness thought. Though there might not be any of them there at all. But if there were and the place wasn't prepped he'd take more casualties getting in, and probably have nothing to show for his blood. The advantages of position, of camouflage and fortification and field of fire, were all with the enemy. He knew of at least two company commanders who had been relieved after such incidents. It was fine to be thoughtful of the civilian population, but not at the expense of the kill ratio.

He called up to the lead platoon, had it withdraw a hundred meters. Within five minutes white phosphorous marker rounds began to drop in the trees and paddies in front. One was short, hit right on his platoon's old position. He adjusted the fire, called in the high explosive.

They brought the wounded back to the captain's position.

Burns had gone forward immediately after the explosion, tied off Walinski's leg. Fraily was a Band-Aid case, a question of picking out a few splinters. Burns gave Walinski two morphine shots, which did not seem to have much effect. He kept trying to clutch the mangled wreckage of his genitals. Every so often the stump of his right calf jerked, as if a doctor were testing his reflexes.

Prissholm watched Walinski in fascination. Walinski was the first seriously wounded man he had seen. Prissholm felt giddy, lightheaded. He was breathing rapidly, through his mouth. Walinski had come only a week before he had. He, Prissholm, had been incredibly lucky to be assigned to HQ rather than a regular squad. He would have to keep in Harkness's favor no matter what.

Leyba, as did the others, with the exception of Burns, ignored the wounded. They were out of it, it did no good to look at them. Leyba sat on a dike top, the radio on his back, connected to the captain by the flexible umbilical cord of the microphone, and hunched over, looked as if he were trying to touch his forehead to the ground between his feet, made himself as small a target as possible. There had been no incomings yet, but there might be any second, or short artillery rounds, or the fucking gunships. Cobra pilots didn't know their dicks from their assholes. Harkness stood beside him easily, map in one hand, the mike in the other, occasionally shading his eyes with the map, giving corrections and instructions to the artillery and then the gunships as casually as if he were conversing in a living room. Harkness was forever exposing himself—he probably thought he had to set a fucking example or something—and Leyba, because he was the radio man, usually got exposed with him. Leyba imagined a short round hitting out in the paddy in front of them, dinging Harkness but sparing him.

While the gunbirds were working, the Medevac came in and loaded the wounded. Walinski was crying and Fraily was grinning.

The gunships expended, flew off, and the artillery started again. Salvos of 105 and 155 alternated. Whole trees were blown up by the 155's, cartwheeled through the air.

"Sock it to 'em," Upshaw said.

"Look at that shit," Blacksides said. "That's beautiful. Beautiful."

"You know Charlie's shit is weak now," Upshaw said.

Prissholm was watching the treeline with the others, but was unable to keep from wincing at each series of explosions. Several fires were started.

"It's burning. Beautiful."

"Burn, baby, burn."

"Fucking arty is O.K."

"Except when they're short. Sometimes those dickheads can't hit a bull in the asshole boresighted."

"They're beautiful today."

When the shoot was over Harkness moved them forward cautiously, placed his machine guns behind the dikes for covering fire, probed with the riflemen of the lead platoon. There was no fire from the trees or huts, no more booby traps. Two of the huts were burning. As HQ approached there was a wild burst of fire and everyone but Harkness, even Himmlemann, threw himself into the mud. Several individual shots. It all seemed to be coming from near one of the burning huts but no one could tell where it was directed.

"Ammo cache," the captain said. He was standing there looking down at them, not haughtily, almost sympathetically. "Get 'em going. Top. It's only some ammo in the roof cooking off."

"Right."

They moved on in. The lead platoon was set up in a fan around the edges of the clearing where the huts were. Occasional rounds kept popping off in one of the flaming hootches and the burning bamboo made loud cracks, like a small caliber pistol. The lead platoon lieutenant showed them several bunkers, and part of a body. There were several clips for an

AK–47 in one of the bunkers. The whole place smelled of explosive, a lingering acrid odor.

Prissholm and Upshaw went to check out a hut at the far corner of the clearing.

"Should we throw a grenade in?" Prissholm asked.

"You fucking idiot," Upshaw said.

"There might be somebody in there."

"You think a goddamn grenade wouldn't blow through these walls and get you too? That's thatch, you asshole, not brick."

Upshaw stood beside the doorway for a few moments, his eyes closed, adjusting them for the dim light inside. Then he pushed through the opening. Along the back wall were bags of rice, gunny sacks filled to the bursting, and several big earthen jars. The hut had been hit many times by shell and rocket fragments, and there were gashes in the thatching that admitted oblongs and sickles of light. Along one wall was a low Vietnamese-style bed, a platform of planks covered with reed mats. Lying on it was a figure. Upshaw turned his rifle on it, index finger taking up the slack in the trigger, thumb automatically checking that the fire selector was off safety, in the full auto position, rock 'n roll. Then he saw the figure was a woman, pregnant and dead, a great rip torn in her throat. The blood was still bright. Flies were buzzing in it.

"Go tell the old man we got a greased dink in here."

A few minutes later the captain, Burns and Leyba arrived. As the captain approached the woman seemed to move, twist slightly.

"I thought you said she was zapped?"

"Let me see," Burns said.

"She's pregnant."

"No shit."

Burns was holding her wrist, feeling for pulse.

"She's gone," the medic said.

"She moved," Harkness said. "I saw her."

"Reflex. I think she may have been in labor."

The woman twitched again, rolled slightly. The flies buzzed away from the wound at her throat.

"My God," Harkness said.

Leyba looked quickly at the captain. It was the first time he could remember seeing a crack in his composure, and he had seen him in and after four or five real firefights, seen him any number of times when anyone normal would have been shitting in his pants. Harkness's composure was one of the things Leyba hated about him most.

"Yeah," Burns said. "She's in labor." He pulled away the blanket that covered her legs. "It's coming out."

The medic stood up, wiped his arm across his forehead.

"Christ. I don't know how to handle something like this."

"It's not alive, is it? The baby?"

"I don't know."

"My God."

"Can you call Battalion, sir?"

"What do I say? That I've got a dead woman having a baby?"

"I guess so. Something like that."

"Leyba, let's go outside."

The body moved again.

"I need some forceps. I can't do a fucking thing without big forceps. I ought to have some boiled water too."

"I'll call Battalion."

The captain and Leyba left.

"It can't be alive," Prissholm said.

"It might be. I've never even read anything about a case like this."

"You could write it up, doc," Upshaw said.

Leyba came back in.

"They'll send out a fucking chopper if you want, but the colonel said he hasn't got any forceps. Upshaw, Top wants you."

"I need forceps," Burns said. "I don't think she ought to be moved."

"The old man didn't say anything about getting you any. Only a chopper."

"Because they haven't got any."

"What do you want me to tell the old man?"

"Tell him let me work on her awhile."

Leyba returned, put his radio set down by the door.

"O.K. Only he says don't take too long. We gotta make the next fucking objective."

"Find me some water," Burns said.

The top of the baby's head was showing. Burns was pushing on the woman's abdomen. Her contractions were not forceful enough to do any good, he thought.

Leyba discovered that the earthen jars held fresh water, filled his helmet. He stood over the medic watching. It reminded him of once at home, at his family's farm in northern New Mexico. They had had a cow that couldn't calve. His father had not wanted to call the vet, had not wanted to have to pay. The cow had grown weaker and weaker. Finally, when it was obviously going to die if something was not done, his father had tied the cow to the corral gate post, put a rope around the neck of the half-born calf. He attached the rope to his saddle and slapped the horse. The calf had been jerked out, its neck broken, but the cow had recovered. He thought of suggesting something like that to Burns, but of course the mother was already dead, and there weren't any horses around.

"It's stuck," Burns said. "I'm going to have to cut."

He stood up again. Sweat was popping out of his forehead. He ought to have boiled water to sterilize his knife at the least, but he didn't think there was time. He drew the knife, a Navy K-bar, an excellent knife that he had traded away from a corpsman for a half pound of good Lao grass. He did not like bayonets, which were what they were issued, because they would not hold an edge. He liked good tools, had promised himself the finest instruments when he got out. He seared the blade with the flame from his zippo.

"That won't sterilize it," Prissholm said. "Lighter fuel is full of grease."

"Shut up, dickhead," Leyba said.

Burns wiped his forehead, knelt, and began to cut. "Throw some water on," he told Leyba.

"Easy. That's enough."

"It ain't bleeding much."

"She's dead. No circulation."

Harkness came in, watched for a moment, and left. Leyba was grinning.

"More water."

Burns worked quickly, but carefully. Once he stopped, wiped the sweat away again. Several times he asked Leyba for water. His first incision was not big enough, the abdominal muscles clamped shut, he could not get hold of the baby.

A crowd gathered outside the hut. Harkness came back, stood just inside the door, prevented the men from pressing in.

"Water."

"That's getting it," Leyba said. "Cut some more sideways."

"Enough water."

The medic pried the slit open, reached in.

"He's taking it out," Leyba said for the benefit of the crowd.

Burns pulled the baby free, tied off the cord with a boot lace, slashed it with the bloody K-bar, and held the form up by the heels in best Ben Casey fashion. He began to slap it.

"It's dead," Leyba said.

"Throw some water on," someone suggested from the door. "Dunk it."

"That's enough," Harkness said.

Burns kept slapping, could not think what else to do, harder now, urgently, as if he could force life into it, but he produced no response. Finally he put it down beside the mother, pulled the blanket over them both. He was still sweating unnaturally, the beads popping out quickly and big on his forehead. He wiped his face on his shirt front, but it was too wet already to absorb much. He felt drained, almost as if he had dysentery. It was the way he always felt after he had lost someone.

"That's it," he said. He started for the door. "That's the ball game."

They formed up, moved through the trees and into the paddies on the other side. There was another treeline barely visible on the horizon.

As they hopped along through the muck Harkness was worried. They had lost a lot of time, would have to press hard to reach the safest position to spend the night. Automatically he checked that the point and flank security was out, that the men were spacing themselves far enough apart.

The war down here was pure shit, he reflected. He had seen more blood spilled in the high country along the border two years ago, but there hadn't been problems with civilians, and up there he'd never seen anything like this today. It had been a cleaner and more honorable war, a soldier's war, with fights between regular units of real armies, without much booby trapping, without the muck and the people. Down here there were limitless complications. It occurred to him that when the enemy came back to the hootches, and they surely would come back, they might take pictures of the woman and child, use them as anti-American propaganda. GI dogs murder pregnant woman, rip infant from womb. If they did that and our own psy war people ever hooked the stuff to his company, he'd have a helluva time explaining what had really happened.

Also, he should have done something about the rice. There had been a ton, maybe more, in that hut. He hadn't even called it in. He had been so involved with the other thing. Next to getting confirmed kills, or weapons, capturing rice was about the best thing that could happen to a commander. He could at least have had the men urinate on the sacks; that was what they did if there was not time or means to haul a cache in. That was a stupid thing to have missed.

Harkness had not had to come back to Vietnam, and he now thought, as he had often the past few months, coming back had been a mistake. After instructing at ranger school he had been an aide to a general at the Pentagon, and the general had been assigned to the mission in Brazil, had wanted to take him along. But he had volunteered to come back here instead. His friends had all come back, and he had felt that somehow it was wrong for him not to. The general, he knew, had been disappointed, thought him a fool. He had thought that when he told the old man he'd understand, would pat him on the back, realize that a job in an advisory mission was not like commanding troops in the field, that an infantry officer should always try to be with the men, had an obligation to them and to himself, to his profession, but the general had only shrugged, told him he was sorry. It was not wise to lose the favor of a general, even an obscure brigadier, and Harkness had tried to explain that he'd learn more on a second tour than he had on the first. He might, the general had said, and gave that cold shrug again. Well, learn he had, especially this today, although what you could not say exactly, or what use it would be.

Leyba was feeling better than he had all day, better than at any time since the last stand-down. He figured they'd had their action for a while, he could scratch this day, which left only two more to be lived through. He was even pretty sure he was going to make them. He could not say why, but for the first time in months he really believed he'd get out of it.

Which did not make him feel any more gently toward Harkness. Maybe he felt so good because Harkness was obviously shaken. Next to seeing the bastard dinged, seeing him blow his cool was the best thing he could imagine. He had already mentioned it to Blacksides and Upshaw. In fact, the only things wrong were that he was still here, and the radio was still cutting down into his shoulders.

Prissholm was horribly, terribly thirsty. The back of his throat was the consistency of stale cotton candy. He had drunk his last half canteen and would have to wait for the next break to get some water from someone. He should have filled his canteens from the earthen jars, but he had been too absorbed. Now he thought that he must not think about what had happened, it was another unreal event, another threat to his imperiled sanity, and he must not dwell on it. If he did not think about it, it would not touch him, and he'd be all right. It was like his fraternity initiation, when they had gang-banged the whore hired for the purpose, everyone very drunk, people sitting and standing in the bedroom watching. He had been very drunk and had climbed on himself finally, when there had been no graceful way left to refuse, surprised at his own potency, that he could even be potent in such a situation—degrading and ludicrous—and even during the act telling himself it did not matter unless he let it matter.

And Burns, the good medic, rolled himself a huge joint, a real bomber, a B-52. He needed it, the real thing, with no menthol or tobacco or filter to cut its effect. He had tried to slip back into his daydream, reconjure the Loach and the house on the cliff and the surf, but he was too tired to make his mind go the way he wanted it to, to force out the woman and the cutting and the slapping, the defeat, so he reached into the side of his bag where he kept morphine and his cache of grass and papers, and stopped on an especially firm clump of rice, standing in plain sight of Harkness and Top Sergeant Himmlemann and anyone else who wanted to look, not really giving a damn, and rolled his bomber, and lit up. No one even cast a curious glance.

Vietnam vet and winner of the National Book Award, Tim O'Brien provides a number of sharp vignettes. This one hurts, even as it shows we were often blind to our cruelty and its costs.

Tim O'Brien

The Man at the Well

He was just an old man, an old Vietnamese farmer. His hair was white, and he was somewhere over seventy years, stooped and hunched from work in the paddies, his spine bent into a permanent, calcified arc. He was blind. His eyes were huge and empty, glistening like aluminum under the sun, cauterized and burnt out. But the old man got around.

In March we came to his well. He stood and smiled while we used the water. He laughed when we laughed. To be ingratiating he said, "Good water for good GI's." Whenever there was occasion, he repeated the phrase.

Some children came to the well, and one of them, a little girl with black hair and hoops of steel through her ears, took the old fellow's hand, helping him about. The kids giggled at our naked bodies. A boy took a soldier's rifle from out of the mud and wiped it and stacked it against a tree, and the old man smiled.

Alpha Company decided to spend the day in the old man's village. We lounged inside his hut, and when resupply brought down cold beer and food, we ate and wasted away the day. The kids administered professional back rubs, chopping and stretching and pushing our blood. They eyed our C rations, and the old blind man helped when he could.

When the wind stopped and the flies became bothersome, we went to the well again. We showered, and the old fellow helped, dipping into the well and yanking up buckets of water and sloshing it over our heads and backs and bellies. The kids watched him wash us. The day was as hot and peaceful as a day can be.

The blind old farmer was showering one of the men. A blustery and stupid soldier, blond hair and big belly, picked up a carton of milk and from fifteen feet away hurled it, for no reason, aiming at the old man and striking him flush in the face. The carton burst, milk spraying on the old man's temples and into his cataracts. He hunched forward, rocking precariously and searching for balance. He dropped his bucket, and his hands went to his eyes then dropped loosely to his thighs. His blind gaze fixed straight ahead, at the stupid soldier's feet. His tongue moved a little, trying to get at the cut and tasting the blood and milk. No one moved to help. The kids were quiet. The old man's eyes did a funny trick, almost rolling out of his head, out of sight. He was motionless, and finally he smiled. He picked up the bucket and with the ruins of goodness spread over him, perfect gore, he dunked into the well and came up with water, and he showered a soldier. The kids watched.

To be sure, the Americans made their mistakes in Vietnam, but more than a few really did try to win the hearts and minds of the people. Charles Anderson, former marine lieutenant, tells the story of one man who understood that the real war was for the support of the Vietnamese people.

Charles R. Anderson

Hearts and Minds

Whether in wartime or peacetime, the arrival of new men in a battalion hardly provokes notice among those already "cranked into" the unit and its routines. Cursory greetings and pro forma offers are made—". . . just call me Jack . . . let me know if you need anything"—and jobs are resumed. That's why I was surprised to get so much attention from one of the established staff officers. I first ran into him on the road between the supply shed and the brig.

"Hi, I'm Bill Thomas. You just report in?"

"That's right. My name's Anderson. What's your job?"

"I'm the S-5."

"What's that?" I asked.

"Come on over to my office and I'll show you."

So I went, but on the way I couldn't help but steal a few sideward glances at Thomas. He was a stark contrast to the image of the marine officer I had gotten used to seeing in stateside training, the image I had been ordered to emulate. When the PR boys in Headquarters Marine Corps look for a model for their recruiting posters and brochures, they quickly pass by officers like Bill Thomas. He had a concave chest and an oversize stomach, and his head never did support a marine cover the way the Uniform Recommendation Committee in Washington intended. But Thomas knew much more about 3d MPs and Vietnam, and so I listened.

"Yeah, this battalion's got a little different organization than outfits back in the World. We've got the standard four sections, you know, S-1 Personnel, S-2 Intelligence, S-3 Operations, and S-4 Logistics. Over here we've got another one: S-5 Civil Affairs. That's me."

Once in Thomas's office I forgot all about public relations imagery. He had the same blowtorch plywood paneling I had seen in every other office in 3d MPs, but most of his was covered with maps and charts. Thomas led me to a large white board overlaid with plastic. On the board was a grid pattern. Down the left side were printed the names of five villages in the vicinity of our compound. Across the top of the board were written the dates for the next two weeks. In about one-third of the date squares there were written project commitments: "17 JUL-MEDCAP, 19 JUL-Begin Well Const., 24 JUL-Deliver Plywood," and so on.

Thomas said nothing to the two men playing blackjack on a desk in the corner and launched right into his briefing.

"Recently we've been running three missions a week to these first three villages. The other two are controlled by Charlie most of the time but we'll be getting back in there pretty soon. The chiefs of the first two vills are rotten corrupt but usually on our side. The third one tries to be honest most of the time and is with us for the most part. The other two chiefs are rotten corrupt and on Charlie's side but they'll take anything they can get out of us."

"What kind of things do you give them?" I asked.

"We've dug a few wells, built a few storage sheds and school classrooms; sometimes we give out food, clothes, and toys for the kids when we can get them. . . ."

"Where do you get the stuff?"

"Some of it comes from Flick, things like cement and grain. Some comes from charities and churches back in the States. But most comes from our own compound here, like used wood. Some of our best stuff comes from the mess hall. Know what it is?"

"No," I said.

"Garbage."

"Is that right?"

"That's right. Just plain old American garbage. Last week I took five hundred pounds of it out to this vill here. Farmers use it for their pigs. Fattens up those porkers faster than anything they got. Unless the hogs got tapeworms, which about half of them do. And the chickens they got . . . you ever seen a Vietnamese chicken?"

"Not yet," I said.

"I laughed my ass off first time I saw one! Look like they're naked—no feathers, real skinny, and they hardly ever give any eggs. But I got a line on some decent feed. We're making progress but it comes slow in this country, it comes slow."

"That's what I hear," I said, looking at the board. "What's a MEDCAP? . . . up there after July 17," I asked.

"That's Medical Civic Action Program. Once a week we take a corpsman out to a vill and give free treatment for whatever we find. There's a lot of skin infections, simple things like that. Villagers can't figure out why they don't heal up but they keep taking baths in the same streams they piss and shit in. We teach them how to use soap but the next time we go back we see the same new bars we gave them. If they got some serious illness or need an operation, we bring them into a hospital in Da Nang. Flick is building a children's hospital over in their compound. Maybe you saw it when you checked in."

"I saw a sign about it," I said.

"Well, you gotta be an optimist to do this job. Most guys around here think the Vietnamese are worthless but I think all they need from us is a little technology and help in setting things up and they'll be on their own in no time. The Vietnamese are hard-working people, I'll tell you. Why, do you know these people can work all day on only two small bowls of rice?"

"No, I didn't know that," I said.

"That's right. Yeah, I think they'll be on their own in no time . . . if we can get the VC off their back and give them a little help setting things up . . . it's just a matter of time."

"Well, I hope so," I said. "Is everything you've just explained what they call the Civic Action Program?"

"Oh, then you've heard of this back in the World?"

"Yes, I read something about it somewhere," I said.

"This is it. At least that's what III MAF and I call it. Other people call it other things. The reporters call it 'the other war.' The embassy calls it 'pacification.' And the politicians call it 'winning hearts and minds.'"

The Civic Action Program answered the crying need in South Vietnam for effective communication and cooperation between Americans and Vietnamese on the local level. CAP was administered by III MAF, the headquarters of all marine units in Vietnam. In its formative period, CAP enjoyed the support of the III MAF commander, General Lew Walt, a semilegendary figure in the Marine Corps at the time and one of the few American field commanders to realize the need for unconventional programs in an unconventional war. The American Embassy and the army used other programs to address the need for assistance at the local level. The basic unit of the Civic Action Program was the CAP team, consisting of fourteen enlisted marines and one navy medical corpsman. CAP team members had the expertise and motivation for working with Vietnamese civilians that regular infantrymen lacked. They were volunteers, which eliminated the chances of

atrocities resulting from the frustration other Americans frequently felt when working with Vietnamese. At least one man
in each CAP team was fluent in the language, and everyone
could speak a few necessary words and phrases. All team
members had civilian work experience that could be applied
directly to the agricultural economy of the rural Vietnamese
village, things like farming, livestock breeding, construction,
and small engine repair.

As soon as Vietnamese villagers realized the value of CAP
marines—the teams had to convince many that they were not
just another gang of plundering foreigners—the teams were
successful. CAP projects were there for all to see—schools,
clinics, roads, wells, pumps, and generators. Better strains of
rice were planted and larger yields were harvested. Better
breeds of pigs and chickens gave more pork and eggs. Farmers
were taught how to form cooperatives, and bought more grain
and livestock. Villagers had more to eat than at any time since
the war in the villages began back in the late 1940s. Most welcome of all to the villagers on a day-to-day basis was the security provided by the marines. CAP team members were
armed, of course, and had been trained as infantrymen. Most
importantly, the marines stayed in their assigned villages
twenty-four hours a day, unlike both the Viet Cong and the
Americans/South Vietnamese. After working with the villagers during the day, they guarded roads and trails and pa-
trolled around their village at night.

The most striking measure of the success of the Civic Action Program was its effect on the marines' enemy, the Viet
Cong. CAP was applied in villages to the west and south of
Da Nang, an area which had a population of about 260 thousand. In the same area an estimated 30 thousand Viet Cong
were active; yet during the one year 1967–68 the VC managed
to recruit only 170 men, not nearly enough to replace losses.
Villagers also began withholding rice from the Viet Cong and
telling their CAP teams when to expect VC attacks. On the
American side, III MAF staff officers proudly pointed to the

efficiency of CAP, and with more than enough justification. The entire Combined Action Program consisted of 15 officers and 1,200 enlisted men. The cost of maintaining CAP was only one-fifth the cost of the same number of American infantrymen engaged in search and destroy or support duties, and only one-third the cost of the South Vietnamese Rural Development Program. The Civic Action Program was also less expensive and much more effective than the U.S. Agency for International Development's pacification program with its generous budget and staff of thousands of experts.

In spite of its obvious success and value to the war effort, CAP labored amid a continuing storm of controversy. Opposition came not only from the Viet Cong but all other directions as well: the South Vietnamese, the American Embassy, even General Westmoreland's headquarters. There was no objection to the idea of helping Vietnamese villagers while at the same time fighting the VC and North Vietnamese. All Americans in Vietnam agreed on the need for that. The objection to CAP was based on the way the marines went about their mission: CAP was an all-marine show; it did not employ any South Vietnamese officials. According to U.S. Embassy policy, the pacification program was supposed to work like this. U.S. Agency for International Development (USAID) personnel, in consultation with U.S. Army advisors in the field, determined what was needed for South Vietnamese development. Most needs were in the areas of food, grain, medicines, and construction materials and equipment. After being ordered through the U.S. Embassy, the goods were sent to Vietnam by plane or ship. The needed food and equipment were to be received at Vietnamese ports and airfields by Vietnamese, then distributed through the Vietnamese bureaucracy, down the organization chart from province chief to district chief to village chief and finally to the hamlet chief, who would see that the people who needed the goods got them.

That was the prescribed, on-paper system. The idea behind it was that while the South Vietnamese, with, of course, mas-

sive assistance from the Americans, were countering the Viet
Cong in the field, they would at the same time be developing a
modern, efficient governmental administration capable of
reaching all corners of the country. In practice, however, the
advisory/USAID concept did not work, though few officials
and advisors would admit it. By sending USAID food and
equipment through the thoroughly corrupt bureaucracy of our
official ally, USAID presented South Vietnamese admin-
istrators and generals with what proved an irresistible tempta-
tion. They stole USAID shipments from docks and
warehouses, sold it to the black market in South Vietnam (or
even Hong Kong), and put the profits in foreign banks. Despite the gross corruption, which everyone knew had a crip-
pling effect on the war effort, the American Embassy and the
army refused to bypass the crooked South Vietnamese administration. To do so, went the official argument, would be to
indicate mistrust of our ally and that would amount to bad
public relations in the host country!

Allowing the whole scandal to continue was the complicity
of most U.S. Army advisors. Few ever blew the whistle on
the corrupt South Vietnamese. To do so would provoke a
complaint from the South Vietnamese command to General
Westmoreland's headquarters that the advisor was not "coop-
erating." The complaint would usually lead to a quick reas-
signment with a bad fitness report, which would ruin the
advisor's career. So, for the sake of good public relations with
one of the least competent governments of the twentieth century, billions of dollars' worth of American food and equipment was turned over to a gang of corrupt leaders who
became rich by selling it on the black market, where much of
it was bought by our enemies, the Viet Cong, and North Vietnamese, who, of course, used it in the field against American
forces. And that was verified by the discovery of much American medicine and equipment in Viet Cong and North Vietnamese positions overrun by American units in the field.

Fortunately the marines were never as concerned as the

embassy/USAID people about public relations. Early in the war the marines decided that if CAP was to succeed, it would have to bypass the South Vietnamese bureaucracy. The result was a lot of bureaucratic infighting in headquarters offices, but one of the few successes of the American effort in the field. Throughout its brief existence CAP was subjected to continuing criticism. CAP was accused of working outside established channels and thereby undermining the U.S.-South Vietnam alliance. CAP leaders were accused of being con-men who juggled statistics to make themselves look good. And anyone who didn't like the marines' program but couldn't think of a specific charge simply said CAP was "counter-productive." But the success of CAP could not be denied, and many an embassy, USAID, and army spokesman had to endure the same embarrassing question from visiting congressmen and reporters: "Why can't you guys conduct your pacification as well as the marines with their Civic Action Program?"

Third MPs was not, of course, a CAP unit. But III MAF policy directed that every marine unit, whatever its primary mission, conduct CAP projects according to its capabilities. Since we had our own compound, and mounting search and destroy operations was not our mission, we were expected to conduct continuing Civic Action projects in five villages. Our S-5 was directed to give special attention to construction projects and agricultural production. To help modernize the five villages, S-5 was allotted one lieutenant, one lance corporal, one Vietnamese interpreter, one medical corpsman for only one afternoon a week, no money, and the oldest jeep in the motor pool. Anyone capable of believing that was an adequate allocation of manpower and resources was also capable of believing in Santa Claus.

Fortunately for our battalion's Civic Action effort, the S-5 officer, Lt. Bill Thomas, wore his commission better than most who carried one. He personified very faithfully an admonition from training: "Do your best in every assignment, whether you like it or not." Thomas had not looked for his job as S-5 officer when he came to Vietnam. Like most officers in 3d MPs, he was trained for the infantry. On his way to the war, he had expected and looked forward to joining a company in the bush. But like many other junior officers in 3d MPs, he was sidetracked into the rear upon his arrival in Da Nang. When he learned he would have to spend six months in the rear before he could transfer out, he asked for the S-5 job. He soon became seriously interested in the Vietnamese people and forgot about going to the bush.

Thomas's full-time assistant, Lance Corporal Farquar, was at first indifferent to his S-5 assignment. He had been sent to Thomas after he had questioned once too often the wisdom of his first sergeant's orders. Assignment to S-5 for him was punishment, and that's the way most of the other junior enlisted men viewed the job, which involved working close to a culture vastly different from their own.

Bill Thomas faithfully personified another admonition from training, "Take care of your men before yourself." Others in the battalion soon noticed that characteristic of Thomas, and our S-5 was more effective than it might otherwise have been but for its considerate officer-in-charge.

One advantage of Thomas's character was that it attracted unofficial help from a few corners of the battalion normally unrelated to S-5. As soon as word got around that Thomas was not Machiavelli reincarnate and was intent on doing more than pleasing the CO, a few junior enlisted men began hanging around the office and volunteering to go along on the weekly trips to villages in the area, "just to see what was happening," as they explained when discovered. Usually after a few such visits, lieutenants or first sergeants from the companies would notice their missing men and drop into S-5 for a surprise visit to pull stray men back to primary duties. But two kept coming around to help Thomas, and their interest served to pull Lance Corporal Farquar out of most of his indifference. One of the part-timers even learned enough Vietnamese to make himself understood by villagers on a few subjects.

There was another advantage to Thomas's attitude, one that helped make up for the lack of supplies given S-5. With neither budget nor requisition forms signed by the colonel, Thomas and Farquar could do no more than beg and barter to get the most basic supplies for their projects—a few bags of cement, a few sheets of plywood, or a trailer to carry it in. For several reasons, most of which were based on a disdain of the Vietnamese, most senior sergeants and officers who had access to any supplies were reluctant to give any of it to Thomas for S-5 projects.

Thomas and Farquar quickly devised a method of bypassing the brick wall they so often encountered, a method which drew heavily on the goodwill Thomas had built up among the junior enlisted men. He would visit the targeted sergeant or officer a few minutes before lunch or dinner and make his pro forma appeal for supplies. When the opposition began his own pro forma recitation of the reasons he couldn't simply give away the precious government property with which he was entrusted by the president, the Congress, and Colonel Palooka, Thomas would glance at his watch, notice it was time to go to the mess hall, and usher his victim out the door. Lance Corporal Farquar, who had been watching from behind a nearby hooch for the opportune moment, would then breeze into the office or supply shed so recently vacated by the authority figure and receive, from a fellow junior enlisted functionary who liked Thomas, whatever it was S-5 needed.

That system worked, but Thomas never stopped hoping for the day when he wouldn't have to use a method so devious, the day when the rest of the battalion would come to see the value of S-5 and give it the support he knew it deserved.

With the necessary supplies safely hidden in the back seat of the jeep or under a tent in the trailer, Thomas and Farquar were ready for the villages. Our villages varied in size, distance from the 3d MP compound, and degree of sympathy to what our S-5 was trying to do. The largest village was home for 2,500 farmers and fishermen; the smallest, for 700. The farthest was eight miles away; the nearest, two miles.

Inhabitants of the friendliest village greeted every S-5 visit by offering Thomas and Farquar the cutest village girls and a private hooch equipped with two thatch mattresses so the great round-eyed bearers of modern ways and gadgets might enjoy an afternoon's respite from their heavy duties of enlightening the darker corners of the planet. Thomas always declined such offers, but only with the greatest reluctance, he later confessed in the club. Farquar cursed his boss's declinations with mumbled expletives the rest of the afternoon.

Inhabitants of the least friendly village greeted every S-5 visit by running inside their hooches, holding doors shut, and making gestures which our interpreter told us meant "Don't talk to us—go away." But even in the two unfriendly villages on his itinerary Thomas usually succeeded in getting the villagers to accept something from his trailer, probably because he had learned early in his tour which brands of American cigarettes and whiskey could melt the resistance of each village chief.

The most disturbing phenomenon Thomas discovered about the reactions of villagers to our efforts was that a considerable number were sympathetic to what we Americans were trying to do, but at the same time they hated the Saigon government and its rapacious army. Since peasants were usually extremely reluctant to complain to foreigners about oppressive authority figures, due to fear of reprisals, the willingness of the villagers to report such feelings to our interpreters indicated not only a serious situation in their lives, but the presence of a definite threat to one of the most basic strategic assumptions of the American presence in Vietnam, the assumption that the Americans should remain allied to Saigon throughout the conflict.

Thomas felt the divided feelings of many villagers were important enough to be reported to commanders and policy planners all the way to the White House. But such facts did not fit anyone's neatly constructed model of what was believed to be really happening in the Vietnam of 1968, so no one listened very closely to what he reported. The few commanders and advisors who did hear what Thomas had to say declined to pass the information up the line. From that time on, the gap between village Vietnam and Saigon, the gap which would eventually prove fatal to the efforts of our S-5 in the Da Nang area, would continue to widen until the time when it could be closed was gone forever.

Subsequent events have shown that not only was the same gap present and widening in other parts of South Vietnam, but a second was operative as well—that between Saigon and Washington. The relentless widening of those two gaps would, only a few years after Bill Thomas and his interpreters identified them, prove fatal to the entire American effort in Vietnam.

Bill Thomas and his tiny section worked under a pervasive atmosphere of opposition to everything the Civic Action Program stood for, and that is why he had gone out of his way to explain his job when I arrived—he was looking for allies in his uphill struggle. The most chauvinistic in the battalion considered it a criminal waste of American manpower and resources to try to help "backward" and "ungrateful" people like the Vietnamese. The most charitable considered Thomas and his staff a collection of naive do-gooders who were only kidding themselves if they thought they were doing anything worthwhile.

In between those extremes were views on cultural distance ("The Vietnamese have their ways and we have ours and they'll never mix them together . . . who was it said 'East is East and West is West and the two will never get together?' ") and the unseemly appearance of some S-5 projects ("It ain't

manly to pass out soap and candy to women and kids—I was
trained to fight!")

Those whose minds were untroubled by more traditional
views of cultural identity, race, and masculinity had what they
felt were more practical reasons for withholding support for
S-5. Depending on their attitude about a military career, members of the battalion considered S-5 either ineffective or dangerous. Those who would not remain in the military thought
S-5 was simply not reaching the Vietnamese. Since the Vietnamese did not understand what the Americans were trying to
do through S-5, these men reasoned, the success of CAP was a
good deal less certain than that of other projects. Other assignments were more interesting than one destined for failure, they
felt. Those who would remain in the military considered S-5 a
dead-end assignment. It was a threat to one's future promotions because it didn't do anything military—it was for civilians. Far better to have an "action" S-2 or S-3 assignment
entered in one's record book. But those in S-5 labored on,
determined to show the Vietnamese that America was trying
to do things other than burning and killing.

About every two months Bill Thomas would give a briefing to all officers and staff NCOs in the battalion on recent S-5
activities and Vietnamese-American cultural differences. The
"suggestion" for such briefings came from the highest Marine
Corps authority in the country, III Marine Amphibious Force.
A "suggestion" from a higher headquarters is always received
as an order, and so the briefings occurred. Our colonel very
professionally covered his true feeling about the "suggestion"
with his official approval, and his dead silence at the briefings.
At the first briefing I saw, Thomas began by showing his S-5
calendar and an area map, and explaining what projects were
scheduled, where the recipient villages were located, and what
the village chiefs' attitudes toward his efforts were. With that
completed he then began an explanation of the different con-
cepts of time held by Americans and Vietnamese, and how
their concept affected the actions of the latter. Thomas's au-

dience accepted the first part of his presentation as they had accepted countless other military briefings with visual aids before it—with less than their full attention and with frequent glances at watches to wonder when the preachy college kid before them would finish so they could get on to more important things at the club.

But when Thomas turned his briefing from a mechanical presentation of numbers and dates to an explanation of one facet of Vietnamese culture, the mood of his audience changed from somnolent acceptance to hostile attention. Slouching bodies sat up straight, arms were folded rigidly across chests, mouths turned downward into frowns, creases came across foreheads. Those in the audience came to look more like bricks in a wall than people in a row. Their posture of resistance was a perfectly faithful manifestation of their attitude of resistance to what their S-5 was telling them.

The staff NCOs and officers in Thomas's audience had very definite ideas about what the words "civilization" and "culture" meant, and about who had those things and who did not. Civilization and culture to these men meant a combination of faith in the latest technology, a desire for material goods, acceptance of Christian moral standards, and a belief in the superiority of white-skinned peoples over yellow-, brown-, and black-skinned peoples. The Vietnamese were found deficient in all categories and were therefore dismissed as lesser beings who did not deserve anyone's tolerance, understanding or sympathy. The cultural attitude of most members of 3d MPs was more appropriate to sixteenth-century builders of colonial empires than twentieth-century warrior-technologists involved in bridging cultural gaps.

The men in the audience believed there was really only one civilization worthy of the title, and it was their own American civilization. Any people who failed to see the superiority of American culture, and declined to emulate it immediately and completely, thereby admitted their own lack of culture and forfeited the privilege of associating with Americans. Any sug-

gestion that the Vietnamese had any culture at all was taken as
not only a lie but an insult to one's own American culture as
well. That was exactly what Thomas was doing and his audience began firing questions right away. "Why can't these
damn people even use a bar of soap?" "Why are the men always holding hands—are they all queer?" "Why the hell don't
they stand and fight the VC instead of running away?"

This was not the first time Thomas had faced this same
hostile audience. He had learned several months before that the
questioners were not interested in understanding the Vietnamese, so they had no desire to really explore such issues.
They were only interested in reinforcing their hurried conclusions based on incomplete observation, and in making it
clear to their S-5 that no amount of logic or reasoning on his
part would shake those conclusions. Thomas didn't even try to
answer their charges; he simply deflected them and moved into
his conclusion.

There was considerable irony in the situation between S-5
and the battalion of which it was a part, as there so often is in
the records of failed projects. Career military members, those
who held positions of responsibility in the 3d MPs and every
other unit in Vietnam, were among the most virulent and
emotional communist-haters. The Civic Action Program was
designed to separate the Viet Cong from the civilian population on which it so heavily depended. The communist-haters
never saw that in denying CAP their support they were giving
passive support to their communist enemy, the Viet Cong.

The organization of the S-5 Section was one of the most
ironic features of the entire concept of the Civic Action Program. Considering the many activities implicit in the mission
given S-5, and the great importance attached to that mission
by commanders at the highest levels and by policy planners,
secretaries of state and presidents, S-5 should have been one of
the three largest sections, along with S-1 and S-4, on the staff
of every rear-echelon battalion and regiment in Vietnam. Instead, it was always the smallest. Because of their mission of

service or support, rear-echelon units had no need for large S-2 and S-3 sections. Units charged with finding and fighting the enemy—the infantry units in the field—needed, and had, large combat intelligence and operations sections. But most S-2 and S-3 sections in the rear were just as large as those in the field. The reason for this situation was to be found in the fact of excess manpower in the rear—nonessential men were frequently "dumped" into S-2 and S-3.

From the point of view of the rear-echelon unit commander, the presence of inflated S-2 and S-3 staffs was desirable. The local commander's first responsibility, of course, was to maintain the security and effectiveness of his unit. In a war without a front, commanders everywhere had to be ready at all times. One never knew when or where the VC would strike. In such an environment, serving the needs of civilians in the area was a secondary consideration. However, from the point of view of senior commanders in Vietnam and Washington and American policy planners, such priorities and headquarters structures were not only undesirable but represented a serious compromise of stated policy. In the structure of rear-echelon unit staffs, the spirit of the Civic Action Program was effectively nullified.

Perhaps the most shocking irony of all is that no one, except Thomas, ever thought to ask any Vietnamese what they thought of the program designed to assist the Vietnamese. The very people for whom the Civic Action Program was conducted were completely closed out of the planning and evaluation of the program. Every day three translator/interpreters, all of course fluent in English, came into the compound and one of them went along on the weekly MEDCAP missions to villages in the area, but no one except Thomas ever asked for their views on the effectiveness of such missions. Thus, no one outside the S-5 staff ever knew how far off the mark the Vietnamese considered many of the CAP projects. Thomas never succeeded in having Vietnamese responses to his questions included in the monthly CAP reports battalion sent to III MAF headquarters. If he had succeeded, I'm sure General Walt would have recognized the potential for subversion of his policies in giving Vietnamese children toys that had no relevance to their culture—ghoulish Frankenstein dolls—or in giving adults food that had been judged unfit for use in American mess halls. But the battalion command was more interested in reporting numbers today than in building understanding and trust tomorrow. They did only what was necessary to fulfil an on-paper commitment from a higher headquarters.

In that entire battalion you could count the people who believed in and were willing to work for CAP on one hand that was missing two fingers. And that situation was not restricted to 3d MPs. Unhappily, it was the norm among American units in Vietnam. All but a few, in 3d MPs and in almost every other American unit in the war, failed to see the tremendous potential of an effective Civic Action Program. It definitely could have increased understanding between Americans and Vietnamese, and thereby reduced the number of atrocities so many American troops committed against Vietnamese civilians, and it possibly could have shortened the war. Both Americans and Vietnamese suffered longer than they otherwise would have.

All S-5 officers in Vietnam, like Bill Thomas, badly needed support to make the Civic Action Program justify the humanitarian phrases in which its mission was described. But they rarely got it, and so in most corners of the war CAP was too little and too late. Most Vietnamese continued to believe that Americans were nothing more than greedy, pushy, loud-mouthed sex maniacs. And most Americans continued to believe the Vietnamese were nothing more than uncivilized, subhuman beggars. What began in the early years of the war as cross-cultural meetings, which both Vietnamese and Americans looked forward to, quickly deteriorated into awkward pro forma gatherings attended out of duty, and, finally, cultural collisions in which there was progressively less interest in creating understanding.

THE
WORLD

Rest & Recreation (R & R) in an exotic locale like Hawaii, Hong Kong, Australia, or Singapore was anticipated, rehearsed, and yearned for in the mind of every man serving in Vietnam. R & R was an opportunity to sightsee, shop, drink, eat good food, carouse, and, most important, enjoy the company of women. More than a few servicemen returned to Vietnam with memories of a one-week romance.

Stan Goff

R & R in Hong Kong

A really tremendous thing happened to me in January of 1969. I was getting an R & R. I had more money then than ever before in my life, about five hundred dollars, cold cash. I was very excited and packed up my little items ready to go. At the R & R center at Cam Ranh, they had all these countries where you could go. A sergeant came and told us about these countries, giving us the whole breakdown, the cultures, everything. He told us about venereal disease; that was the big thing. "Now, we gotta talk about VD. I know you guys have been without women. I know the first thing you're going to do—those of you that go that way. Only deal with the girls that have a medical card."

All my life I'd seen movies with Clark Gable and Vivien Leigh about Hong Kong. So I said, "Well, I'm going to go there."

I never will forget approaching Hong Kong. Suddenly I saw a huge cliff emerging from the ocean, like a city sitting on the edge of an island. The water was beating up the edge of this rock cliff. And then all of a sudden, we were landing. I don't know how the pilot actually landed; I never did see a strip, myself. We were there. Wow! I was getting off and my head was about twenty feet high.

I heard the guys talking about what they were going to do, but I didn't make any friends on that flight. We got on a bus and they took us to a large auditorium that was part of the city municipal center. They told us *again* about VD and gave us the names of good hotels. So it was not a bad orientation. They were doing it to help us, because they told us, "Once you're out there, you're on your own. If you get your heads knocked in, killed, anything . . ." Then he finally said, "Okay, now, we'll turn you loose." When he said that, boy, chairs rolled over, guys climbed all over themselves.

I hailed a taxi. I told this guy the name of the hotel that the instructor had recommended. It was a moderate hotel, not very expensive, but very, very clean, a very stately type of building. I admired the Chinese for the quality of their workmanship. I looked at the table, the hard wood floors—everything was handmade.

After a bath and some tea, I was back out on the street and saw this place called the Old Savoy Club. I got to Hong Kong thinking about Clark Gable and Vivien Leigh. Now I thought, wow, Billie Holiday used to sing at a club called the Old Savoy. So I walked in. Upstairs they had a lot of entertainment; downstairs at the bar was where the girls were. So I went downstairs. I was sitting there, having a drink, when mamasan approached me, "Hi, GI. You want a girl, GI? You want a girl?" I said, "Yeah, that's a good possibility." She say, "Oh, I got a girl for you, GI." She showed me one girl. She was a little skinny; I thought, not enough chest on her. Then she showed me another girl whom I didn't like at all. Then there was only one that wouldn't come or smile at me either. But she was really fine. I looked at her, and she looked at me, and then she started to take her hair down. Mama-san fussed at her in Chinese. Finally, this girl reluctantly came over.

But I said, "Naw, that's OK," and she went back. I knew she was reluctant. Then I thought, what the hell, I liked her, and told mama-san she was the one. "You want *her?*" "Yeah, I want her. What's her name?" "Suzanne."

When Suzanne appeared after about five minutes, I began asking her, "What have you heard about black GIs? It's obvious you have heard something about black GIs that is causing you not to want to meet me." She said, "Oh, no, you got me all wrong. I like everybody. I'm not prejudiced." And immediately when she said that, I knew. They weren't familiar with that word; somebody had crowded that idea into her mind.

"Oh, you buy me a drink?"

So she got off the subject. I bought her a drink and we started talking. She said, "You like music?" I said, "I love music." She went over to the juke box and played a song by Esther Phillips—her first big hit, a love ballad. That became our theme song. We always played it, she and I.

We got to drinking. I knew nothing was in her drink, but as we drank I became more loose and canny, too; I wanted to collect my thoughts and not be anxious to let my physical desires overrule my good sense.

She said, "I'm very expensive, Stan. Can you afford me?" "Aw, come on, what do you mean, you're expensive? What are we talking about?" She said, "Oh, well—you interested?" "Sure I'm interested. Do you think I'd have you over here, talking with you? I could be down the street." She said, "OK. I go with you and we talk price in your room. You have to pay mama-san money to take me out." So I paid her five bucks just to get Suzanne out of the place.

I took her on back to my place and saw how really beautiful she was. Then I thought, wait a minute, don't get carried away and blow everything—I was getting to be a gullible mess here. She sat over on one side of the room, which pleased me. I sat back on the other side, watching her crossing and uncrossing her legs, letting me see what I wanted. We started talking about price. After a lot of dickering, we agreed on thirty dollars a night for the whole week.

It was a gentle love-making though it was all night long, very gentle, because I really took it very slow with her. I wanted it to be slow, because I wanted to it be good, to myself, as well as to her. It was a great experience. I'd heard all kinds of stories about prostitutes myself—that they had no feeling and stuff like that, and that was all bullshit.

The next morning she awoke about nine o'clock. She awoke with a start, like she didn't mean to really stay that long. She said, "Oh, nine o'clock? I've got to get home." She said, "Oh, Stan," but I knew she liked me, when she talked to me like that, and even when she stayed that long and forgot herself as Suzanne, professional prostitute, and became Suzanne, the woman. She was only about twenty, my age. I was very impressed with her.

When she was ready to go, she said, "You're a real nice guy, Stan." I said, "Well, will I be able to see you tonight?" "I don't know, Stan; you don't pay me enough money, I need more money. Tonight you talked me out of what I need to get. But you're a real nice guy. If you want me, you come down there. Then I know you want me." She was serious about that, looked at me hard as she left. I thought, wow, I had to come all the way to Hong Kong to fall in love! She was getting to me, just that quick. I didn't want any other woman then. She had spoiled me.

So I crashed, and couldn't even fall asleep. Seven o'clock, I couldn't hardly wait. I knew I didn't want to go there too early, so I made myself stay away until about seven-thirty or eight o'clock. But when I got near the Old Savoy, I almost ran to that place, I was so anxious. As I got downstairs mama-san came over and said, "Hi, GI, I heard. Suzanne called me. She likes you." I said, "Really?" I'd gone all to pieces now, waiting and waiting. She said, "I don't know where Suzanne is." I thought maybe she hadn't showed up for work or something. Finally about 9:30 P.M., like magic, I looked up and there she was, smiling just so beautifully: "Where have you been?" "Oh, I've been out—I hear you're looking for me." She got in the booth and sat right beside me and squeezed my hand.

Suzanne and I decided to party that night. I wanted her to show me Kowloon before going to my place. First she took me into plush night clubs where all the English were. There was a singer up there singing Dinah Shore-like tunes, sort of boring. We ate dinner and drank a little wine. She said, "You don't like, huh?" I said, "Oh, no, it's OK." She said, "No, you don't like. I take you to other club where there is a band." But this place really didn't have a lot of blacks either. I thought I would see other black GIs. Then she said, "I know. I know where to take you, Stan."

We went to a disco where I saw nothing but dark-skinned Chinese girls, and it blew my mind. My mouth fell open. I had never seen any dark-skinned Chinese girls. They were really getting down. I saw other black GIs. "Hey, what's happening, man? What's going on?" I was really coming loose. "Why didn't you take me here first?" She was giddy with laughter now, "Oh, I just wanted to save the best for last." But I thought to myself that she wasn't comfortable here. She was used to going to the other places. But she sat there. That was when I knew Suzanne liked me. She was so light-skinned, not white, but her skin was very pale. I could see the other girls were cutting her down. It was like they knew her or something. They were just staring at her, hard. I was having a good time, but she said, "We go, huh?" I started to say, "What do you mean? We just got here." We had only been there for an hour, and things were really getting bopping. I smelled a little smoke, and I thought maybe I might be able to angle around here, but since she was talking about going, we left. She really made love to me that night.

The next morning she asked about more money. She said,

"Listen, Stan, I guess you know I've agreed to go ahead and stay with you all week. Yeah, I stay with you, Stan. I don't like the money that you're paying me. Why don't you pay me more?" I said, "No, Suzanne. There's no way I will do that. I'll pay you what we agreed every day, or at the end." She said, "OK, you pay me every day."

The next morning after I paid her, she said, "Maybe you want to be alone one night; maybe you want to go out and see some things on your own." I was sort of tired out. She was telling me she had something else to do.

I went out and started walking down the street again, looking at jade and jewelry. I passed some clubs and heard this soul music, saw a lot of cuties, but wasn't interested. I couldn't bring myself to pick out another woman. I stayed out to about eleven o'clock and suddenly remembered, Suzanne was supposed to call me.

I got back to my room and waited until the phone rang. "Stan, I'm coming over; you want to see me tonight?" "Sure, I want to see you. You know that." She stayed with me all the rest of the time, and I was very sad about leaving her. I even thought about going AWOL.

When I returned to the Nam we wrote each other for a full three months. Each time I'd write her, she'd write me back, telling me things going on in Hong Kong. Finally, I saw the opportunity for a leave. I had a good rapport with the officers, especially Major Williams. I told him I would like to have another leave.

When I got back to Hong Kong, I picked up the phone and called the Old Savoy. Before I even hung up the phone, I was down in the lobby, waiting. She came running down the sidewalk right into my arms. I just picked her up. "Oh, Stan, I'm so happy to see you here, I'm just so happy!" I was happy, too. Tears were in my eyes. She really didn't believe I was coming. She said, "You told me you were coming, I just didn't believe it."

The second time I left, it was a tear jerker. We were both

crying. She said, "I'll never see you again, I know, I know . . ." I said, "I'll write you. I'll write you and I'll send for you. But I want you to make sure that it's a decision you really want. Once you're in the states it's hard as shit to get back." She said, "I know. I want to go. I want to go." I wrote her several letters later at the Old Savoy, but never got a response. I said to myself, "Well, I guess you can hang it up, Stan." But when I got back home, sure as shooting, a big package was waiting for me at the post office, all the way from Hong Kong. It had five suits in it, half-a-dozen shirts, another half-a-dozen ties. She sent that to me, but there the story of Suzanne ended.

Some might think that the generals and the colonels had all the power, but anyone who served in Vietnam knows that the clerks often held destiny in their hands. We all knew one or two Specialist-4 Wetzels.

Thomas Parker

Troop Withdrawal—
The Initial Step

The position that Specialist 4 Wetzel had assumed in a morning formation in Southeast Asia was not one covered in Army Regulation 122-156, "Dismounted Drill," Section 2, "Inspections and Formations." It was, in fact, a position not covered in any Army Regulation and was therefore unauthorized, an infraction of the military rules for body member placement. Wetzel's legs were not shoulder-width apart "at ease," nor were they together from crotch to heel at "attention," with the toes canted outwards forming an angle of not more than forty-five degrees. Only a single leg of Wetzel's touched the ground at all, while the other was elevated flamingo-like behind him. And each time inspecting officer First Lieutenant Ernest Bauer clicked his heels in a left face in front of one of the men standing at "attention" in Wetzel's platoon, Wetzel clapped his hands in a short burst of praise.

Men to his right and left glanced at Wetzel out of the corners of their eyes, some with disdain, others with amusement, all, however, wondering what 1st Lt Bauer's reaction would be to Wetzel's nonmilitary behavior, to such an undisguised flouting of an officer's authority by an enlisted man.

Wetzel himself wondered how Bauer would react. Along with the clapping and his lack of "attention," would Bauer also ignore the tarnished brass belt buckle, the boots that had taken on the color of the hundreds of things that Wetzel had kicked, tripped over, and stepped into since the last inspection; would Bauer, for his own sake, for his own protection, pass Wetzel by without a word? It was a fair possibility. Wetzel had calculated that, despite Bauer's learning disabilities, by this, the third week of Bauer's conditioning, he would have caught on. The officer clicked his heels in front of Wetzel, looked him over, and, with a queasy smile, clicked his heels again and went on to the next man. Wetzel was pleased; it seemed that his Pavlovian experiment with Bauer was finally succeeding.

Lately, Bauer had been struck down by an epidemic of shots. Following some reprimand to Sp4 Wetzel, who was in charge of Company Personnel, his official shot record would be lost and he would once again have to undergo the full battery of inoculations specified in AR 134-161, "Health in the Sub-Tropics." In the last month alone, Bauer had had sufficient immunization to guarantee the enduring good health of a sperm whale.

Wetzel's antagonism toward Bauer was not an immature one. It had been nurtured over the past year, growing through infancy, childhood, and adolescence, and finally reaching adulthood as their fifth month together in Vietnam was about to end. It was an antagonism which germinated from Wetzel's experiences with Bauer at Fort Polk, Louisiana, where the two of them had gone through Basic Combat Training together, forced by circumstance to be "buddies," communally eating sand and dirt, drinking rain, sleeping on rocks, and following impossible trails at double time to get to useless objectives, where, if they got there fast enough, they could take a five-minute-long "ten-minute break," to sit in the snow and smoke and fart to keep each other warm.

About three weeks into Basic, Wetzel realized with impassive understanding that he and Bauer were star-crossed. There, in an olive-drab mural of arms and legs, he among 250 men would run a hundred yards into the hand-to-hand combat sand pit, where, by the rules, the arbitrary man standing to his left would be his opponent for the lesson. Wetzel would turn and, without a single prayed-for exception, there would be Bauer glaring at him, frothing from the run, eager to try out a new twist of the rear-takedown-and-strangle. When Wetzel was the "aggressor," he took it very easy, dummying the kidney punches, letting the "enemy" fall gently to the ground, and then applying a minimum amount of pressure to the throat and larynx. But then Bauer was the aggressor, smashing his fist into Wetzel's kidneys, taking him down so Wetzel would hit the sand like a sack of ballast, and applying sufficient pressure to the throat and larnyx so that Wetzel's eyes would bug, his lips would begin to turn purple and the color would disappear from beneath his fingernails.

Also, in bayonet drill, prefaced by a card shuffle of 250 men counting off, calling out numbers, where men whose numbers equaled twice plus six the square root of each other became partners, it was always Bauer's number that would fit Wetzel's equation. Wetzel, when he performed as aggressor in the long-thrust-hold-and-parry-horizontal-butt-stroke, thrust short, parried half-heartedly, and the horizontal swing of his weapon was a good two feet away from Bauer's head. Bauer, true to form, as aggressor, made incisions into Wetzel's web-belt, parried so zealously that Wetzel's weapon dropped from his hands to the ground, and performed a horizontal-butt-stroke with such gusto that the sand embedded in the heel of Bauer's stock would scratch Wetzel's nose.

But the greatest single contribution to Wetzel's growing antagonism toward Bauer was made by their Mexican drill in-

structor—a man whose name started with "F" and ended with
"o," whose name no living man could pronounce, but whose
name was shortened and simplified out of desperation by the
men in his platoon to Sergeant Frito—who matched Bauer and
Wetzel as bunkmates and buddies. It was a match that forced
complete responsibility for the other man, a match which en-
tailed making bunks together and making sure your buddy
was dressed in time and wearing the right gear. It was a per-
verse marriage between men who never shared anything sacred in their nine weeks together other than air, water, and
cigarettes and the fact that neither of them had been circum-
cised.

It became increasingly evident to Wetzel as Basic painfully
dragged on, that Bauer had something going with Frito.
Whenever anything had to be done for your buddy, Wetzel
seemed to be doing it: cleaning Bauer's weapon, taking notes
for classes Bauer missed, making Bauer's bunk, polishing
Bauer's brass. Bauer cleaned his own weapon only once during Basic and that was in front of the entire company as a
demonstration. "It was," said Sgt Frito, "the cleanest weapon
in five platoons."

During range fire for record, Bauer was in sick bay, but
nevertheless led the company qualifying as "expert." While it
was unlikely that squinty-eyed Sgt Frito could even see as far
as 350 meters, much less hit a target the size of a large man
perched at that distance, it was nevertheless true, unless there
was something that Frito had going with the cardboard silhouette as well.

So it seemed to Wetzel that truly, Bauer's trophy for soldier of the training cycle, Bauer's medal for M-16 firing, and
Bauer's commission had been a mistake, the result of logical
fallacy like so much else he knew existed in the Army. While
death may have been a great leveler, leveling all men to zero,
the Army leveled live men to an IQ of 85. Halfway through
Basic, Wetzel resigned himself to sailing forever in Bauer's
torpid wake, at least while they were both in uniform.

★   ★   ★

It came as no surprise to Wetzel then, when he was finally sent to Vietnam after two months of typing school at Fort Tara, Virginia, where, when he entered the course he could type seventy-plus words per minute and, upon leaving, was cut to a more moderate thirty-minus words per minute—under the theory that typing so fast demoralizes the other men—that he and Bauer were to be in the same company. For his efforts with Sgt Frito and whoever else's palm he greased in OCS, Private Bauer became 2nd Lt Bauer, and then miraculously, 1st Lt Bauer, stationed with a hospital company of almost a thousand men.

On the outside, Bauer had driven truck for a large fruit concern and had recently made the transition from fresh to quick-frozen produce. It was a status job, a bigger truck, ten feet longer, a foot wider, and the latest in cabin design. When he stopped at cafés with the new truck, he took little or no shit from anyone except maybe the Mayflower guys. Even then it was all in good fun, although Bauer once had his nose broken by a stainless-steel cream pitcher being used as brass knuckles by a guy with a small laundry truck who didn't seem to give a damn what anyone was driving. This code violation was a mystery to Bauer, who, without ever considering what it meant, thought that fair was only fair.

Because of his specialized background, Bauer was made Ground Transportation Officer in the company, a job that involved trucks and similar vehicles. Since the hospital was a permanent Army hospital near Saigon, the only real ground transportation that Bauer was called on to regulate was an eight-times daily bus to the city and an occasional ambulance to pick up American survivors who were injured in terrorist attacks. Usually however, the attacks were thorough and there were no survivors. At that point, the Vietnamese police would deliver to the hospital any bodies that seemed American. It was a "hands-across-the-sea" program that Bauer himself had instituted. There were only problems when it was impossible to tell whether the victims were Vietnamese or American or when they were not quite dead. Bauer put a thirty-mile-an-hour governor on the ambulance so that it would take just about a half-hour to make it into the city, and by that time, things would have, in his own words, "worked out one way or another."

All in all, Bauer didn't mind the war much. It was a way of passing the day. Enlisted men assigned under him kissed-ass and he responded by giving freely of absurdly long passes, which Wetzel, in Personnel, would find reasons to tear up and then send the men back to Bauer for others. In this way they would miss at least one bus, although sometimes Bauer would run an unscheduled charter for his men alone, which Wetzel, in Personnel, would find out about and feel obligated to mention to Colonel Schooner, who, in turn, would be duty-bound to mention it back to Lt Bauer. It was then that Bauer would mete out what he considered just punishment and Wetzel, as a result, would spend a series of weekends on KP and consecutive nights as Charge of Quarters. The fabled shit rolled downhill from rank to rank until it hit Wetzel, who, in Personnel, having no one under him, did what he could for vengeance and protection, destroying Bauer's official shot record, and then, as a dutiful Sp4, notifying the proper medical authorities.

On the other hand, Wetzel *did* mind the war. Before he was drafted he had been working as an accountant in a branch bank in San Francisco, where, other than an occasional holdup which would cut into his two-hour lunch break, he led a quiet, safe, and unobtrusive life. In Vietnam, what quietness there came to him was inner, his unobtrusiveness was the result of his rank, and safety was a thing of the past.

And then there was the problem of the sounds. He had very poor filtering devices and the constant going off of claymore mines, rockets, and other forms of ammo would get on his nerves, and often, before a day would end in the building where he went over officers' and enlisted men's records, he would stutter and show other visceral signs of psychic disorder.

In his room in Saigon atop a small barbershop, Sp4 Wetzel lay on his bed listening to the rockets and claymore mines go off. It was a drag, he realized, more than a drag, a colossal mistake for him to be here. He would have to leave at the soonest time possible. Why, he wondered, didn't he leave right now? The answer he came to, he had arrived at before and before that; he lay too close to the half-inspired middle of mankind. He was neither smart enough nor stupid enough to desert; and also, he didn't have the guts.

On his bureau in olive-drab cans marked with black letters which read, "10 Weight US Army Oil," "20 Weight US Army Oil," "30 Weight US Army Oil," and "10×30 Weight US Army Multipurpose Oil," Wetzel kept his different blends of grass. The fact that he turned-on did not necessarily distinguish him from the thousands of other enlisted men in Vietnam that did also. For Wetzel though, the grass provided neither a good stoning nor an orgiastic trip. It was merely a component in his survival kit, used to abstract, to make things disappear, things which ordinarily imposed themselves on his being with the bluntness of telephone poles. It worked: it kept him from harm and didn't seem to be doing him any harm.

It was anyway only the officers, medical and otherwise, who feared the stuff and they would drink themselves into a puking stupor every day, sometimes so far gone by noon that they would disappear into their posh quarters, leaving the enlisted men in the hospital to perform reasonably delicate operations and to zip up the plastic bags which contained the newly dead patients. Wetzel could only guess how many of them weren't really dead when they were zipped. The fresh corpses simply didn't show the life-signs that the enlisted men were taught to look for: a certain level of heartbeat, breathing, pulse, the ability to cloud mirrors, etc. Zip! Off to the States, dog tags hanging from the zipper tabs on the outside, the

name inked-in on the chest of the returnee. An early-out, Wetzel realized one day in the zipping room—a thought.

Wetzel, along with every other man in the entire United
States Army, was allotted by Army Regulation 14-198, "The
Billeting of Troops," Section 1, Paragraph 2, a minimum of
300 cubic feet of living space, which, when broken down,
yielded approximately 6 feet by 6 feet by 8 feet. He did, in
fact, have at least that much living space in the five-hundred-
man barracks, but other than make his bunk there the first day
he got to Vietnam, the 300 cubic feet went almost completely
unused. Like all the other enlisted men in the company who
had space allotted and a bunk assigned them in the barracks,
Wetzel didn't live there. Only when it rained, when it was
impossible for him to maneuver his motor scooter through the
shellpocked streets from the hospital compound to Saigon,
would he have to spend a night; and then it would be a night
completely alone, for Wetzel was the only man not to qualify
for Bauer's emergency transportation to the city. The last bus
would leave Wetzel in the barracks among millions of cubic
feet of space.

Appropriations for the maintenance and upkeep of the barracks, Wetzel found out one day reading Colonel Schooner's
memo to First Army Command, was over $800,000 a year.
This included the substantial maintenance and upkeep of Captain Ellsworth, Officer-in-charge—daily changing of sheets,
Vietnamese maid service, and what seemed to Wetzel an inor-
dinate amount (3 miles) of mosquito netting. Once a month a
barracks inspection with all five hundred men present would
be held and Colonel Schooner, nearly blind in both eyes but
much in need of a year's active service for retirement points,
would walk through followed by a retinue that included all the
field-grade officers in the company along with a certain first
sergeant named Horzkok.

"Horzkok," the colonel would ask, "are these men getting
their sheets changed?"

"Yes, sir," Horzkok would reply, writing something down on a clipboard whose top sheet hadn't changed since Wetzel had been in the company.

"Horzkok, are the maids coming in daily?"

"Yes, sir."

"What about the netting? Do you need more netting?"

"Probably more netting, sir."

The colonel grinned and winked at Horzkok.

And so the retinue would eventually make their way past Wetzel's bunk, grown men, some of them making more than a thousand dollars a month, inspecting a barracks that no one lived in, checking to make sure that all the special niceties in these barracks for the hospital personnel, who lived twenty miles away in hovels and brothels, were being carried out.

In the beginning of his Vietnam stay, all that made life bearable for Wetzel were the menial tasks he performed while working in Company Personnel. There he could create his own order; there, all his antagonists existed only in paper files, on green and yellow cards, and on sheets of paper stapled to forms that, Wetzel realized one afternoon, in a company of a thousand men, only *he* understood. In realizing this, he realized also in a clouded way, that whatever power he as a Sp4 had, lay in his sole understanding of the forms.

In these first few months, Wetzel did little with his recognition until one night in his Saigon room after some moderate smoking, the idea came to him in a raw but almost crystalline form. As Wetzel looked up to study the contours of his thatched ceiling, Bauer appeared out of the smoke of Wetzel's burnt-down joint, the genie of Wetzel's high. But this ethereal Bauer was not the singular Bauer of the past; rather, Bauer took on the face and dimension of all the men in Wetzel's basic platoon, all the typical American fighting men that Wetzel had known. Here was Bauer with his Army sense of fairness and morality, his self-righteousness; of a certain breed of man, Bauer became their everyman. As the smoke dispersed and the ceiling came back into focus, Wetzel remembered the forms.

Why not, he wondered? Why not, if Bauer is indeed what I see him as, why not de-form him, re-form him, change his being, make him into a more agreeable human. Or why not change his duty station? But then Wetzel realized that by making small changes on Bauer's forms he would be just playing with him. It would be no different than destroying his shot record. It was in this second, as Wetzel recognized the pettiness of merely toying with Bauer's file, that the missing card meshed with the computer tabs in Wetzel's brain and lodged itself resolutely there, leaving nothing else to be considered. Why not plainly murder Bauer, eliminate him entirely, take him out of the war? After all, it would be simply a matter of form, of a form, to wound Bauer in action and have him captured, to make him a hero, a coward, to ship an unidentified body with Bauer's name on the chest along with a copy of Bauer's dog tags, which Wetzel could cut with the machine in his office, back to the States. All the Army would need would be the correct forms and the body would be buried in some military cemetery and his insurance policy paid.

What it came to with the imposition of the reality of the next morning was that Bauer was far more than just Bauer, and to eliminate him would be the initial step. It would be ample, sufficient, for Wetzel to know that while Bauer was harassing him in some formation, that the Army was concurrently paying off $10,000 to Bauer's beneficiary and inactivating his file in St. Louis—where it is said (and probably lied) that every man's record exists in duplicate.

If every day Wetzel weren't witness to the same idiocies of men whose actions were outlined by the cumbersome regulations—the brains behind the men who had given up their own—if every day he didn't feel that the Army, with him included, was digging deeper and deeper into the soggy Asian soil, if a hundred other things he had witnessed, noted, and forgotten hadn't happened, the idea would have never entered his head. But lately, as he sensed things getting worse around him, he turned-on with greater frequency and was beginning to stutter.

Somewhere also, Wetzel knew, if he kept after it, he would run down the regulation that would simply provide for his own release, the one that would send him legally back to the States. There, if things were not truly better, at least there was a semblance of order and peace and the Bauers were back on their trucks and not directly, at least, foisting their guerrilla tactics, their self-respected killer instincts, on those that had no desire for or interest in them. Wetzel didn't have it in for teamsters or even Bauer anymore, really. Only symbolically did his war concern these people.

The morning following Bauer's nocturnal visit, his tragic story began to take form. Wetzel never felt as justified, as sure, in anything else he had ever begun. Using the regulation method, he changed Bauer's record to show that the Ground Transportation Officer had orders releasing him from the hospital company and transferring him to a small infantry unit a few hundred miles north of Saigon, where daily confrontations with the enemy produced a high rate of casualties. Now it was simply a matter of how and when it would happen. Would Bauer be a hero or a coward when he died? It was a decision that Wetzel could make without any more real concern than flipping a coin. He decided to wait before he actually killed Bauer off. Let him get used to his new surroundings, he thought. Let him get the feel of his new duty station before he died defending or running away from it.

Wetzel cut a set of the phony orders on the office mimeo machine and distributed copies to all officers that were in some manner concerned, but not in any position to care or to do anything about them. One thing was definite: everyone believed printed orders, and orders anyhow, were orders. Among the recipients would be the United States Army Records Center in St. Louis, Missouri.

The hospital mail clerk hoisted the bag with the bogus or-

ders from the office floor. It seemed to Wetzel that the first
budging of the huge boulder that he himself had been called on
to push was, that second, taking place. Now it was merely a
matter of momentum. As in any large organization, minor errors would become major errors, would become glaring errors, would become more than errors, lofting themselves into
the fields of absurdity until finally, a frantic hush-hush would
become their epitaph.

Wetzel felt as he watched the mail clerk leave Personnel
and make his way to Captain Ellsworth's bunker to pick up
the never-existent barracks mail, that his decision to end
Bauer's involvement in Vietnam, even in an advisory capacity,
was doing more for his private antiwar effort than if he himself had deserted, gone on extensive AWOL, or lied his way
into the hospital with phony meningitis symptoms. It was to
be something finally done; in his life, something he embarked
on that soon would be completed, something he could actually
be proud of, Bauer's paper-death. Through his mind flashed
an image of Bauer doing a short-thrust-vertical-butt-stroke.
"You're a grand old flag, Bauer, but you're a big boy now."

Wetzel did wonder, weeks before and even now, who was
he, Wetzel, to be deciding the number and frequency of
Bauer's inoculations and now his death. His own was not a
history of unblemished service in the progress of mankind.
Hadn't he frittered away a quarter of a century in self-in-
dulgent sloth and leisure? In ways, didn't he share Bauer's
guilt; was there really that much difference between negative
action and inaction, Wetzel wondered.

For an accountant, he had done very little accounting in his
lifetime, none actually until he was hit with the reality of the
sounds of mines and rockets. But Wetzel also realized the afternoon the orders were sent, his part counted for nothing.
One felt experience, one significant understanding in a lifetime, sometime, and you're on your way; and all that could be
said about it was, if it happened, it happened. And now Wetzel
felt that he was nearing the point of its happening.

If it was Bauer who had provided the emotion for Wetzel's homicide plan, it was the zipping room that contributed reason. Whenever anyone was zipped, Wetzel had to bring down the ex-man's 201 personal file to the zipping room and check his dog tags with his file for spelling, blood type, religion, and serial number. If any one of these things was off, Wetzel would have to cut a new set, then bang them up a little for authenticity and hang them on the special hooks at the top of the zipper. Accounts checked this way: St. Louis was happy, Colonel Schooner had no reason to be unhappy. But even when things ran smoothly in the zipping room, Wetzel was unhappy about the entire situation; more than unhappy. Each trip to the room took him further and further away from believing that he actually saw what he saw. The eerie, overlit room with its plastic cleanliness and its antiseptic pink and black bodies made imperfect by bullet holes and missing chunks, became unreal to him; part of a white light-show that he was forced to participate in and then leave, spent and drawn, as if he had danced over there too long. When Bauer was in the room, as he often was, overseeing a delivery, Wetzel's anxieties became directed and plain to him: clearly Bauer was in some way responsible.

The door to Personnel opened. Bauer stood in the doorway for a second, attempting, what seemed to Wetzel, a certain effect, and then walked in. Wetzel stood up, mentally discovered, his thoughts detonated and scattered. Immediately as he was faced with the man, Wetzel was sorry that he was so mercilessly, so whimsically, so self-righteously plotting his demise. It was impossible in the intimate situation of two men standing right next to each other without weapons, for Wetzel not to bridge the span between men, and, for an instant, make himself that other man. But his feeling changed the second he saw the glint in Bauer's eye. This was not the glint that would save Bauer from death. Had he come with sorrow, with reverence, with a question or a runny nose, with anything other than the look of a man thinking that what he was doing was unquestionably justified, Bauer might have been saved, Wetzel might still have relented and had him transferred back to the hospital company.

"What's this dickin' around in formation, Wetzel? I want to know about that. I let it go today. You know why?"

Sure. Wetzel knew why. It was the shots. Bauer was actually tired of the shots, the side effects, the vaccinations that must have pocked his arms like craters. Bauer had ground the gears in his sturdy but simple brain and had finally made the connection between the shots and Wetzel.

"Well, Wetzel, I'll tell you why. Your attitude here is the shits. It demoralizes, it pisses-off the men. They look at you and figure, 'Why not, if Wetzel can do it, why not me?' And when there's a war going on, there isn't any room for that sort of crap. So today I decided I wouldn't draw attention to you by yelling in front of a whole platoon, but believe me, you better change your whole way of life around here. I'm telling you that personally, here and now, so that you know I'm not just jerking you around as an example. It's you and you alone I'm going to get, unless you change that high-and-mighty garbage of yours. Believe me, Wetzel, I'll have you out of this cozy office, working your ass off permanently for me, if you don't cut the shit. Do you understand that, Wetzel? Understand?"

The man would have to die, Wetzel then decided with all his heart. Bauer had just turned Wetzel's half-formed, fairly definite whim into an irrevocable mission. He had to see Bauer's file sent away, he had to see the look on Bauer's face on payday when he didn't get his cash to buy his prophylactics, beer, and ugly trinkets. Revenge asserted itself back into Wetzel's plan. He now knew, that in order to stay in Personnel in the weeks pending the final processes of Bauer's demise, that he would have to be careful, that he would have to stay away from Bauer's shot record altogether. It was unfortunate, but a necessity. It was something in Bauer's tone that indicated this to him, something that tipped him off to the fact that Bauer would literally kill him if there was a way of making it seem in the line of duty.

"Wetzel, I asked you a question. When an officer asks you a question, you answer. Do you understand *that*, Wetzel?"

It was then, at that very instant, the second that Wetzel was to come out with his servile apology to keep him safe in his job in Personnel, as Wetzel understood the meanness of means and the glory of ends, that the hospital compound was hit soundly, initially and accidentally by a squadron of American planes launched by the carrier *Wendell Willkie* to fly cover for some marines about to walk into the range of at least a half-dozen machine guns guarding VC mortar implacements, a few miles from the non-city side of the hospital.

The plan to paint the roofs of the various buildings that made up the compound white with huge red crosses like the other hospitals in Southeast Asia, had failed when 1st Sgt Horzkok had ordered the wrong color paint from Supply. Colonel Schooner, in an attempt to cover up for Horzkok's error, pointed out at a high-level staff meeting that the crosses were not necessary. The hospital had excellent natural camouflage; having been built by a youthful and recently drafted group of Engineers, it was a masterpiece of integrated structure and terrain. It was impossible, the colonel assured his men, to spot the sprawling bunkers from the air or even from any distance on land. Colonel Schooner had called it right, but unfortunately the perfect camouflage was not working in his favor.

The entire out-patient clinic was destroyed with the first impact. With the second went the enlisted men's barracks. The building made a decent little puff and then, after a few seconds of limbo, burned itself to the ground; just minutes before, all the sheets had been changed. The zipping area was hit and the building in which Wetzel and Bauer stood facing each other with hate, then with questioning, and finally—and Wetzel noted it distinctly in Bauer's face—with fear, collapsed around them. Filing cabinets vomited out drawers full of papers and then the cabinets themselves fell. The wooden roof collapsed, raining down thin slats and shingling, and finally, the sides, no longer feeling any responsibility for the roof, bowed and quit. In the middle of the tangle of typewriters, paper, and Army Regulation pamphlets, Bauer and Wetzel lay pinned beneath a bookshelf, bodies crossed. Wetzel had hit the ground first, covering his head, having attended that particular class in Basic, and Bauer followed, not having attended the class but having been told about it later by buddy Wetzel.

"Get the hell off of me, Bauer." Bauer didn't respond. Wetzel heard further impacts off in the distance. Possibly by now Radio Operator Keyes, whose knowledge of international code was limited to a few words and catch phrases, would have awakened and shot a quick message to the United States Navy or the United States something to ask for a bombing halt.

"Come on, Bauer, get the hell off!" Still no answer, but then Wetzel heard a moan. Bauer was alive! Big deal. Of course Bauer was alive. All that had actually landed on him were some AR pamphlets and a bookshelf which had fallen on Wetzel a few days before when he had attempted to move it and the regulations outside the building.

Wetzel managed to crawl out from under the Ground Transportation Officer. Off in the distance he could see a fire in one of the wards, backlighting crafty Marines as they snuck up on the unsuspecting VC. There were bursts of machine-gun fire, lots of lights from flares, tracers, and flames and huge explosions from someone's heavy artillery. The war arena had invaded the sanctity of the hospital compound. Bauer pulled himself up next to Wetzel, looking out to the left and the right as he did.

"Jesus! Come on, Wetzel. We got to do something. We can't just stand here. Follow me to that fire!"

Wetzel ran behind the man. As he ran, all he felt was

the movement of his legs and his face heating from the blaze he neared. Bauer spotted some men in beds behind the flames and ran through to them. Wetzel didn't have time to decide, running through a few steps behind him. If he had stopped for just a second, he would have never done it. In the pulsating orange light, he saw Bauer pick up a man from one of the beds and run out of the building with him. Wetzel looked around, picked someone up himself, felt the weight on his shoulders, ran with it, was outside, and dumped it off. He started back in after another, but this time he stopped for a second and thought. He hesitated at the edge of the flames. In the meanwhile Bauer had torn through and dumped another body.

"See what you can do for these men, Wetzel. I'm going back for another."

It was the perfect reason not even to think about going back in, realized Wetzel. Bauer had given an order and now the idiot was running back in himself. Wetzel looked down at the men on the ground in front of him; all three of them were dead. The one Bauer was running in to get would probably be dead also. But Bauer couldn't know that; he was this second too busy being a hero. Wetzel wondered, how many rights did Bauer have to do to make up for his wrongs? What went on in that plodding mind that could transform Bauer from what he ordinarily was to the man who just ran back into a burning building to save what he thought was someone's life. As Wetzel looked again at the men on the ground and heard the machine-gun fire of the Marines or the VC, he realized that it was Bauer's wrongs that, by contrast, would put him in a position to make his rights seem great. If Bauer really thought about the humanity he was lugging out of the fire, he wouldn't be here in the first place: not in this hospital, in this fire, in this war or this Army. It hit Wetzel that way, but he knew it wasn't that simple, although he wished it was.

The fire went on for most of the day and into the night before it was finally put out by equipment that Bauer, in his official capacity, commissioned from Saigon, where it was always vitally needed. The equipment was not returned the next day or the day following. Wetzel knew it would go the way of all equipment that had been borrowed by the hospital. During an inspection, Colonel Schooner would spot it, declare it obsolete, and insist it be dismantled for parts.

Personnel was rebuilt in a day. It took three days for Wetzel to straighten out all the records. In that time he re-resolved that Bauer would have to die, but it became increasingly clear, as Wetzel relived the moments of Bauer's running into the burning ward, that to have him die a coward would be a lie. It was an option that circumstance had stolen from him. It bothered him to have to admit this. What death, then, would he himself have to die? What sort of man was he, Wetzel, who would choose cowardice over almost anything else dangerous or painful? He thought and all that came to him was that the heroes must be the men who didn't attach any worth to life—what did that make them: stupid, insensitive, unappreciative, or great, vital, keyed even more to life because they were that much more close to death? Whatever, the world needed these men; Wetzel decided that he was not one of them. Most people, though, were or wanted to be heroes.

After Bauer's file had been located and carefully arranged, Wetzel made his way to the zipping room, carrying with him the file along with a newly minted copy of Bauer's dog tags. A large hole in the room's ceiling, still not repaired from the attack, admitted the sun and rinsed everything in the room in natural light. Boxes of the zippered plastic bags sat on one side of the room on shelves labeled "small," "medium," and "large." One entire wall of the spacious chamber held the deep drawers that contained the bodies that had been recently zipped. Because the bodies would never spend more than a day in the hospital before being lifted off by helicopters to landing strips where airplanes would take them back to the States, these drawers were not refrigerated. In the latest *Army*

Digest, Wetzel read in an article entitled, "The Wonders of Body Evacuation," that the body of a United States serviceman killed in Vietnam could be evacuated from a given battlefield and be back in the States in less than twenty-four hours. Implicit in the article was the message that the Army profited doubly by this efficiency: first, by not having to refrigerate the filing cabinets which held the bodies and, second, by always having empty drawers in the case of a major enemy offense.

On a smaller wall, though, there was a group of the drawers that were refrigerated. In these drawers doctors would keep such perishables as sandwiches spread with mayonnaise, beer, mixer, etc. These would usually surround the "no-names" that were also in the drawers and were bodies being held for positive identification. Occasionally, during a rush, semi-positive identifications were made by Colonel Schooner or some other high-ranking officer, and the bodies would be zipped and shipped, telegrams sent and policies paid. All in all, it was a lot cheaper than expanded refrigeration.

Wetzel opened one of these drawers. A man lay on his back in a torn and burned fatigue uniform. His face had been scarred to a charcoal anonymity and next to his left arm was some onion dip with a few pieces of potato-chip shrapnel in the center of the bowl. The no-name's uniform had no identifying patches other than the one which read "US Army," black on green so that he couldn't be spotted by the enemy during nightfall. There were no dog tags; they had probably been destroyed in the same fire that the man had died in, obliterated in the heat.

The second before he decided anything, Wetzel noticed in the sunlight how very calm the no-name looked; the pressure was off. The only thing left for him to do was to lie there and eventually decompose. Compose, decompose, he thought; no matter; there was work to be done. "Well, Bauer, it may be better than you deserve; I'm not really sure. But I'll do my best for you." He wrote Bauer's name on the man's chest with the regulation pen, zipped him in the plastic bag on which he lay, and, with his own heart beating with notable panic, transferred him to a slot in the non-refrigerated section. In less than two hours there would be another lift-off; in less than ten the body would be on its way back to the States. Bauer, as his file had indicated, had no living family, no loved ones. The beneficiary on his Army insurance policy was a Teamsters local in Detroit, who, when they found out about Brother Bauer's demise, would cancel his card, take the $10,000, and have a wake with the corpse in absentia. Wetzel affixed Bauer's dog tags to the bag.

Then he went back to Personnel and cut orders to the unit that Bauer was supposedly transferred to, to drop Bauer's name from the morning report and all other rosters. To the Army Records Center in St. Louis and to the Pentagon, Wetzel sent the following letter:

> Sirs:
> 1st Lt. Ernest L. Bauer, 0967543, a short time in my command as Unit Transportation Officer, was fatally wounded when trying to drive a burning truck away from our ammunition dump. Through his courageous action, the lives of our entire company are in his debt.
> I therefore recommend that Lt Bauer receive commendation for his valor, hopefully in the form of the Distinguished Service Cross. Lt Bauer lives in our minds as an example to us all.
> WILFRED KRIEG, MAJ, INF–USRA 045328
> 6789th Inf Reg, Quo Hop, SEA

Major Krieg, Wetzel had learned in the *Vietnam Newsletter*, had been recently captured by the VC, so there was little or no official way to check the story out. Besides, there was no time to check stories out. In the meanwhile, Wetzel knew that with the receipt of this letter, Personnel at Quo Hop would be desperately dummying-up records to show that Bauer *had* been there. It was far better than trying to deny it. If they did, there would be investigations, the Inspector General would insist on auditing all the reports filed in the time of Bauer's supposed presence. It was better, far better, to change a few records, to forge Bauer's signature in a few places. Wetzel also sent Quo Hop a belated copy of Bauer's phony original orders, those that transferred him there in the first place. With them, Quo Hop would have nothing to worry about. It was now only a matter of hours before the Teamsters local would be notified.

With the death of Bauer completed, Wetzel who had been short of breath ever since he had lifted the no-name from the "pending" to the "out" file, sat and slowly mused over what he had done. And indeed, it had been done. In its execution, he realized its infallibility. The huge wheels, though held on by plastic cotter pins, would run true; turning and churning, they would soon eliminate a member. Somewhere in St. Louis, Bauer's duplicate file would be pulled and put into another container; somewhere in the Pentagon, the decision was being made about Bauer's decoration. Wetzel had done what the negotiators had been trying to do. And he did it without violence, without more destruction, and, the second he actually zipped the bag, without any personal hate.

He wondered; if one man could be so easily eliminated, what about a platoon of men, a company, an entire regiment? It would be a graceful and honorable withdrawal. The Army had actually provided the framework for it to be done, what with each man's complex file, the mass of orders and orders countermanding orders, the regulations that by their mere volume would have to lead to a notable contradiction—a massive one that could bring the Leviathan crashing from the sea. He would have to study it all more carefully before he went on.

In the rearranging of the files, Wetzel did run into the regulation that earlier he had expended so much energy looking for, the one which quite clearly outlined his way back to the States. It would work if he changed a few things on his own file. Other than that, it involved having a stateside contact locate an old man dying in a hospital and having the man claim that Wetzel was his son, his only family. The Red Cross would be notified and, in turn, would notify Personnel in Southeast Asia for verification. If the stories checked, in less than twenty-four hours, Wetzel could be at the old man's bedside. And possibly the man would grab at the last of life—and the choice of the old man would have to be wisely made— leaving Wetzel at his bedside for the duration of his active obligation. It would be time well-spent, Wetzel conjectured; he would give an old man, who may well have been in a war himself, some solace by telling him that, indeed, he was dying in vain, but that we all did. "The world didn't improve between our wars, old man, it just got a little more complicated."

But Wetzel decided to forego this loophole. He was onto something bigger, something far more worthwhile. Now, as he read through the regulations to see what else there was to do, he anxiously awaited the initial correspondence that would be crossing the Personnel desk. It was inevitable that the note would come from St. Louis, a response to Bauer's urgent request. It would state as succinctly as possible, composed and typed by someone in Personnel:

> Dear 1st Lt Bauer:
> The reason that you were not paid on 1Jul68 was because you were killed in action a month preceding your request. You have been awarded the Purple Heart and the Distinguished Service Cross for your heroic service.
> Further explanation of this matter will be found in AR 167-18, Sec. 3, para 4, "Payment

Procedures." Any further correspondence should be taken up with:

> AM-AGAP, 67543
> APO San Francisco
> Sp5 Giles Blanchey
> Personnel Specialist

The long-awaited flight back to the World.

Tim O'Brien

Don't I Know You?

The air is still, warm. Just at dusk, only the brightest stars are out. The Southern Cross is only partly there.

The curved bosom, a long, sterile tunnel, opens, and a man rolls a gate open and you walk carefully onto a sheet of tar. You go up eighteen steps.

The airplane smells and feels artificial. The stewardess, her carefree smile and boredom simmering like bad lighting, doesn't understand. It's enraging, because you sense she doesn't want to understand.

The plane smells antiseptic. The green, tweedy seats are low-cost comfort, nothing at all like sleeping in real comfort on top of the biggest hill in the world, having finally climbed it. Too easy. There is no joy in leaving. Nothing to savor with your eyes or heart.

When the plane leaves the ground, you join everyone in a ritualistic shout, emptying your lungs inside the happy cave of winners, trying to squeeze whatever drama you can out of leaving Vietnam.

But the effort makes the drama artificial. You try to manufacture your own drama, remembering how you promised to savor the departure. You keep to yourself. It's the same, precisely the same, as the arrival: a horde of strangers, spewing their emotions and wanting you to share with them.

The stewardess comes through the cabin, spraying a mist of invisible sterility into the pressurized, scrubbed, filtered, temperature-controlled air, killing mosquitoes and unknown diseases, protecting herself and America from Asian evils, cleansing us all forever.

The stewardess is a stranger. No Hermes, no guide to anything. She is not even a peeping tom. She is as carefree and beautiful and sublime as a junior-high girl friend.

Her hair is blond; they must allow only blonds on Vietnam departures—blond, blue-eyed, long-legged, medium-to-huge-breasted women. It's to say we did well, America loves us, it's over, here's what you missed, but here's what it was good for: my girl friend was blond and blue-eyed and long-legged, quiet and assured, and she spoke good English. The stewardess doesn't do anything but spray and smile, smiling while she sprays us clean, spraying while she smiles us back to home. Question. Do the coffins get sprayed? Does she care if I don't care to be sterilized, would she stop?

You hope there will be time for a last look at the earth. You take a chance and try the window. Part of a wing, a red light on the end of it. The window reflects the cabin's glare. You can't even see darkness down below, not even a shadow of the earth, not even a skyline. The earth, with its little villages and bad, criss-crossed fields of rice paddy and red clay, deserts you. It's the earth you want to say good-bye to. The soldiers never knew you. You never knew the Vietnamese people. But the earth, you could turn a spadeful of it, see its dryness and the tint of red, and dig out enough of it so as to lie in the hole at night, and that much of Vietnam you would know. Certain whole pieces of the land you would know, something like a farmer knows his own earth and his neighbor's. You know where the bad, dangerous parts are, and the sandy and safe places by the sea. You know where the mines are and will be for a century, until the earth swallows and disarms them. Whole patches of land. Around My Khe and My Lai. Like a friend's face.

The stewardess serves a meal and passes out magazines. The plane lands in Japan and takes on fuel. Then you fly straight on to Seattle. What kind of war is it that begins and ends that way, with a pretty girl, cushioned seats, and magazines?

You add things up. You lost a friend to the war, and you gained a friend. You compromised one principle and fulfilled another. You learned, as old men tell it in front of the courthouse, that war is not all bad; it may not make a man of you, but it teaches you that manhood is not something to scoff; some stories of valor are true; dead bodies are heavy, and it's better not to touch them; fear is paralysis, but it is better to be afraid than to move out to die, all limbs functioning and heart thumping and charging and having your chest torn open for all the work; you have to pick the times not to be afraid, but when you are afraid you must hide it to save respect and reputation. You learned that the old men had lives of their own and that they valued them enough to try not to lose them; anyone can die in a war if he tries.

You land at an air-force base outside Seattle. The army feeds you a steak dinner. A permanent sign in the mess hall says "Welcome Home, Returnees." "Returnees" is an army word, a word no one else would use. You sign your name for the dinner, one to a man.

Then you sign your name to other papers, processing your way out of the army, signing anything in sight, dodging out of your last haircut.

You say the Pledge of Allegiance, even that, and you leave the army in a taxicab.

The flight to Minnesota in March takes you over disappearing snow. The rivers you see below are partly frozen over. Black chunks of corn fields peer out of the old snow. The sky you fly in is gray and dead. Over Montana and North Dakota, looking down, you can't see a sign of life.

And over Minnesota you fly into an empty, unknowing, uncaring, purified, permanent stillness. Down below, the snow is heavy, there are patterns of old corn fields, there are some roads. In return for all your terror, the prairies stretch out, arrogantly unchanged.

At six in the morning, the plane banks for the last time and straightens out and descends. When the no-smoking lights come on, you go into the back of the plane. You take off your uniform. You roll it into a ball and stuff it into your suitcase and put on a sweater and blue jeans. You smile at yourself in the mirror. You grin, beginning to know you're happy. Much as you hate it, you don't have civilian shoes, but no one will notice. It's impossible to go home barefoot.